THE FOOD OF
OMAN

THE FOOD OF
OMAN

Recipes and Stories from the Gateway to Arabia

FELICIA CAMPBELL

FOREWORD BY JAMES OSELAND
PHOTOGRAPHY BY ARIANA LINDQUIST
RECIPES BY DAWN MOBLEY

Andrews McMeel
Publishing®

Kansas City • Sydney • London

This book is dedicated to the people of Oman who invited me into their kitchens, homes, and lives, introducing me to a world that captivated my imagination and my heart. As the flavors of this singular place transformed my palate, their graciousness, hospitality, patience, and rootedness in the world transformed my life.

CONTENTS

Foreword by James Oseland . . . ix

Introduction . . . xi

Quick Facts . . . xvii

Key Dates . . . xviii

Omani Map . . . xix

A Brief History of Oman . . . xx

Ancient Fusions: Muscat's Food Scene . . . xxvi

I
THE OMANI PANTRY:
FROM MUSCAT TO NEW YORK   1

CHAPTER 1:	Identifying, Purchasing, and Substituting Ingredients	3
	Visual Ingredient Glossary	4
	Shopping Guide: Where To Find Specialty Ingredients	11
	"As You Like": Notes On Substitutions	12

II
OMANI MEALS:
FRIENDS, FAMILY, AND SACRED SPACES   15

CHAPTER 2:	Grilled, Smoked, and Charred	21
CHAPTER 3:	Savory Porridges, Stews, and Soups	45
CHAPTER 4:	Rice: The Main Meal	67
CHAPTER 5:	Meat, Seafood, and Marak Mains	93
CHAPTER 6:	Produce and Legumes	125

III
BETWEEN MEALS   139

CHAPTER 7:	Savory Bites	143
CHAPTER 8:	Omani Breads	161
CHAPTER 9:	Omani Sweets	189
CHAPTER 10:	Beverages	215
CHAPTER 11:	Omani Pantry Basics and Condiments	233

Acknowledgments . . . 245

Metric Conversions and Equivalents . . . 247

Index . . . 249

Artist Biographies . . . 257

FOREWORD

Some people enter your life with a bang. Others saunter in more quietly, on cat's feet. Felicia Campbell came into mine by way of the latter method. She'd been an intern for a number of months at *Saveur*, where I was editor in chief. But her presence hadn't registered too intensely for me until one day I needed help with the most menial of tasks: pinning page proofs to my wall. As Felicia and I worked together, we got to talking.

She was from California, she told me. Her parents were academics. She had moved with them to Colorado, where she dropped out of high school (like me) and enrolled in college early at CU Denver, where she had begun a pretty typical first semester. Then September 11, 2001, rolled around. And for Felicia, as for so many others, everything changed.

"I was so upset by what I watched on TV that morning that I decided that I had to do something— though I didn't know what, at first," she said. "The thing that came to me over and over again was: Join the army."

I stopped pinning proofs. I listened to her recount the extraordinary tale of joining the military at seventeen; learning how to repair helicopters; and, just after her nineteenth birthday, being sent with the first deployment of American soldiers to Iraq, where she—counter to all expectations—fell in love with the Middle East.

Against all odds, Iraq—its people, its history, its food—resonated profoundly with her. After her tour of duty, a college education, and a stint in the restaurant industry, Felicia earned a master's degree in food studies, specializing in Arab foodways. The cultures and extraordinary cuisines of the Middle East became the focus of her work.

In the years after that first conversation, I've gotten the chance to know Felicia much better: She was hired after her internship as my assistant and then graduated to a more senior position. Throughout it all, she continued to develop her knowledge of the Middle East, traveling there at every opportunity and championing the coverage of its diverse foods and culinary history in our pages.

On one trip, she made her first visit to Oman. I remember vividly her animated state when she returned.

"Jim, it's an amazing place," she said. "And the food! Each dish practically tells the story of the ancient spice routes."

In the multiple trips Felicia made to Oman after that first one, her enthusiasm and knowledge for its cuisines blossomed and deepened. What would take most people decades to acquire in terms of culinary knowledge, Felicia packed into a few extraordinarily dedicated years.

I knew she was onto something profound when she invited me to spend a day testing recipes for some of the dishes that appear in this book. A group of dedicated Felicia fans gathered one chilly fall morning to help out. I was given the job of cooking the complicated Zanzibari Biryani (page 88)—a recipe that required each element, from the spice blend to the rice to the rich sauce and pan-fried chicken, to be prepared separately and then layered before being finished with saffron-infused rose water.

I won't lie: It was a daunting task. But as I got deeper into the process, simmering the chicken in a spiced broth, frying onions, and toasting spices, I fell into a kind of wonderful trance. I began to see the biryani start to come together, what made it function, why it worked the way it did.

As we cooked, the kitchen filled with the most miraculous aromas. It was as if the shores of the Arabian Sea were drawing near, lapping at the door of the New York City kitchen. It was intoxicating.

At the end of the day, we sampled a dizzying array of foods: a savory chicken and rice porridge called *Madrouba* (page 50); grilled lamb (page 29) and chicken kebabs (page 30); *Musanif Lahm* (page 154), a kind of meat-stuffed, pan-fried dumpling; and creamy spinach simmered in coconut milk (page 129). While I'm proud to say the biryani was extraordinary (really, insanely delicious), so was everything else. I understood then what I know for certain now: Not only has Felicia crafted an essential book about a remarkable cuisine relatively unknown outside its native place, but she has also captured that culture's beautiful soul in its recipes.

—James Oseland, editor in chief of Rodale's Organic Life
and author of Cradle of Flavor

INTRODUCTION

Oman is not merely a place; it is an immersive, sensory experience. After the warmth of the sun and sultry ocean air, smell is perhaps the first sense ignited upon arrival in the capital of Muscat. Sweet vanilla- and orange-scented Abyssinian roses grow wild on the roadsides; woodsy oud, bright citrusy musk, and dark amber perfume and *bahoor* incense linger on the clothes of the people; and from crowded souks to the receiving rooms of homes throughout the country, frankincense smoke lends its ancient, velvety cover. In the kitchens tucked in the rear of cavernous villas or in the courtyards of mountain homes, bouquets of sizzling onions melting in oil, cardamom simmering in coffee and curries, and pungent cloves dancing in a medley of hot chile, coriander, ginger, and musky dried black lime play against the subtle backdrop of coconut milk bubbling with spinach or mashed green bananas.

The cursive sound of Arabic, from gentle murmuring at urban cafés to the cacophony of laughter, children happily shrieking, and women talking over one another in village kitchens, is interrupted only by the echo of the call to prayer, sung five times a day from minarets in cities and towns from Salalah in the south to Musandam at the northern tip of the Sultanate.

As singular as the sounds and scents are the visual juxtapositions: Jagged, black slate mountains jut out of the flat beige earth at sharp 45-degree angles; crisp, white adobe houses overlook the dark blue sea; golden sand dunes stretch to the powdery horizon; and in the south, rolling green hills are wedged between the flat, white desert of Rub'al Khali, the Empty Quarter, and Salalah's lush, green oceanside cliffs.

The people themselves—men in starched white, ankle-length *dishdasha* and colorfully embroidered *kuma* caps or wrapped *mussar* turbans and women in brilliantly colored *dishdasha* and scarves from India or elegant black abayas with delicate, sheer *sheila* scarves—look as diverse as the landscape, with complexions and features that reflect ancient trade connections between Arabia, East Africa, South Asia, and Persia.

The tastes of Oman reflect both Bedouin pragmatism and hospitality, and the curiosity and adventurousness of the ancient Indian Ocean seafarers. Typical *Khaleeji* (the Arabic word describing people and things from the Arabian Gulf) rice dishes are enlivened with ginger, cloves, cardamom, and tart black lime; Indian biryanis are subdued, becoming mild, more subtle versions of themselves; East African vegetables in coconut milk are made using richer, malty coconut milk powder. These tastes are reminiscent of many places, but distinctly Omani. I was seduced by the incredible distinctiveness of this place and the people there, whose food felt vaguely familiar somehow but was unlike anything I'd ever had before.

When I set off for Oman for the first time in 2013 to report a feature, I was simply looking to tell an interesting story about a little-known subset of Middle Eastern cuisine. I certainly wasn't expecting to find an answer to that unnamed longing that had been scratching at the inside of my chest since I returned from serving in the war in Iraq in 2004.

The Iraqi desert, which had at first appeared so empty, had been filled with howling winds and fierce sunsets and a people who knew how to patiently weather its fits and furies. In that wild, ancient place, as a restless 19-year-old, for the first time I learned to be still. In Iraqi cafés I was welcomed by those I thought were my enemies, their warmth and graciousness softening my carefully guarded heart, humbling me. With them, I learned to sit and simply be, savoring the minutes or hours spent with my platoon, my tribe, safe from the brutal loneliness that lay beyond our encampment. But, despite their kindness and my own curiosity, I remained afraid of the local people, and before I ever learned much about those who gave me refuge as mortars fell and time crept on through blistering heat and freezing storms, it was time to go. I never learned their names. We redeployed to America and we all went our separate ways, to our separate houses, getting down to the business of building our separate lives. There was no more time for sitting.

Over the years since, I'd learned how to ignore the haunting emptiness I returned home with, filling the space with raw ambition, with work, the distraction of relentless pursuit. New York City is the perfect place for that kind of compulsion.

And it worked, kind of. The ache faded to a tickle, and I began to wonder if that haunting desert, or the girl who sat and sipped sweet glasses of tea in those makeshift Iraqi cafés, ever really existed at all.

As a graduate student and then a journalist, I returned to the Middle East many times after the war, eating and learning and writing about the fascinating region etched in my heart. I loved every return to the warm embrace of Arabia: the food, the people, the ancientness of the place, coupled with the enthusiasm of young Arabs for anything new. But the Mediterranean seaside cities of Lebanon and the towering skyscrapers of Dubai hardly echoed that desert or the intimacy I had found there. So, when I got on a Muscat-bound plane from JFK, heading for the picturesque Sultanate just south of the Emirates, east of Saudi Arabia and across the sea from Iran, I thought I already knew what to expect.

On a whirlwind culinary tour of the capital city, I ducked in and out of catering halls, fish markets, stylish fusion restaurants, and a gracious home where I enjoyed tart turmeric fish soup, mild beef curry, and molasses-rich date chapati in an opulent outer dining room. The foods of Oman were a wonderfully bizarre mash-up of Bedouin rice and meat, South Asian curries, and East African vegetables spiked with coconut milk, hot chiles, and lime. It was thrilling to find something so new, different, unexplored in a world where I'd come to believe everything was Google-able.

I was excited and returned with a photographer a few months later. On that second trip to Oman, something began to shift inside of me. I went out from the capital city, leaving behind my carefully crafted itinerary, accepting my Omani acquaintances' generous offers to stop everything they were doing to take me further into their worlds. I was humbled by the time they gave so freely to help me, as I was taken to ancient mountain villages, beyond *majlis* receiving rooms and into home kitchens, and, two days before I left, back to the desert.

Amid the dunes of a region called Sharqiyah, I crouched under a violently flapping tarp with a tribe of Bedouin women as they fried dough and drizzled it with thick date syrup; boiled rice in a heady stock spiced with cloves, cardamom, cinnamon, and coriander; and crisped paper-thin rounds of Omani bread, *khubz ragag*, on a metal plate placed over burning palm fronds and cinder blocks.

When the cooking was complete, I followed an old Bedouin woman to a woven palm frond hut at the top of a hill. In her vibrant, emerald *dishdasha*, floral *lahaf* scarf, and pointed black *burqa* facemask, she looked like an exotic bird. She motioned for me to sit. We ate together and then, sipping light cardamom-scented Omani coffee, I spent hours listening to the musical intonation of their voices, watching them dance and laugh. I felt at home for the first time in years.

I returned to New York, but my heart and mind continued to drift back to Oman: obsessing over this place so different from the countries that surround it; captivated by the gracious, diverse people I'd met; and intrigued by the foods I'd only just begun to discover.

I tried to learn more, devouring the two self-published English-language Omani cookbooks I'd found in Muscat and reading everything I could find about the Indian Ocean trade routes, but then, there was nothing more to be found. There were only a handful of recipes for Khaleeji specialties on Emirati home-cooking blogs, and I found that the trade histories, even those on the spice routes, typically ignored food altogether in favor of stories of war and commerce. As I told friends and colleagues about my experiences in Oman, they would nod excitedly, then ask, "Where is Oman exactly?"

So I enlisted the help of my best friend, Dawn Mobley, a brilliant cook, researcher, and recipe developer, and together we traveled back to Oman half a dozen times over the twelve months that followed. One Omani friend would put us in touch with another friend, people willing to let us into the private sanctuaries of their homes and kitchens, where we would spend hours: Dawn standing over the hot stove, carefully chronicling every spice and step, while I spoke to the women about their foods, families, and lives. I wanted to capture, in some small way, the essence of this incredible place with the first internationally available, English-language Omani cookbook, a love letter of sorts to the people and place that reawakened my heart.

As we learned to cook *Luqaimat* (page 192), fried balls of dough soaked in thick, local honey, alongside *nicab*-clad women in the northern border town of Buraimi; made Tuna *Kabuli* (page 77) with young Omani men camping in the desert; and watched mountain people in the far southern province of Dhofar turn out perfectly charred chickens using nothing but hot river rocks, fire, and salt (see page 37), I learned about far more than food.

Over the past twelve months, watching in Oman and cooking Omani dishes in New York, I learned about patience that can transform creamed coconut greens, edible after about 15 minutes, into a lusciously savory dish after 45, in the same way that the Omani style of greeting, taking an extra moment to respectfully say, *Salam alaikum, Kefak? Allah Yasalmik* ("Peace be upon you, how are you? May God keep you well"), rather than the more succinct *Marhaba* ("Hi"), gives the sense of an unhurried culture that values respect and honor over efficiency. And in some ways, I slowly began to learn new ways of dealing with the unpredictable winds of life, as I watched the incredible people who had become my friends savor the good times for as long as they lasted and accept the bad as *dunia*, a part of life.

The deliberate, leisurely daily meals we shared throughout our time in Oman were expressions of what was most important: love and family in all its forms. During those meals in Oman, I learned how to sit and be still again, to care and allow others to care for me, to connect with a terrifyingly uncertain world instead of running from it.

This book is an invitation to explore a place you might never have heard of through the foods of Oman and the people behind them. This is not an exhaustive catalog of every Omani dish, but an introduction to flavors and techniques shared with Dawn and me by home cooks and chefs, as well as dishes inspired by the styles of eating we experienced throughout the Sultanate.

The book is arranged to reflect the way Omanis eat, with a section about the menagerie of distinctive and commonplace ingredients that make up the Omani pantry, and two recipe sections. Part II covers Omani main dishes. *Al gha'ada* is the main meal of the day, taken at lunchtime, and it almost always includes rice, the cornerstone of Omani cuisine. Other mains reflect the diverse influences of the Indian Ocean trade routes, with rich coconut curries and slow-cooked, caramelized beef braises that may be served with rice, bread, or East African polenta. Rich porridges are Omani comfort foods eaten after

sundown during the holy month of Ramadan, when mealtime is turned on its head, with nothing eaten between sunrise and sunset. And many celebratory mains are grilled, as cooking outside is a favorite way to entertain. All other meals in Oman orbit around the hearty, late-afternoon lunch, or post-sundown Ramadan *iftar* supper. Many dishes can be eaten for breakfast, dinner, snack, or dessert, so I began to think of recipes like delicious Omani flatbreads smeared with savory white cheese and egg (page 162), fried chile-potato puffs (page 147), and luscious crêpes drizzled in date syrup (page 181), as "in-between" meals. Part III covers these bites and sides.

Many of these recipes were developed in the absence of any written instructions, conveyed to us through demonstration, and though some of the steps may seem strange or unnecessary, after many rounds of testing during which we tried to simplify as much as possible, we came back again and again to the methods we were taught in Oman. The techniques are there for a reason, often because the magic happens in the last few minutes of a long simmer, when seemingly disparate flavors suddenly harmonize.

QUICK FACTS

COUNTRY NAME: Oman, Sultanate of Oman

GOVERNMENT TYPE: Sultanate (monarchy) with a popularly elected legislative body, the Majlis al Shura

POPULATION: 3.9 million, 1.15 million in the capital, Muscat

LANGUAGES SPOKEN: Arabic (official), English (taught in school), Swahili, Urdu, Lawati, Baluchi, as well as Jabali and other local dialects

RELIGION: 86 percent Muslim (majority are Ibadhi/Ibadiyah, a moderate local sect of Islam, some are Sunni and Shia); 6.5 percent Christian; 5.5 percent Hindu, Buddhist, or Jewish; 2 percent unaffiliated

SIZE: 119,498 square miles, a little smaller than the state of Kansas

Geography:

SEA: Eastern and southern borders comprise 1,299 miles of coastline, feeding the coastal plains that account for 3 percent of Oman's geography

DESERT: 82 percent desert, including the beginning of Rub'al Khali, the Empty Quarter, the largest desert in the world at 250,966 square miles, extending into Yemen and Saudi Arabia

MOUNTAINS: 15 percent mountainous areas, in the north and far south, with the largest range being Jabal Akhdar, the Green Mountains, whose highest point (snow covered in the wintertime) is 9,776 feet

KEY DATES

- **700s** Introduction of Islam
- **800s** Ibadiyah sect and rule by hereditary Imamate begins
- **1507** Portuguese take Muscat and capture the Omani coastal cities
- **1650** Independence with expulsion of Portuguese
- **1698** Portuguese expelled from East Africa, Zanzibar becomes part of the Sultanate of Oman
- **1737** Persian invasion and rule
- **1749** Persians expelled and current Al Bu Said dynasty established
- **1800s** Expansion period and Indian Ocean trade domination
- **1832** Oman's capital moved from Muscat to Stone Town, Zanzibar, for 8 years
- **1856** Zanzibar and Oman divided into The Sultanate of Zanzibar and The Sultanate of Muscat and Oman
- **1913** Rebellions by Imams of the interior split the country
- **1932** Sultan Said Bin Taimur comes to power and moves the capital from Muscat to Salalah

- **1959** Sultan Taimur imposes harsh restrictions and violently stomps out the rebellions in the interior
- **1962** Oil is discovered in the Ad Dhahirah region by Petroleum Development Oman (PDO)
- **1965–75** Civil war breaks out in the southern Dhofar region
- **1970** Sultan Qaboos bin Said Al Said overthrows his father in a bloodless coup and begins modernizing Oman
- **1981** Oman is a founding member of the Gulf Cooperation Council (GCC) along with Bahrain, Kuwait, Qatar, Saudi Arabia, and the United Arab Emirates
- **1997** Women are decreed eligible for election to the consultative council and two women are elected
- **2002** Voting privileges are extended to all citizens over 21
- **2011** Oman begins mediating talks between the United States and Iran

A BRIEF HISTORY OF OMAN

Sultans and Seafarers

The story of modern Oman dates back only to July 23, 1970, when the current sultan, Qaboos bin Said Al Said, overthrew his father, Said bin Taimur, in a bloodless palace coup and established a modern monarchy. He appointed a cabinet and an elected consultative council and set about pumping the country's new oil wealth into building public schools, roads, and hospitals as part of an aggressive modernization campaign. The story of the great Omani empire, however, is thousands of years old.

Since 500 BC, Oman's position at the intersection of Asian and African maritime trade routes, as well as overland caravan routes to the Eastern Mediterranean,

was vied for, and in 1514 the Portuguese succeeded in gaining control of coastal Oman after a bloody seven-year war. Despite an Ottoman- and Persian-supported uprising, the Portuguese remained in power through brutal rule for over a hundred years, until Sultan bin Saif Al Arubi expelled them in 1650. Omani forces went on to drive the Portuguese out of their East African trade ports as well, taking control of Mombasa in 1698, then, finally, the entire coast of Mozambique and Zanzibar. Omani expansion continued for the next two centuries, Omani trade from the Far East to Western Europe flourished, and by the early 19th century, Oman was the most powerful state in Arabia.

The first sultan from the current ruling Al-Busaidi family came to power in the 18th century, after a civil war weakened the empire and Oman briefly fell under Persian occupation. In 1749, a provincial governor, Ahmad ibn Said, led the uprising that liberated Oman and he was elected Imam. He then established the hereditary sultanate that continues today.

The early 20th century saw continued upheaval in both Arabian Oman and Zanzibar. The ruling sultan in Muscat, Said bin Taimur, violently quelled rebellions in the interior and moved the capital from Muscat to Salalah in 1932, where the current Sultan Qaboos was born in 1940. In 1964, Zanzibar gained autonomy after a sudden, violent uprising. Taimur sought to maintain strict control in Arabian Oman, imposing increasingly extreme social and economic restrictions, which led to widespread poverty and greater discontent and instability.

Taimur's son, Qaboos bin Said Al Said, gained the support of the army and eventually of the tribal leaders of the interior, taking over the Sultanate in 1970 and moving the capital back to Muscat in 1971. Over the past forty years, the country has been transformed through opportunities for economic growth, universal education, and increased international engagement.

Maintaining Omani heritage and culture has been as important to Sultan Qaboos as modernization, as demonstrated in regulations like building codes that require traditional, low-story white- and beige-washed buildings in the capital to the government dress code of *dishdasha*, the national dress, for all male employees to the massive government investments in heritage, arts, and historic preservation. Oman has managed to maintain a traditional feel and aesthetic, with a capital city whose horizon, dominated by jagged mountain peaks and the crisp blue of the Gulf of Oman, stands in stark contrast to the glittering skyscrapers of neighboring Dubai, Doha, and Riyadh.

The Spice Routes on a Plate

To get a true sense of the vastness of the Omani trading empire in the 19th and 20th centuries, you need look no further than Omani kitchens, whose pantries reflect an intricately tangled web of connections between the

The subsequent 18th-century Al Said family continued to expand the empire, establishing trading ports in Persia and along the Makran Coast, in what is now Pakistan and India. In 1840, the capital was moved to the prosperous coconut and clove plantation island of Zanzibar.

In 1856, the ruling sultan, Said bin Sultan Al Busaid, died and conflict over his succession broke out between his sons. They decided to divide the state, with one ruling East Africa from Zanzibar and the other ruling Arabian Oman from Muscat, which weakened the empire.

Middle East, South Asia, East Asia, and East Africa. Ingredients were transformed in Oman: East African coconut milk was dehydrated, Malaysian fresh limes blanched and dried in the sun, and local fresh fish salted and preserved to make perishable goods transport-ready for long caravan journeys into the heart of the Middle East or for maritime expeditions. Preserved ingredients were also incorporated into Omani cuisine with dried limes adding a distinctive, sour-bitter tang to rice dishes, coconut milk powder stirred into curries to cut the fiery edge, and dried dates added to everything from South Asian chapati bread to lime-date juice. Beyond these foods born out of utilitarian adaptation, a menagerie of international ingredients brought in aboard trade ships became staples of the Omani pantry. The origins of each seasoning paint a vibrant picture of Oman's adventurous maritime heritage.

Much of the history of the Indian Ocean spice trade is hazy, thanks to the fantastic stories traders invented to protect the sources of their precious goods and perhaps to drive up the prices, like with cinnamon and cassia. Used throughout the East, cassia, from the Moluccas Islands (Indonesia), is a more subtly flavored relative of the "true cinnamon" that came from Ceylon (Sri Lanka). In the 440 BC *Histories*, Herodotus recounted stories the Arab traders told of the way they sourced the fragrant bark, which they claimed was used by giant birds to build their nests. When traders offered the fowl heavy chunks of meat, the greedy bird would bring the treat back to its roost, but being too heavy, the nest would break, sending the cassia branches tumbling down to earth where the traders could collect them. In actuality, the bark was taken from Southern China and Indonesia to be sold and transported north from the so-called "cinnamon country" that stretched along the East African coast from Zanzibar to Madagascar.

Cloves have had perhaps the most dramatic place in Omani-Zanzibari history. As one story goes, an Omani Arab, Harameli bin Saleh, was banished from Zanzibar after he committed a murder. Sailing through the Indian Ocean, he ended up in the Dutch-controlled Moluccas Islands, and risked his life smuggling out a live clove plant to offer as a form of atonement. He returned to Zanzibar with it in 1818, and the sultan granted him a pardon and issued a decree that required all Zanzibari landholders to grow cloves and made removing live plants from Zanzibar punishable by death, an edict that stood until 1972. This broke the Dutch monopoly on the wildly popular spice, which was used the world over for medicinal purposes and as a flavoring agent, and it became one of Oman's most important exports from the island.

Coconuts, on the other hand, came from the island's indigenous coconut palm groves and groves of the shorter dwarf palms that were brought to Zanzibar from the Tamil region of India by Omani Arabs in the mid 1800s. They are used extensively in the cuisine of the Swahili and Arab Zanzibaris, but the island's coconuts were not exported in any significant quantity. Most of the coconut groves of Oman are concentrated on small plots in the southern Dhofar region, where the flesh and milk of the fresh fruits are regularly used in sweet and savory preparations, like Dhofari Coconut-Eggplant Chutney (page 241). But in the rest of Oman, it is most common to this day to find nonperishable, less expensive coconut milk powder, produced mostly in South and Southeast Asia, on Omani shelves.

Another nonperishable staple, black limes, were initially imported *Citrus aurantifolia*, or "true limes," from Malaysia, introduced to Oman in the Middle Ages through Muscat, where merchants shrewdly began drying the perishable fruit to preserve them

for up to two years. In the process they created a new ingredient: black limes or *limoo Omani* (see page 4). The whole dried limes were simmered in stews and soups; the gummy, black flesh added to rice dishes; and ground black lime powder sprinkled on dishes to impart a distinctive tangy, dry-earthy flavor, which gained popularity along Oman's maritime spice route, especially in Iran and the Iraqi port of Basra.

Spices and ingredients that originated in the Middle and Near East—cumin, coriander, saffron, rose water—share space in the Omani cupboard with spices from distant lands like the Far East. Ginger, for example, was brought on junks from China; nutmeg and cassia from Indonesia; and sesame and cinnamon from Ceylon, and from the other side of the globe,

New World hot chile peppers seem to have come to Oman by many routes: Scotch bonnets from Africa, bird's eye and round peppers from India, and bell peppers and various hot peppers with the Portuguese during their brutal 17th century reign.

Perhaps the most significant sources of key Omani ingredients, both historically and in contemporary times, are India and Pakistan, just across the Gulf. Black pepper and cardamom largely come from the Malabar Coast (though cardamom was introduced to the Middle East in 7000 BC, so this ingredient also could have originally been traded in Oman via overland caravans from Iraq), coconut and coconut milk powder from the southern coast of India, and basmati rice, a staple without which Omani cuisine

would be unimaginable, comes from northern India and Pakistan.

Another essential Omani staple, Arabic coffee, was introduced to the Middle East in the early 1500s from Ethiopia via Yemen, where much of the coffee consumed in the Gulf was then grown. Typically sold green or as a lighter roast than in the Levant, Arabic coffee traditionally has cardamom added to the beans before grinding.

Other signature Omani ingredients are home-grown, like tamarind from the southern Dhofar region, Damascus roses from Jabal Akhdar that are distilled into smoky rose water, and *ghar*, a mild, local bay leaf, though most of what is grown and produced in Oman is of too small a quantity to export and is

supplemented with imports from Iran and India. A few major exceptions to this are the fish (grouper and tuna) and huge, succulent prawns that are prized throughout the region. Famously, since the time of the Queen of Sheba, and of the greatest significance historically, dried dates were exported from the northern regions and frankincense, the sweet-smelling sap of the Boswellia tree, was traded from the groves in the south.

Mysteriously, there is one spice that didn't really seem to take hold in the Sultanate except in the ancient *dhow* (Arab trading ships) building port town of Sur. Licorice-flavored fennel, originally a Mediterranean crop, was disseminated through the Saharan spice routes of Africa and was perhaps introduced exclusively to Sur, where it is crushed and added to breads and rice dishes, from Zanzibar, which is directly connected to the Omani port town by the summer and winter monsoon trade routes, though no one seems to know for sure how the spice arrived in Oman, and why its use never spread throughout the Sultanate, like so many other exotic ingredients. The complex, global history of the Omani pantry is reflective of the Omani heritage of exploration and engagement with the world, a heritage that comes through in both the culture and the cuisine.

ANCIENT FUSIONS: MUSCAT'S FOOD SCENE

Forty years ago, Oman was a very different place, without many of the modern amenities and infrastructure that are in place today. Women spent much of their time cooking for their families, spending hours stirring pots of *harees* or preparing rice and meat dishes, but with modernization and new oil wealth came waves of immigrant workers ready to take low-paying jobs in construction and domestic labor. Today, most young Omani women in urban areas like the capital, Muscat, spend their time pursuing higher education and building careers, and most have little interest in spending time in the kitchen. Many of their mothers learned Omani recipes from their grandmothers, but there are perhaps even more who didn't, instead employing cooks to take over the laborious task of daily cooking.

This led to an interesting phenomenon of cook-trading, in which the Indonesian, South Asian, and Filipino household cooks are taught a few recipes, and if a family likes a dish they are served at another house, they send their cook to learn that recipe from the other household's cook.

Many new Omani brides, suddenly put in the position to cook for their new families because they are between housemaids or because they want to give it a go on their own, don't know where to begin. So, in 2007 Fawziya Ali Khalifa Al Maskiry, who moved to Muscat from Zanzibar in the early 1970s, decided to write a basic cookery book for Omanis based on her years of experience feeding her own family. Self-published in English and then translated into Arabic, her book, *A Taste to Remember*, offers instructions for cooking many of her family favorites, from Zanzibari grilled fish in coconut sauce to garlic cheese bread and pizza. In almost every Muscati kitchen Dawn and I visited, the women had a well-worn copy of her book.

Lamees Abdullah Al Taie also saw the need to chronicle the cooking of her homeland so that historic regional dishes would not be lost as modernization changed Omani tastes and habits. She spent years compiling recipes from throughout the country, from obscure recipes for tripe and pluck with vinegar from the northern province of Musandam to every imaginable variation of classics like Omani coffee and *aseeda*, and her work was published locally as *Al-Azaf: The Omani Cookbook* by Oman Bookshop LLC in 1995, in honor of the twenty-fifth anniversary of the reign of Sultan Qaboos. These passion projects are the only English-language texts in existence about the cuisine of Oman, and they are vital resources for young Omanis who are returning to kitchens with renewed interest in their national cuisine.

The National Hospitality Institute in the Ruwi neighborhood of Muscat is training the next

generation of Oman's professional cooks, and one of the NHI alums, Issa Al Lamki, went on to become the most prominent Omani chef in the region. After his training in international cooking, he spent years working in luxury hotels owned by the Saudi royal family before deciding to return to Oman. He realized that his own culinary heritage was in danger of being lost, so he set out on a mission to preserve and elevate the food of Oman. He went door to door in the old neighborhood of Mutrah, asking the elderly women there if they would be willing to teach him to cook classic Omani food. Many doors slammed in his face, but even more were opened, and he was invited back to cook.

He began teaching Omanis to cook both international and Omani dishes on his Ramadan cooking program on Oman TV, and in 2009 he went on to open a fine-dining restaurant with restaurateur Ghada Al Yousuf, called Ubhar, which specialized in Omani fusion cuisine. He put creative twists on classic dishes like *paplou* seafood soup, using prawn dumplings in place of tuna, and developed entirely new creations, like chewy, fragrant frankincense ice cream. He left Ubhar and in 2013 opened Al

Mandoos, a casual restaurant that serves authentic Omani cuisine that he prepared using the techniques from his continental cooking background, like adding mirepoix to sautéed dishes or adding fresh mango and herbs to *qasha*, dried fish, for a fresh, modern Omani salad. Tireless in his mission to elevate and promote the foods of his country, he sold his restaurant in 2014 to pursue the possibility of opening the first Omani restaurant outside Oman.

Other chefs have begun to follow Lamki's lead in Muscat. Many new Omani restaurants have opened over the past five years, from the Omani fine-dining restaurant Al Angham, housed in the exclusive and opulent Royal Opera House, to everyday Omani food joints. For years the Bin Atiq restaurants in Muscat, Nizwa, and Salalah have been serving cheap Omani fare to the many Omani men from the interior regions who came to Muscat to find work during the week and returned to their family homes on the weekends. However, a new crop of Omani entrepreneurs have begun to specialize in high-quality, moderately-priced Omani takeout and catering for the many parties, events, and weddings that are held throughout the capital. One such pair of entrepreneurs, Adnan Al Balushi and Souad Al Jabriya Aghsan Al Barakah, are an unusual Omani couple in that they are also business partners. They decided to expand their home catering business into a takeout shop in 2013, and less than a year later, they expanded to include Aghsan Al Barakah Omani Foods restaurant in the suburb of Mabellah. They serve specialties from around the country, like Muscati *Madrouba Malleh* (page 54), a fish and rice porridge, and *Kalia Kabuli* (page 78), a fried beef and rice specialty from Dhofar.

These new Omani restaurants are an interesting addition to the vast international dining scene that food-centric Omanis already enjoyed in the capital city. In 2006, Riyadh Al Balushi began "Omani Cuisine," the first comprehensive review blog in the city, in which he reviews and profiles restaurants from the authentic Japanese sushi house tucked away in the Al Falaj hotel in Ruwi to the immensely popular Slider Station in the posh Qurum neighborhood.

Interest in both Omani and international dining continues to grow among the young professional generation, with many young women launching home-based baking businesses or stand-alone shops, like the Al Khusaibi sisters, who kept their day jobs but opened their own European-style café, K's Cafe, as a passion project for a year. The chef of the family, Samar Al Khusaibi, plans to open another bakery when she retires from her position at the bank, but in

the meantime, she continues to take special orders for her luscious desserts, like the walnut-filled Date Cake (page 207) she shared with us.

The Omani appetite is part of the cultural heritage of the Sultanate, from the desire for the flavors of the world that drove adventurous traders to take to the sea in their *dhows* to the traditional home cooking techniques developed long before the comforts and wealth of oil money by women who innovatively found ways to make basics like rice and dried fish into feasts that could satiate a crowd. Despite the proliferation of international dining, from fantastic Turkish and South Asian restaurants to fusion cuisines, the growing interest of Omani youth in the traditional foods of their homeland echoes the internal compasses of their ancestors, who knew how to take the best the world had to offer while never forgetting their way home.

THE OMANI PANTRY: FROM MUSCAT TO NEW YORK

When I finally came to stay in an apartment in Oman, after many trips living in hotels and guesthouses, it was time to stock my own pantry, but before Dawn and I could make our first trip to LuLu Hypermarket, friends arrived with some of what they considered to be the essentials: basmati rice, ground Arabic coffee, dried dates, a bag of dried black limes, and dried spice blends. Dawn and I headed to the store later to pick up bags of red onions and garlic, canned tuna, fresh chicken, and a few condiments to have on hand.

Our Omani pantry back in America had come to look like a well-stocked suburban supermarket, with nothing too exotic or difficult to find on our shelves aside from dried limes and coconut powder. This section is a guide to Omani pantry staples, from what they are to where to look for them while shopping. In the States, we make our own condiments, from Spicy Mayo (page 239) to Omani Mango Chutney (page 242) to jars of ghee, or clarified butter (page 243), since there is no LuLu in Brooklyn for us to purchase them from. We've even taken to having some limes drying out in our fruit bowls. If you want to try and make your own basics, see chapter 11.

CHAPTER 1

IDENTIFYING, PURCHASING, AND SUBSTITUTING INGREDIENTS

Past the rows of South Asian hawkers selling pashmina scarves, incense, and "I Love Oman" T-shirts along the main corridor of the Mutrah souk; past the little coffee stand at the rear entrance selling fried snacks, milky tea, fresh orange juice, and cups of bright pink strawberry milk; just up an unassuming side street from the iconic, blue-domed Shia mosque, the old spice grinders of Muscat still practice their craft. They sit in plastic chairs in front of their bins of whole spices and coffee beans, surrounded by bags of dried limes and Zanzibari cloves, and when a customer arrives, asking for just the right blend for chicken *kabuli* or grilled fish, the old men will take handfuls of the spices inside their shop for a quick turn in the roaster before grinding them and pouring the custom blend into an old jar that might have once held processed cheese spread or Indian pickles. Likewise, coffee might be ordered: light, medium, or dark roasted, ground with or without whole cardamom pods. They sell prepackaged bags of Omani masala blend made with whole sticks of cinnamon bark, bright red round chiles, cumin seeds, cardamom, and dried fingers of ginger.

Though many of the spices are familiar, the sheer variety on offer can be overwhelming. This chapter is a guide to the spices and ingredients that make up the Omani pantry, from a visual glossary to tips on where to look for some of the more unusual ingredients, along with a section on substitutions. Omani cuisine was built on exploration and adaptation, so I hope you will embrace a sense of adventure and curiosity as you stock your own pantry and explore the recipes for which these spices are so essential.

VISUAL INGREDIENT GLOSSARY

Arabic Coffee (Kahwa) Green coffee beans are often purchased and roasted to order at rotisseries or at home, sometimes with whole cardamom added before grinding. The resulting brew is light in color, with flavor ranging from delicate to intensely bitter. It is served from a coffeepot with a long, curved spout called a *dallah*, to which rose water or saffron might be added. It is poured into small, handleless cups called *fenjan* and it is customary to only fill them part of the way, so that the coffee remains hot and the host can continue to refill the guests' glasses as an act of hospitality. Served without sugar or milk, this style of coffee is a perfect accompaniment to dried dates or the Omani sweet *Halwa* (page 210). We call for Arabic coffee, found at Middle Eastern or Indian markets, which has a finer grind, akin to espresso.

Bay Leaf (Ghar) Grown wild, bay leaf takes on different flavors depending on where it is found in the world. In Oman the "tree leaf" is called *ghar*, and it is smaller with a slightly subtler flavor than the bay leaves found in the United States.

Black Limes (Limoo Omani) Known as black limes, these whole dried limes are more commonly light brown in color and may also be sold as Persian dried limes or *limoo Omani*. The color makes little difference in flavor; the main things to look for are limes that are completely dry with no soft spots and that sound a bit hollow when tapped. Once broken open, they should be free of mold and should not be hollow, but have gummy or slightly papery flesh. This distinctive ingredient lends a unique, subtle tartness and musky, almost fermented tang to dishes. Historically made by blanching "true limes" from Malaysia in saltwater and laying them out to sun-dry, this

Omani ingredient keeps for up to two years. There are a few ways to use them:

Whole. Whole lime can be tossed in a pot to add a slightly bitter-tartness, but be sure to scrub your limes well before adding.

Whole Pierced. After washing and soaking briefly to soften the skin, a single hole can be poked into the lime to allow more of the bitterness from the seeds and sour flavor of the flesh to seep into a dish.

Broken or Halved. Halving the limes and, in some instances, removing the bitter seeds allows the flavor of sweet-tart flesh and skin to be fully released.

Flesh Only. After breaking the lime with something blunt and cutting it in half, the gummy black flesh can be removed (the dry skin and seeds discarded) and added to dishes like Tuna *Kabuli* (page 77), where it will melt into the dish.

Ground. The entire lime can be ground in a spice grinder for a black powder that adds a deeply layered citric flavor to soups, stews, and our Omani-style potato chip seasoning (page 158).

Black Peppercorns (Filfil Aswad) One of the oldest spices traded from the Malabar Coast of southern India, a touch of ground black pepper finds its way into almost all savory Omani dishes.

Cardamom (Heel) Native to the Western Ghats of southern India, cardamom was introduced to the Middle East via Babylon as early as 7000 BC, so it could have come to Oman from either Basra or Gujarat. No matter its origin, the fact is, Omani cuisine would be sorely lacking without this spice, which is thrown whole into *kabuli*; ground and added to coffee, breads, and desserts; and simmered in sweet milk with black tea for a signature breakfast drink (page 223).

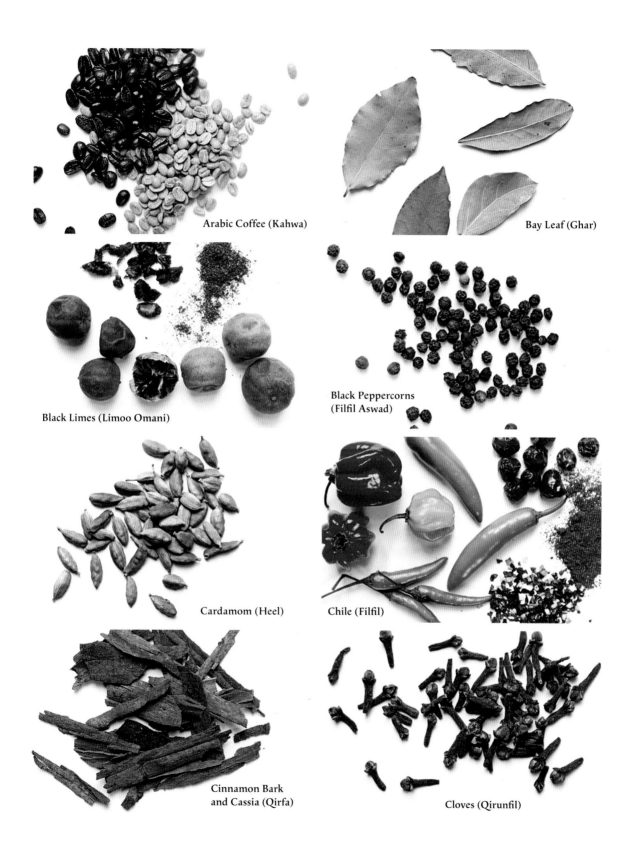

Arabic Coffee (Kahwa)

Bay Leaf (Ghar)

Black Limes (Limoo Omani)

Black Peppercorns
(Filfil Aswad)

Cardamom (Heel)

Chile (Filfil)

Cinnamon Bark
and Cassia (Qirfa)

Cloves (Qirunfil)

Chile (Filfil) The huge importance of chiles in this relatively mild cuisine is one of the things that distinguish Omani food from other Middle Eastern fare. These New World ingredients came to Oman by way of Africa, India, and with the Portuguese. Long, fiery bird's eye chiles were introduced by Indian traders and are almost always found on the vegetable plate that accompanies a meal for those who want to add a kick. Scotch bonnets were brought back from Zanzibar and are simmered whole in creamy coconut milk–laced beans and removed before they split, so as to add their aroma but not their heat. Dried red chili powder or red pepper flakes are added to nearly every spice blend, and dried whole, round red peppers are simmered with chickpeas for the simple breakfast food *Dango* (page 134). The amount of chile used, and whether or not they are split, seeded, or removed after cooking, depends entirely on the tastes of the family or the cook. Some Omanis love chile-rich dishes with a fair amount of piquant heat, while others prefer more subtle flavors and associate hot chile flavor exclusively with Indian food. Whether used for mild or fiery flavor, chiles remain a universally important ingredient in the Sultanate.

Cinnamon Bark and Cassia (Qirfa) Cinnamon and its more subtly flavored cousin, cassia, came to Oman via Zanzibar, where winter monsoon winds allowed traders to make the trek to Sri Lanka, China, and Indonesia, where they are historically grown. The sweet, spicy, woodsy flavors lend warmth to meat marinades and desserts alike.

Cloves (Qirunfil) Introduced to Zanzibar from the Moluccas Islands in 1818, this intense, earthy, bittersweet spice flourished and became one of Zanzibar's most important exports. Both ground and whole cloves feature prominently in Omani spice blends, and its exotic sweet-hot flavor is more pronounced in Omani cooking than in other Middle Eastern fare.

Coconut Milk Powder Unlike flaky desiccated coconut, coconut milk powder is a rich, malty powder made from dehydrated coconut milk that can be rehydrated using varying ratios of water to add richer or more subtle coconut flavor to curries, stewed vegetables, and breads. It is also toasted before being rehydrated for some preparations.

Coriander (Kuzbara) A native ingredient to the Middle East, in Oman toasted whole or ground coriander seed adds a distinctive savory, nutty, orange essence to meat and rice dishes, vegetables, and *maraks*. Though used much less frequently than the seeds, the fresh leaves, known as cilantro in the United States, are also called *kuzbara*, and are sometimes used to add a fresh finish to dishes like rich *Shorbat Harees* (page 63) soup.

Cumin Seed (Kamoon) Cumin, the most widely used spice on earth, was in use in the Near East even before the rise of Egyptian and Mesopotamian civilizations. It was introduced to the subcontinent by early Arab traders and to the West by North African Berber seamen. Adding a savory earthiness and a subtle bittersweet finish to dishes, it is a vital component of all Omani spice blends.

Dates (Tamr) Dates have long been one of Oman's main culinary exports. They are eaten fresh and dried out of hand, soaked and squeezed into juices, or added to bread dough for a subtle molasses-like richness. Sometimes they are reduced to make thick, luscious date syrup that can be drizzled over delicate Omani crêpes called *Khubz Mahallah* (page 181).

Fennel (Shumar) This anise-flavored Mediterranean spice isn't used in much of Oman, but in the port town of Sur it is crushed and added to breads like *Muraduf* (page 187) and to rice dishes.

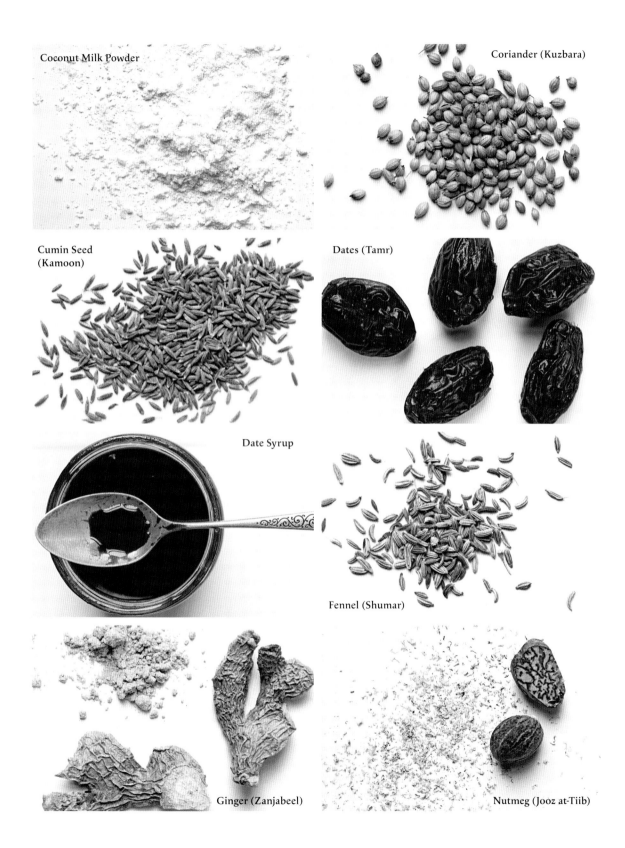

Coconut Milk Powder

Coriander (Kuzbara)

Cumin Seed
(Kamoon)

Dates (Tamr)

Date Syrup

Fennel (Shumar)

Ginger (Zanjabeel)

Nutmeg (Jooz at-Tiib)

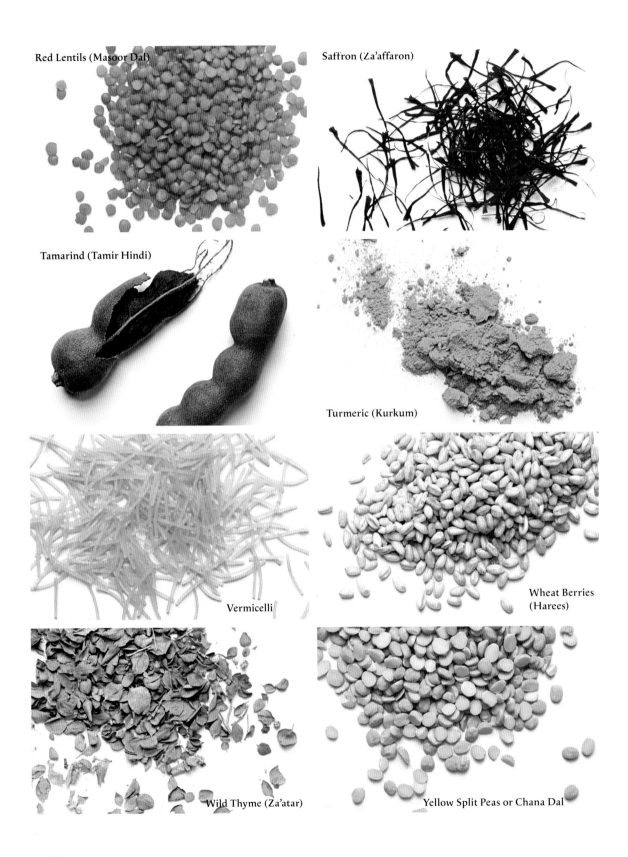

Red Lentils (Masoor Dal)

Saffron (Za'affaron)

Tamarind (Tamir Hindi)

Turmeric (Kurkum)

Vermicelli

Wheat Berries (Harees)

Wild Thyme (Za'atar)

Yellow Split Peas or Chana Dal

Ginger (Zanjabeel) Dried ginger can be found in whole fingers in masala blends in Oman but is most often used in ground form, adding a background note of sweet-hot bite to spice blends. Fresh ginger is simmered in water to make a restorative tea and is minced and added to marinades.

Nutmeg (Jooz at-Tiib) Native to the Moluccas Islands, nutmeg is one of the warming spice elements of the Omani *baharat*, or spice blend, used in many savory meat and rice dishes, like the peppery, pan-fried beef and rice specialty *Kalia Kabuli* (page 78).

Red Lentils (Masoor Dal) Small red lentils cook quickly and add a nutty heft to simple basmati rice and make a great base for cardamom-spiced Omani *Marak Dal* (page 126). Though they look red or orange, they become a light beige color when cooked.

Rice (Arooz) Basmati, grown only in northern India and Pakistan, is the rice of choice for most Omani dishes, from intricately spiced Zanzibari Biryani (page 88) to simple steamed rice with red lentils (page 70), and it is a staple that is eaten daily by most Omanis. The fragrant grains must be rinsed to remove excess starch so that the grains stay separate and tender after being cooked.

Rose Water (Maa' al Urid) Traditional rose water is imported and used to finish biryanis, the dumpling-like mash *Aseeda* (page 56), and the signature Omani dessert *Halwa* (page 210), and it is even added to Omani coffee. The Damascus roses that grow in the mountains of Jabal Akhdar are distilled into a smoky rose water that is used locally for both cooking and as a beauty product.

Saffron (Za'affaron) Saffron of varying quality, from fine Persian tins to bottles of the stuff from Spain sold inexpensively at the Mutrah souk, always finds a way into the Omani cupboard. It is added to some rice dishes for the distinctive rust orange color and earthy flavor, as it is in Persia and South Asia, and it's also used to flavor creamy *karak* tea (page 219) and the traditional Omani sweets made of sugar and ghee called *Halwa* (page 210).

Tamarind (Tamir Hindi) Literally called "Indian dates" in Arabic, tamarind pods contain seeds covered in a tangy paste that, when soaked and mashed, can be added to sauces and marinades for a fruity, earthy tartness that can take the place of vinegar in some cases.

Turmeric (Kurkum) A staple of the South Asian pantry, this savory spice comes from a rhizome. In whole form it looks a like a smaller, darker version of ginger, but once cut open and dried, the brilliant orange flesh becomes a bright yellow dried powder. It adds an unmistakable yellow-orange hue and slight bitterness to dishes and is a key ingredient in Omani seafood spice blends.

Vermicelli These noodles, which we refer to as the Middle Eastern variety, are sold as bags of short, broken pieces of thin noodles. Found in Middle Eastern and South Asian markets, they are used in soups, toasted with sugar for signature desserts like sweet and salty *Balaleet* (page 197), or simmered in rose water and milk for *Saweeya* (page 205). Most Italian angel hair pasta does not work in these recipes; Goya brand broken angel hair pasta is the best substitute we have found.

Wheat Berries (Harees) White wheat berries are cooked down with meat or poultry and then mashed for the traditional savory porridge of the same name, or tossed into soups to absorb the rich flavor of the broth and add pleasant pops of texture. It is important to use pearled, as the unpearled, with the husk still on, will never become soft enough to break down. Also go for the white variety, rather than the red, which doesn't have as much starch and will behave differently.

Wild Thyme (Za'atar) The wild thyme that grows in the Middle East has larger leaves and a more floral fragrance than the thyme found in the West, and it makes a wonderful addition to sweet *karak* teas.

Yellow Split Peas or Chana Dal Though they look nearly identical, split yellow peas are different from *chana dal*, which are actually made from hulled black chickpeas and have a slightly firmer texture. Either will work in our recipes, and though *chana dal* is used more frequently in Oman, yellow split peas are much easier to find in the West and work great for recipes like Chicken *Kabuli* (page 71).

SHOPPING GUIDE: WHERE TO FIND SPECIALTY INGREDIENTS

When looking for some of the harder-to-find ingredients in this book, you can always order online (Amazon carries both black limes and coconut milk powder), but there are likely places in your area that have them as well, and I've always found hunting for spices to be a fun adventure. Coconut milk powder can typically be found at Caribbean markets and some Southeast Asian markets. Black limes, also called Omani limes, *limoo Omani*, Basra limes, Persian dried limes, and dried lime, can be found at many Middle Eastern and Persian shops. Tamarind and ghee can usually be found at Whole Foods and are available in any Indian market. Nice plump dates like the ones found in the Middle East can sometimes be found at Whole Foods as well, but are also likely available at co-ops, natural food stores, or Middle Eastern shops. Super-ripe sweet plantains that have turned black can be found occasionally at Whole Foods, but they usually are not ripe, so you can buy them and keep them in a paper bag until they blacken; otherwise look for them at African, Caribbean, or Latin markets. Better za'atar, with larger, more fragrant leaves, can be found in specialty spice shops and Middle Eastern markets. Hibiscus, also known as Jamaica or sorrel, is available at Mexican, Caribbean, and Asian supermarkets. While basmati rice is now available at almost all supermarkets, you can usually find better quality at a better price at Middle Eastern and Indian shops.

"AS YOU LIKE":
NOTES ON SUBSTITUTIONS

In every kitchen we entered in Oman, I asked the home cooks about the "right" combination of ingredients. In the kitchen of the Buraimi Women's Association, on the Oman–United Arab Emirates border, I watched Noorah add a handful of dried spices into a sizzling pot of oil and caramelizing onions for chicken *kabuli*. I asked her what spices they used in *kabuli* in Buraimi. "As you like," she replied.

"Yes, but what do *you* like to use?" I pressed.

She paused, then began listing spices: "*Qirfa, kamoon, filfil aswad. . . .*"

I nodded, scribbling down notes. Remembering another version I'd eaten in the desert, I asked, "What about *qirunfil*? Do you use cloves here?"

"As you like! Some people, they like it, so they add. Some people want more spicy, so more *filfil*. To your taste. As you like."

Farther south, in our friend Thuraya's Muscati kitchen, her cook, Shaymeena, had forgotten to buy ghee. She thought for a minute, then shrugged and reached for a bottle of vegetable oil and got back to her chapati. Again and again, in kitchens throughout the Sultanate, Dawn and I came to understand the general Omani sense of adaptability and flexibility. So, don't let a missing spice or a hard-to-find item or a particular flavor you don't like stop you from trying a dish. If you can't find coconut milk powder, then use coconut cream, or coconut milk if you can't find that. Meat dishes in Oman typically call for *lahm*, which literally translates to "meat," demonstrating the general interchangeability of lamb, beef, and goat (even camel, especially in the Dhofar province). If you don't care for lamb, use beef in the lamb dishes. The spicing of Omani food is generally mild; that said, if you are particularly sensitive to chili powder or peppers, leave them out, or add more if you love heat. These recipes are guides, a starting point to a highly individualized cuisine, so follow the methods carefully, as some of the long cooking times or counterintuitive steps are essential for the magic of these flavors coming together. But when it comes to the seasoning and ingredients, read these suggestions, then do "as you like."

Suggested Substitutions:

Black Lime: There is nothing like this spice! I have included a recipe for making your own in the pantry section (page 236), and though you can still make the dishes that call for black lime without, it really does add a distinctive tart earthiness that is inimitable and well worth a trip to your local Middle Eastern market or placing an online order (see Shopping Guide, page 11). Otherwise, just add a squeeze of fresh lime or some lime zest to the dish.

Coconut Milk Powder: Use the same liquid amount of coconut milk, or the same amount of coconut cream, as the liquid called for in the coconut powder–water slurry. The powder has an extra layer of intense coconut-y, malty richness, so you may want to add a touch more coconut cream/milk to finish your dish.

Ghee: Ghee, or clarified butter, lends a distinctively rich flavor to many dishes and is relatively simple to make (see page 243). It is available at Indian markets and many grocers like Whole Foods or Trader Joe's, but if you start a dish and find yourself in need of a cooking fat, you can substitute butter, especially in porridge recipes, like the mashed chicken and rice dish *Arseeyah* (page 47), and you can use a neutral-flavored oil

like vegetable, canola, or corn for many of the pan-fried breads, like Date Chapati (page 169). Just steer clear of margarine or flavorful oils like olive or peanut.

Fish: When a firm-fleshed fish, like swordfish, tuna, or kingfish, is called for, any of these can be used interchangeably. In general, only saltwater fish, not freshwater fish, are used, the most popular of which are tuna, hamour, and shari, the latter two members of the sea bream or grouper family. We use tuna in the recipes in which it is called for, and for all others we typically use red snapper, branzino, porgy, or sea bass. For saltfish, salt cod or salt pollock can be used, but using the highest-quality saltfish (only marginally more expensive) makes for an even tastier dish. Shark is shark, and we found no substitute for it in *Rabees* (page 110).

Lamb/Beef: They can be used interchangeably, but even the most avid lamb haters in our recipe-testing crew were won over by the lamb dishes in this book, whose spicing and preparation methods remove any hint of gaminess.

OMANI MEALS:
FRIENDS, FAMILY,
AND SACRED SPACES

In Oman, life moves at a different pace and on a different schedule than in the West. In much of the Gulf, days have historically revolved around the elements, which meant avoiding the harsh afternoon heat. Workdays in cities like Muscat reflect that ancient habit, with government and many private offices opening around 7:30 a.m. and closing around 3:30 p.m. Souks and small shops open early, close in the afternoons, and reopen from around 4:00 p.m. until 10:00 p.m. or so.

Meals are likewise taken at different times than in the West, with early morning breakfast often consisting of no more than strong Omani coffee scented with cardamom and rose water and a few plump dried dates, a snack that continues to be consumed throughout the day. Lunch, *al gha'ada*, is the main meal of the day, and many families still gather for the meal in the late afternoon when work lets out, and with extended family at one of the elder family members' homes on Fridays after the Salat Al Jummah prayers. Whether dining at home with family around a huge platter of *kabuli*, eating biryani out with friends, or getting *mendi* takeout, for most Omanis, it wouldn't be a proper lunch without rice.

There are some exceptions, of course; lunch will occasionally include an Omani curry called *marak* served with Zanzibari polenta called *ugali* or alongside rice or bread.

While rice forms the heart of Omani cuisine, there is an entire canon of dishes that were introduced by the diverse ethnic groups of the Sultanate that can be eaten with bread or another starch at lunch or dinner. Zanzibari Omanis, who trace their lineage to East Africa, brought coconut-rich dishes to Oman, like spinach simmered in coconut milk (page 129) and whole baked fish in coconut sauce (page 104), which might be served with fresh Chapati (page 174). Lawatis, who trace their ancestry to a community of traders in Muscat, Persia, South Asia, and Iraq, and Balushi families, whose ancestors hailed from South Asia, both lay claim to the popular Omani dish *Paplou* (page 107), a bright turmeric seafood soup that can be served on its own or with a scoop of basmati rice.

Dinner is taken late, sometimes 9 p.m. or later, and will sometimes consist of light, sweet dishes that are also consumed at breakfast, like Crêpes with Date Syrup (page 181) or Sweet Vermicelli with Eggs (page 197). Otherwise, sandwiches and a salad or Western-style casseroles might be served, but rice is generally not eaten for the evening meal.

During celebrations (see page 40), from wedding parties to Eid al Fitr, which marks the end of Ramadan, and Eid al Adha, celebrating the end of the Hajj, the centerpiece of the feast is often *shuwa*, one of the most beloved dishes in the Sultanate, made with lamb, beef, or goat slathered in oil and spices, wrapped in banana or date palm leaves, and placed over hot embers in an underground pit for a day until it becomes meltingly tender. It is considered by many to be Oman's most famous dish. For more casual celebrations or gatherings, grilling out is a favorite way to entertain, from Muscati beachside barbecues to *madhbi*, a specialty of Southern Oman, for which smooth river rocks are fashioned into a blazing hot cooking surface to char everything from camel to chicken.

Savory porridges made with wheat berries or mashed rice are particular to the Gulf region and are considered quintessential comfort foods, not to mention staples during the holy month of Ramadan when nothing is consumed between sunrise and sundown. Each evening the fast is broken with an *iftar* dinner and just before sunrise the *sahoor* meal is the last (or first) meal taken before the day of fasting begins at sunrise. These late suppers and early breakfasts make for an extreme change in dining routine for those used to having their main meal in the daytime.

The importance of food in Oman cannot be overstated. Omanis take great pleasure in eating and sharing meals, and dining is not seen as a solitary experience, but a daily celebration and reinforcement of relationships.

LADIES WHO LUNCH

One afternoon, Dawn and I drove north from Muscat along the seaside corniche to the Seeb neighborhood to visit with our friend Thuraya, the niece of the last Sultan of Zanzibar. Her housemaid let us in, and we settled into plush, embroidered couches in her sitting area and soon were joined by a group of stylish young women, one dressed in jeans and a sequined jacket that matched her loose gold scarf, another in an abaya, her thick black bangs peeking out from a crystal-hemmed *sheila* scarf, and three Lebanese girls, with their thicker scarves, luxurious swaths of colorful fabric, wrapped like elaborate updos on their heads. We greeted with kisses all around. Then Thuraya herself came in. Her long black hair was flowing down her shoulders and she was dressed simply in a pair of skinny jeans and a cardigan with a few gold bracelets and rings.

We caught up for a few minutes and then it was time for lunch. Shaymeena, the longtime family cook, came in and we waved at each other as she began arranging platter after platter on the table and sideboard. Dawn and I had spent many mornings in the kitchen with her, learning dishes like Zanzibari Biryani (page 88), *Arseeyah* (page 47), and sweet Fried *Mandazi* bread (page 172). I was starving, but I wondered if these perfectly coiffed ladies would just nibble daintily.

"Felicia! You must eat everything," Thuraya said. "Come."

I followed her to the side table and she added fried *kachori*, *misanif*, and *sambusa* and some stuffed grape leaves to my plate. I took a seat at the table and she appeared over my shoulder, putting a scoop of a creamy spinach, chicken, and potato casserole on my plate.

"Shaymeena makes this so nicely. We love it for dinner," she said.

The other ladies added snacks to their plates and sat down. A yogurt-topped fatoush salad was passed, and we all got quiet as we focused on the food in front of us. Thuraya suddenly jumped up and walked over to the other two Omani women, taking a huge scoop of chicken *kabuli* and piling it on one plate and then the other.

"They want to start with rice, it's lunchtime so it has to be rice, but they're being shy," she said with a laugh.

She made another pass around the table, putting fried shrimp on everyone's plates. "I think she is related to my mother," one of the girls joked. "Always with the 'eat more, eat more'!"

I watched as all the women dug in, going back for seconds and thirds. Everyone loves to eat in Oman, even the glamour girls.

"You know, if we were Omani men, I think we could have finished it all," she said, giggling.

In every setting, food is shared and offered and pushed, from men trying to give each other the bigger piece of meat from a platter of *mandi* to wives pushing extra rice toward their husbands and husbands picking a choice morsel for their wife or child. There is a sense in Oman that eating is a shameless pleasure that is meant to be shared. Free from puritanical impulses, Muslims see the earthly pleasures of the table as a gift from Allah and a foreshadowing of the pleasures to come.

With a sizeable dent put in the lunch spread, we all sat back. Thuraya stood, smiling. "So, Arabic coffee and dessert now or later?"

As friendly as people are in Oman, they are also quite private, so being invited to someone's home is a very nice thing. Being invited beyond the *majlis*, or receiving room, is intimate. Entering the kitchens, the inner sanctuaries of the homes of the women in this book, from our beloved friends in Muscat, like Miad Al Balushi and Thuraya Al Said, to the kitchens of friends of friends in the mountain village of Jabal Akhdar and in the coastal city of Sur, to the small kitchen of the Buraimi Women's Association, Dawn and I found ourselves transported to a world of women, filled with lightness, laughter, and relaxed intimacy. In Oman, as in many places in the Arabian Gulf, there are female spaces, male spaces, and family spaces, and these spheres do not often overlap. As American women, we were in the unique position to comfortably pass among them.

I was taken by the vital depth of the relationships in every area of Omani life. Men sit with each other and talk for hours at coffee shops and village *majlis*, or dance together around raging campfires. Women gather in cafés, but more often in their beautiful homes, and for frequent celebrations—weddings, births, engagements—at home or in opulent party halls decorated with flowers and crystal chandeliers, dressed like fairy-tale princesses in shimmering, vibrant dresses. In villages, families of women who don't employ cooks sit around flat *tawa* griddles, searing rounds of thin Omani Bread (page 162) and stirring large pots of *Harees* (page 52) porridge, passing the time with stories and teasing banter.

The place in which the worlds of men and women merge is often around a meal. In many restaurants there are two areas: the main dining room where single men sit and separate family rooms where female or mixed-gender groups have the option of eating privately. Dawn and I came to love these rooms, leaning on pillows on the floor around a plastic tablecloth on which a spread of rice dishes, curries, sauces, and snacks were laid out for all to share. And at home when the family gathers, like at Omani celebrity chef Issa Al Lamki's mother's home, the space echoes with the boisterous energy of brothers, sisters, in-laws, and children who spend the better part of the afternoon or evening together savoring both the food and the opportunity to be together one more time. When I find myself craving Omani cuisine, it is not only the flavors I long for, but also these moments of intimacy and togetherness.

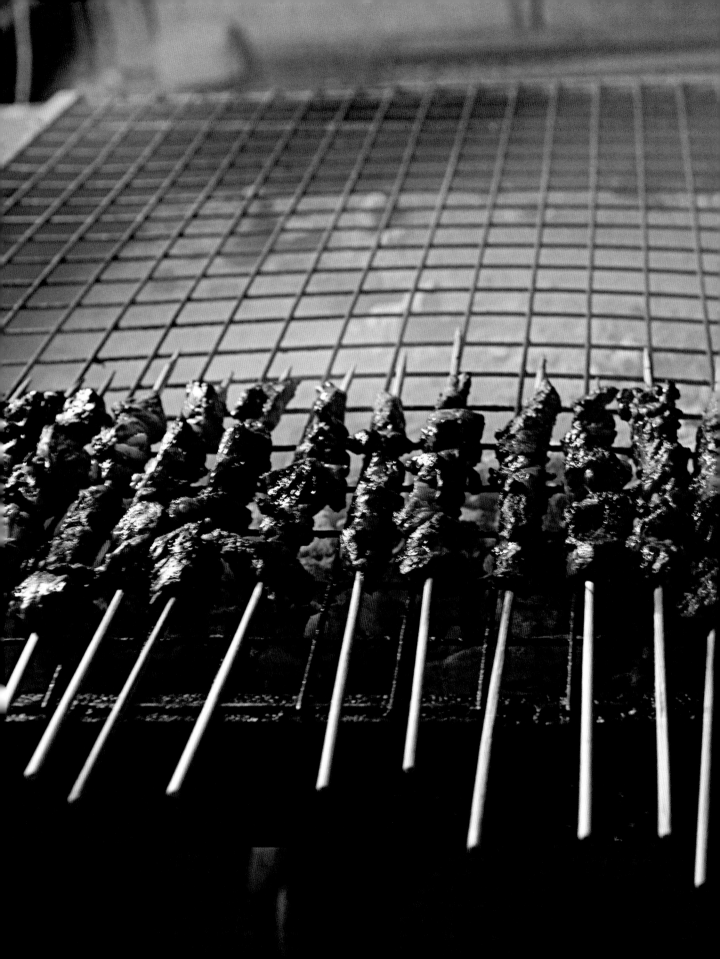

CHAPTER 2

GRILLED, SMOKED, AND CHARRED

Grilling out is an essential pastime throughout Oman, and from luxurious beach parties in which upper-class ladies like Thuraya lounge in rented tents and gossip while hired grill men turn out kebabs and fish to rustic Bedouin meals prepared using only palm fronds and cinder blocks, a kind of casual simplicity is at the heart of this cooking method. The food is served and eaten in rounds as it comes off the fire and there is unbounded flexibility in seasoning, from basic salt and lime to thick, spicy marinades. No matter how the food is prepared, there is always enough of everything to go around twice. The regional methods of cooking and eating outdoors that we learned in Oman transformed the way I cook, both in my kitchen and on the grill.

Every day while we were down south in the Dhofar region, in the former capital city of Salalah, my friends and I would head to the roadside *madhbi* grillers for takeout containers of rice and foil-wrapped whole chicken for lunch or dinner, sometimes both. The Dhofari specialty *madhbi* may be one of the world's simplest ways to cook meat and poultry: Smooth, white river rocks are cleaned and then placed over the hot embers of a fire lit the night before, then

spatchcocked chickens and every imaginable cut of lamb, goat, even camel, are heavily salted and placed directly on the stones to cook.

Tearing richly flavored chicken from the bone, I simply couldn't believe that there were no other seasonings. I pestered the grillers with questions, but they continued to insist it was just salt and the stones from the *wadi* (a dry riverbed) that were responsible for the taste.

Upon returning home, I came to appreciate the near magical cooking property of stone. Through capillary action, porous rock, whether natural pebble from a *wadi* or a manufactured pizza stone, will wick away moisture and allow for perfectly even caramelization and just the right amount of char without a drop of oil. Shockingly, without any seasonings other than salt, this method consistently produces some of the most flavorful chicken I've ever eaten.

In the Wahiba Sands desert in the Sharqiyah region of central Oman, I watched Shanaliza of the Al Wahiba tribe as she cooked. Dressed in a vibrant embroidered frock that looked vaguely Indian and a traditional facemask called a *burqa*, she looked like a bejeweled falcon. She rubbed the cavity and the outside of a whole large fish—scales and fins and all—with coarse salt and placed it directly on a pile of palm fronds on the sand.

A younger woman, Jamilah, paused to wipe her brow with the emerald green sleeve of her dress before bending to light the fronds, piling more leaves on top to cover the fish. The blaze flared as she quietly washed her hands, slowly rose, and made her way back to the nylon canopy of our tent.

I followed her and a gust of wind slapped the orange plastic against me. I crouched under the furiously flapping tarp and watched the skilled hands of the other women as they prepared crisp *khubz ragag* Omani Bread (page 162); *saloonat*, a stew of chicken and vegetables; and a medicinal combination of the *khubz* bread soaked in date syrup and seasoned with black pepper and garlic that is thought to speed a woman's recovery after childbirth. Their makeshift kitchen consisted of little more than pots balanced on cinder blocks. By the time they finished cooking and we made our way to the square palm hut overlooking our makeshift tent kitchen, I had all but forgotten about the fish.

I slipped off my sandals and took a seat on the mat floor. Naheemah poured cups of bitter Omani coffee. Dates were passed. Then, old Shanaliza appeared in the doorway, carrying the blackened fish on a platter. She peeled back the incinerated skin, which had protected the moist, snowy flesh, and poured a simple mixture of lime and onion over the fish along with a sprinkle of coarse salt. She pulled off a flaky piece and passed it to me. Like the *madhbi* chicken, this subtle, fire-licked fish tasted like the most savory version of itself, its delicate sweetness enhanced by the smoke and citrus. Conversation ceased as we sat, picking the fish with our fingers.

Omani grilling, while a casual and forgiving cooking method, is not usually so Spartan when it comes to seasonings. One of the most ubiquitous Omani snacks is grilled *mishkak*—skewers of peppery beef, or sometimes squid or even quail, that are marinated in spices and finished with a tangy tamarind hot sauce. Driving south from the ancient port city of Sohar toward Muscat one night, we swerved off the road to join a group that had gathered around the yellow light of a long burning grill. Two young boys turned skewers of beef, heavy with black peppercorns and cumin and perked up with a thick crushed red pepper and tamarind sauce. Men in traditional white *dishdasha* called out numbers and waited for their requested newspaper-wrapped skewers to come off the grill. Cooked in backyards for *iftar* during Ramadan, served at most every celebration, and on offer at roadside stands like that one throughout the country, *mishkak* are a quintessential staple of Omani barbecue.

Though I enjoyed the simplicity and surprise of all the cookouts we had in Oman, it was on the beaches of Muscat on the northeastern coast where I truly fell in love with Omani grilling.

As night falls over the capital city, caravans of cars pull off the highway onto the sandy beaches. Woven mats are laid out, bonfires are built, and portable propane cooktops are fired up. The rhythmic lapping of waves muffles the happy sounds of the gatherings, and the gentle breeze is redolent with the smell of caramelizing meat.

Late one night on Athaiba beach, I sat in the sand and watched our young Omani friends cook. The light

from the moon reflected off the foil-lined grill where ground lamb and chicken kebabs sizzled alongside charring onions and tomatoes.

When the kebabs were almost done, rounds of pita were placed over them to warm. My friend Ameer, dressed casually in shorts and a polo shirt, sat barefoot on his heels manning the grill. He pulled one of the kebabs off the barbecue with a warm round of pita, slathered it with spicy mayonnaise, and handed it to me. A blackened tomato was cooling on a plate on the woven mat. I looked at the others for a cue as to how to go about eating it with no utensils in sight. Ameer glanced up and came to my rescue, tearing off a piece of the soft, tart fruit with his fingers and handing it to me. I added it, along with a petal of charred sweet onion, to my wrap and took a bite. The pillowy bread gave way to a symphony of sweet vegetables, spicy mayonnaise, and salty, rich meat. Throughout the night, more wraps were made, and the feasting continued until the morning sun began to peak over the mountaintops.

We returned to the beaches for midnight barbecues many times, enjoying other meals, from simple *mishkak* and chopped salad to aluminum pans of fresh fish, prawns, and vegetables steamed directly in the bonfire: Every dish was as special as the last and each leisurely gathering as satisfying as the first.

The casual, celebratory act of grilling mirrors the laid-back, hospitable people behind the flame, always ready to welcome another guest and happy to put together a party at a moment's notice. Take cues from this relaxed approach at your next outdoor gathering. Don't worry about timing everything for a seated meal; eat and serve as you go. Keep it simple. Don't worry about scaling whole fish or elaborately spicing your grilled chicken: Take advantage of the power of fire and stone to transform foods in delicious ways. Adjust the seasonings to suit your tastes and those of your guests, but whatever you do, be sure to make more than you think you'll need; that way you'll never have to turn away an extra guest or leave a plate empty.

BEDU SAMAK MASHWI
(BEDOUIN WHOLE CHARRED FISH)

Kosher salt

1 medium (2 to 3 pounds) whole striped bass or any other mild saltwater fish, cleaned, head and tail on

Juice of 2 limes

Lime wedges, for serving

SERVES 4

This rustic Bedouin method for preparing fish comes from Sheikha, the head of the Sharqiyah region's women's association, Binat al Bedu, and the women of the Al Wahiba tribe. Skip the tedious task of scaling and simply place the entire cleaned fish directly into the embers of your fire to cook. The skin keeps the flesh moist and clean, making this one of the easiest and most forgiving ways to cook whole fish. Peel back the charred skin and enjoy the sweet, snowy white meat tinged with subtle smokiness, enlivened by a final squeeze of lime and sprinkle of salt.

Rub the salt on the outside of the fish and in the cavity.

Prepare your coals in a fire pit or barbecue grill, letting them burn until the flame dies down and the embers are glowing and ashy. Place the fish directly on the hot embers and cook; flip after 15 minutes. Let char 15 minutes more. Alternatively, bury it directly in the hot embers and leave it to cook 25 to 30 minutes, until the fish is cooked through and the skin is completely charred and blackened.

Carefully remove the fish from the embers with long tongs or two spatulas. Let cool slightly and then use a knife to peel off the charred skin. Sprinkle additional salt and lime juice over the flesh, and serve whole with lime wedges, alongside rice or bread.

MISHAKIK
(PEPPERY BEEF SKEWERS WITH SPICY TAMARIND SAUCE)

MARINADE

1 (2½-inch) piece tamarind paste

½ cup boiling water

1 teaspoon ground cumin

½ teaspoon red pepper flakes

½ teaspoon ground black pepper

½ teaspoon ground cardamom

¼ teaspoon ground cinnamon

2 teaspoons kosher salt

1½ pounds beef steak, such as sirloin, flank, or round, cut into 1-inch pieces

SAUCE

½ plum tomato

2 cloves garlic

½ teaspoon kosher salt

½ teaspoon red pepper flakes

⅛ teaspoon ground black pepper

1 teaspoon distilled white vinegar

14 to 16 bamboo skewers, soaked in water 10 minutes

MAKES 14 TO 16 SKEWERS

Simple to make, these smoky beef skewers offer a big flavor payoff thanks to a unique marinade of cinnamon, cardamom, black pepper, and red pepper flakes along with a final dash of tangy tamarind sauce. Eaten throughout Oman year-round, they are especially popular during Eid al Fitr, the annual celebration that marks the end of Ramadan. Great eaten off the skewer, they are also delicious served with a flatbread such as pita or Chapati (page 174).

To make the marinade, place the tamarind paste and boiling water in a small bowl and soak 15 to 20 minutes. Mash the tamarind in the water, breaking up the paste well by hand. Strain into a bowl or measuring cup through a sieve, using a wooden spoon to press and mash the pulp, extracting as much liquid as possible. Reserve the liquid for the marinade and sauce; discard the pulp and seeds.

Combine the cumin, red pepper flakes, black pepper, cardamom, cinnamon, salt, and 2 tablespoons of the tamarind juice in a medium bowl to make a thick, paste-like marinade. Add the beef and mix well by hand to coat the pieces evenly. Cover with plastic wrap and chill 20 minutes.

To make the sauce, in a blender, purée the tomato, 3 tablespoons of the tamarind juice, garlic, salt, red pepper flakes, black pepper, and vinegar. Add up to 2 tablespoons water if necessary to thin out. Pour the sauce into a shallow baking dish.

Heat a grill or a cast-iron grill pan to medium-high. Thread 5 or 6 pieces of marinated beef onto each skewer; grill 2 to 3 minutes per side, depending on thickness, until the beef is charred and tender. Roll the cooked beef skewers in the tamarind sauce to lightly coat and serve on their own or with a flatbread, such as Chapati (page 174).

LAMB KEBAB SANDWICHES WITH CHARRED TOMATO AND ONION

1½ teaspoons kosher salt

¾ teaspoon ground black pepper

¾ teaspoon ground coriander

¾ teaspoon ground cumin

¾ teaspoon ground ginger

¾ teaspoon ground cinnamon

¼ teaspoon ground nutmeg

¼ teaspoon ground cardamom

¼ teaspoon cayenne

⅛ teaspoon ground cloves

1½ pounds ground lamb

¼ cup roughly chopped fresh parsley

2 tablespoons minced fresh cilantro

½ cup finely minced red onion (about 1 small onion)

3 cloves garlic, finely minced or mashed into a paste

3 or 4 plum tomatoes

Vegetable oil, for brushing (if using cast-iron grill pan)

2 small red onions, halved

Pita bread or flatbread, for serving

Spicy Mayo (page 239), for serving

MAKES 12 KEBABS

These simple casing-free lamb sausages are laced with fiery cayenne, savory cumin and coriander, ginger, and a hint of cloves, along with finely minced onions and garlic. The juicy kebabs are perfect plucked warm from the grill with warm pita bread and topped with char-roasted tomato and onion and a smear of Spicy Mayo (page 239).

In a medium bowl, mix together the salt, black pepper, coriander, cumin, ginger, cinnamon, nutmeg, cardamom, cayenne, and cloves. Add the lamb, parsley, cilantro, minced onion, and garlic to the bowl. Gently mix to distribute the spices and herbs evenly, being careful not to overwork into a sticky paste. Divide the mixture into 12 oval patties about ½ inch thick and 3½ inches long; cover and chill until ready to use. Wrap each whole tomato in aluminum foil.

Line a grill with foil and heat to medium-high. Alternatively, heat a cast-iron grill pan to medium-high and brush with vegetable oil instead of lining with foil. Place the tomato foil packets and the onion halves on the outer edge of the grill to cook until tender and charred in spots, 15 to 25 minutes. Grill the kebab patties over direct heat in the center of the grill, flipping once, until charred and cooked through, 15 to 20 minutes. When ready to serve, throw the bread over the cooking kebabs or directly on the grill to warm.

To assemble the sandwiches, smear a dollop of spicy mayo down the center of the flatbread and top with a grilled lamb kebab, some charred tomato, and petals of grilled onion. Wrap and eat while hot.

OMANI-SPICED GROUND CHICKEN KEBABS

1½ teaspoons kosher salt

½ teaspoon ground turmeric

½ teaspoon ground coriander

½ teaspoon ground cumin

¼ teaspoon ground cinnamon

¼ teaspoon ground black pepper

¼ teaspoon ground cardamom

¼ teaspoon ground ginger

¼ teaspoon red pepper flakes

⅛ teaspoon ground cloves

⅛ teaspoon cayenne

1 pound ground chicken

⅓ cup finely minced red onion (about 1 small onion)

2 cloves garlic, finely minced or mashed into a paste

1 tablespoon finely minced fresh parsley

3 or 4 plum tomatoes (optional)

Vegetable oil, for brushing (if using cast-iron grill pan)

2 small red onions, halved (optional)

Pita bread or flatbread, for serving (optional)

Spicy Mayo (page 239), for serving (optional)

MAKES 10 KEBABS

The chicken version of the Omani ground meat kebab is enlivened with ground cardamom, a pinch of turmeric, and a hint of cinnamon for distinctive, flavorful chicken sausages that stand up to their lamb counterparts in a pita with charred vegetables.

In a medium bowl, mix together the salt, turmeric, coriander, cumin, cinnamon, black pepper, cardamom, ginger, red pepper flakes, cloves, and cayenne. Add the chicken, minced onion, garlic, and parsley and mix gently with a wooden spoon until the spices are distributed and everything just comes together. (Warning: If you overmix the chicken, it will turn into a sticky paste and the texture of the grilled kebabs will be reminiscent of chicken nuggets.) Cover with plastic wrap; chill 30 minutes or up to 2 hours. Wrap each whole tomato in aluminum foil.

Divide the chicken into 10 oval patties about ½ inch thick and 4 inches long. Line a grill with foil and heat to medium-high. Alternatively, heat a cast-iron grill pan to medium-high and brush with vegetable oil instead of lining with foil. Place the foil packets of tomatoes and the onion halves on the outer edge of the grill to cook until tender and charred in spots, 15 to 25 minutes. Grill the kebab patties, flipping once, until cooked through and charred on the outside, 10 to 14 minutes. When ready to serve, throw the bread over the cooking kebabs or directly on the grill to warm.

To assemble the sandwiches, smear a dollop of spicy mayo down the center of the flatbread and top with a grilled chicken kebab, some charred tomato, and petals of grilled onion. Wrap and eat while hot.

THE CHEDI'S YOGURT TANDOORI-SPICED SHRIMP

2 cloves garlic

1 (2-inch) piece fresh ginger, peeled and sliced

½ to 1 whole serrano chile

1 tablespoon plus 2 teaspoons mustard oil

2 teaspoons freshly squeezed lime juice

⅔ cup plain yogurt (preferably full-fat)

1 tablespoon garam masala

1½ teaspoons ground fennel

1½ teaspoons ground turmeric

1 tablespoon ground cumin

1 teaspoon ajowan (carom) seeds, toasted

½ teaspoon kosher salt

1½ pounds large, tail-on shrimp, peeled to tail and deveined (40 to 50 shrimp total)

10 to 14 bamboo skewers, soaked in water 10 minutes

MAKES 10 TO 14 SKEWERS

The romantic Chedi hotel in the Al Ghubra neighborhood of Muscat is a local favorite for fine dining, due in part to the gorgeous grounds overlooking the sea, but also because of Chef Sebastien's sophisticated preparations of Omani seafood. His subtle, spiced yogurt marinade is wonderful on shrimp, which he cooks in a tandoor oven but also works great on the grill. Just be sure to blot the shrimp before grilling, as excess marinade can lead to a mushy texture.

Make the marinade by placing the garlic, ginger, chile, oil, lime juice, yogurt, garam masala, fennel, turmeric, cumin, ajowan seeds, and salt in a blender or food processor and pulse until just smooth. Transfer to a large bowl, add the shrimp, and stir to coat. Cover with plastic wrap and chill 3 hours.

Heat a grill to medium-high. Alternatively, heat a cast-iron grill pan to medium-high or set the oven to broil. Thread the shrimp on skewers, 4 pieces per skewer, being sure to pierce through both the thickest part and the tail and leaving space between each piece; wipe off excess marinade.

Cook on the hottest part of the grill until the marinade is cooked off and slightly charred and the shrimp are cooked through, 3 to 4 minutes per side. (If broiling, place the skewers on an aluminum foil–lined baking sheet and broil, flipping once, 3 to 5 minutes per side.)

FIRE-STEAMED SEAFOOD AND VEGETABLES

1 to 1¼ pounds seafood, such as large shell-on shrimp, squid, cleaned small whole saltwater fish (porgy, snapper, or sea bream), fillets of any white, flaky fish, or a combination

Juice of 1 lime

1 dried lime

1 teaspoon kosher salt

¼ teaspoon ground turmeric

¼ teaspoon ground coriander

¼ teaspoon ground ginger

¼ teaspoon ground cumin

¼ teaspoon red pepper flakes, or more

Pinch of ground black pepper

Pinch of ground cinnamon

Pinch of ground nutmeg

Pinch of ground cardamom

4 cloves garlic, halved

½ medium red onion, quartered and pulled apart into petals

1 plum tomato, cored and cut into 1-inch pieces

½ small green bell pepper, cut into 1-inch pieces

2 medium zucchini, cut into ¾-inch coins

3 or 4 bird's eye chiles

1 lime, halved, plus wedges for serving

Pita bread, for serving

SERVES 4

Sitting on a woven mat by the beach, Ameer assembled aluminum trays of chopped vegetables and seafood: whole hamour, *samak beed* (a giant fish roe), sharri fish, and prawns. He sprinkled on a handful of his own custom blend of ground spices, gesturing for me to bring him some of the black lime flesh, which he added to the pan. He gently mixed the seafood, vegetables, and spices with his hands, then, after rinsing his hands with a bottle of water, he tightly wrapped the trays in foil before carrying them to the bonfire to cook along the edges of the flames. An hour later, as the fire waned and our hunger grew, the silver trays reemerged. The prawns were sweet in their shells, the vegetables soft and tender, and the fish was laced with subtle hints of smoke, garlic, and a tingle of chile. Rustic and forgiving, with endless options for variations, this may be the ultimate campfire meal. It can also be made in the oven, but is best as an outdoor feast.

Rinse the seafood and place in a small, disposable aluminum pan if making outdoors; alternatively, place in a small roasting pan or baking dish and preheat the oven to 400°F. Pour the lime juice over the seafood.

Remove the flesh of the dried lime: Crack the lime with the bottom of the handle of a heavy knife, cut the lime in half where pierced, then pull out the thin, papery flesh and discard the seeds and dried outer rind. (If the inside of the dried lime is dry and hollow or moldy, discard and use a new one.) Place the lime flesh in a small bowl with the salt, turmeric, coriander, ginger, cumin, red pepper flakes, black pepper, cinnamon, nutmeg, and cardamom and mix well.

Add the garlic, onion, tomato, bell pepper, zucchini, and chiles to the pan with the seafood and sprinkle everything with the spice mix; toss by hand, rubbing the spices into the seafood and vegetables to distribute evenly. Wrap the pan with aluminum foil at least two times all the way around in both directions to seal completely (this will allow everything to steam). Place the pan directly on the hot coals in a barbecue pit or on the perimeter of a bonfire. Alternatively, place on the middle rack in the oven. Cook until the vegetables are tender and the seafood is cooked through, 45 minutes to 1 hour.

Remove from the fire or oven and let sit 10 minutes, then remove the foil and squeeze half a lime over the top, sprinkling with salt to taste. Serve with lime wedges and eat by hand with pita bread.

MADHBI DJAJ
(HOT STONE DHOFARI CHICKEN)

1 medium (about 3½ pounds) whole chicken

2 tablespoons kosher salt

SERVES 4

Ask anyone about the cooking of Salalah in southern Oman, and they will describe *madhbi* (MA-th-bee), or river-rock grilling. Flat smooth stones from the *wadi*, or riverbed, are cleaned and placed over the embers of a fire, and meat, seasoned only with a generous lashing of salt, is set on the hot rocks to slowly cook. Cooking a heavily salted, spatchcocked chicken on a very hot pizza stone on the grill or in your oven yields similar results, for ridiculously simple and incredibly flavorful crisp-skinned chicken.

Place a pizza stone on the middle rack in the oven and preheat to 500°F.

To spatchcock the chicken, place the whole chicken breast side down on a cutting board, cavity side facing up, and use kitchen shears to cut along either side of the backbone to remove. Discard the backbone. Flip the chicken over and press down on the breasts to flatten. Rinse the chicken and pat dry.

Rub the chicken with salt. Place the chicken, breast side down, directly on the preheated pizza stone and cook until the skin crisps and releases easily from the stone, 25 to 30 minutes. Using long kitchen tongs and a spatula, carefully flip the chicken over and cook 25 minutes more, until golden all over and cooked through. Remove carefully from the oven, as tender chicken may easily come off the bone.

NOTE: To clean your pizza stone, remove it from the oven once it is cool and sprinkle with water and plenty of salt. Let sit at least 1 hour and then scrub with a scouring pad.

MARINADE AND SAUCE RECIPES

Leaning over the grill station at the Petroleum Development Oman (PDO) private beach, we watched as Iman turned hunks of beef and chicken quarters over hot charcoal. He handed me a charred drumstick and I took a bite. The chicken was tinged with the fresh bite of ginger, savory garlic, and a subtle hot-tart tang. The *riash*, lamb chops, came off the grill next and were redolent of the same intense flavors, which cut nicely through the fattiness of the meat. Next to me, Waleed Salim Al Harthy grinned and said, "This marinade is unique, it's good on meat and chicken, and you know, we usually use different spices for meat and chicken." He handed me a pan of burgundy sauce. "I know you like spicy, so I added extra chiles to the sauce today," he said. I dipped a piece of chicken in the mixture of cooked-down tamarind paste, hot chiles, and sugar. It was tart with a nice, fiery finish. I devoured my chicken and spent the rest of the evening dipping vegetables and pieces of pita bread into the addictive mixture and begging Waleed for his secret recipes. Miraculously, he agreed to share them. We adjusted Waleed's recipes slightly to account for the slightly less potent tamarind we get in the United States. The resulting marinade is the only one I use when grilling now and I use his amazing tamarind-chile barbecue sauce on grilled foods and as a glaze for oven-roasted meats.

GINGERY TAMARIND YOGURT MARINADE

¼ cup packed seedless tamarind paste

¾ cup boiling water

1 small (5.3-ounce) container plain Greek yogurt

¼ cup cold water

1 tablespoon vegetable oil

1 (1½-inch) piece fresh ginger, peeled and mashed into a paste or grated using a Microplane

3 large cloves garlic, mashed into a paste

¼ teaspoon black lime powder

2 teaspoons kosher salt

MAKES ABOUT 2 CUPS (ENOUGH FOR 2 TO 3 POUNDS OF MEAT OR CHICKEN)

Break the tamarind paste into pieces and place in a small bowl; pour the boiling water over it and let soften and cool, about 30 minutes. Mash the tamarind by hand in the water to break it up.

Using a fine-mesh sieve, strain the tamarind concentrate into a bowl, a little at a time, using a wooden spoon to firmly mash and press the pulp to extract as much liquid as possible, occasionally scraping the pulp on the underside of the sieve into the bowl. This will take a few minutes. Discard the mashed fibrous pulp in the sieve and set the liquid (about ½ cup) aside.

Whisk together the yogurt, cold water, oil, ginger, garlic, black lime powder, and salt in a medium bowl; stir in the tamarind liquid and adjust the seasoning with salt to taste. Use as a marinade for chicken or meat, allowing the proteins to marinate at least 1 hour. Shake off any excess marinade before grilling.

FIERY TAMARIND BARBECUE SAUCE

1 (400-gram) block seedless tamarind paste

10 bird's eye chiles, minced or grated

2 cloves garlic, finely minced or grated

7 tablespoons sugar

1½ teaspoons kosher salt, plus more

MAKES ABOUT 1½ CUPS

Break up the block of tamarind into a few pieces and place in a medium saucepan with 3 cups water; bring to a boil over medium-high heat, lower the heat to medium, and simmer, stirring constantly with pressure to break up the tamarind, until the tamarind has softened and the mixture has thickened, 5 to 7 minutes.

Using a fine-mesh sieve, strain the tamarind concentrate over a small saucepan, a little at a time, using a wooden spoon to firmly mash and press the pulp to extract as much liquid as possible, occasionally scraping the pulp on the underside of the sieve into the bowl. This will take several minutes. Discard any mashed fibrous pulp in the sieve.

Add the chiles, garlic, sugar, and salt to the tamarind liquid and bring to a simmer over medium heat, then cover (as it will sputter), decrease the heat to low, and cook 10 to 12 minutes, until thick and darkened. Turn off the heat and let sit 5 minutes. Adjust the seasoning with salt and sugar to taste, and add a little water to thin the sauce out, if desired. Serve alongside grilled chicken or meat or atop roast meat or vegetables. If the sauce becomes too thick before using, reheat over low heat, adding a little water as needed.

OMANI CELEBRATIONS

When it comes to celebrations in Oman, there has to be rice and meat. Eid al Fitr and Eid al Adha are the most important holidays for Muslims around the world. Eid al Fitr, or Feast of Breaking the Fast, marks the end of the holy month of fasting known as Ramadan, while Eid al Adha, or Festival of Sacrifice, comes at the end of the annual Hajj, or pilgrimage, to Mecca. It is a celebration of Ibrahim's willingness to obey Allah and sacrifice his beloved son Isma'il. Allah spared Isma'il at the last minute, allowing Ibrahim to sacrifice a lamb instead, so often a lamb, goat, or cow is sacrificed for this meal. The meat is then split three ways among family, friends, and the less fortunate. In Oman, entire villages, neighborhoods, and clans gather to prepare for the celebrations by making *shuwa*.

The men dig a deep pit in the earth and fill it with hot embers, while the matriarchs of each family coat the meat in their own special *shuwa* spice blends before placing it in bags made of woven banana leaves or palm fronds. Each family adds their sack to the pit, which is then covered so the marinated meat can slowly roast over 24 to 48 hours, until it is meltingly tender and each piece is infused with intense flavor. Typically it is on the third and final day of Eid al Adha that the succulent meat is hoisted out of the ground and enjoyed in one of the most anticipated meals of the year.

Shuwa is also a popular choice for wedding parties, along with the gelatinous ghee, sugar, and saffron dessert *Halwa* (page 210), which is said to give men "strength for the wedding night." In Oman, wedding celebrations and feasts are held separately for men and women.

The men have a more laid-back affair, going to the mosque for a quick ceremony overseen by the Imam, dinner, *halwa* and coffee, and sometimes dancing. For ladies, it is a totally different story. Whether held at home with female relatives or at an opulent hotel like the Al Bustan Palace, the bride will be decked out in either traditional, colorful Omani attire, embellished with crystals and intricate embroidery, or a lavish, Western-style dress and lots of gold jewelry from head to toe.

Dressed in floor-length gowns, Dawn and I joined a crowd of women at the Al Bustan Palace one night. The ladies sported all manner of sparkly, shimmery, vibrantly colored dresses that might have been just as appropriate for a beauty pageant as for the wedding of our friend Thuraya's cousin. We found Thuraya, dressed in a chic gold and jade abaya from Dubai, and she began pointing out her friends and family who were in attendance. Music played, a ballerina came out and performed. Then, the bride walked in, covered in henna from hands to elbows and toes to calves, wearing a Cinderella white wedding dress that gleamed with embellishments. She took her seat on a stage decked out with pink roses and hanging

crystal chandeliers. Friends and family formed a line to congratulate her and take pictures, and then the crowd migrated toward the buffet.

There were Arabian mezze and smoked salmon canapés; cheesecake and a luscious sticky date pudding (page 202); and at the end of the line of shining silver chafing dishes, past the penne in mushroom cream sauce and roasted rosemary potatoes, was the main event: *shuwa*. The ladies bypassed most of the other dishes in favor of this celebratory favorite. We took our plates and returned to the glowing hall to listen to music and watch the performer dance until, just before 10 p.m., the groom arrived. The ladies donned their headscarves and abayas, though I imagined that they didn't really need to, as the groom's eyes remained transfixed on his smiling bride as he walked purposefully toward the stage. He wore a coral *dishdasha* and matching embroidered *mussar*, the same color as the bride's floral arrangements. His matching *bisht*, a cummerbund of sorts, was wrapped around his hips, a silver *khanjar* dagger tucked in it. He leapt onto the stage and kissed his wife, and the room filled with the "lalalalallalalalaleeeh" of the women's ululations. Photos were taken and he whisked her away. We went back to the buffet for dessert. A few canapés remained, but the *shuwa* was long gone.

SHUWA
(PIT-ROASTED LAMB WRAPPED IN BANANA LEAVES)

SPICE PASTE

¼ cup cumin seeds

3 tablespoons coriander seeds

8 to 10 cloves garlic

1 tablespoon plus 1 teaspoon red pepper flakes

1 tablespoon kosher salt

1½ teaspoons ground cinnamon

1½ teaspoons ground black pepper

1¼ teaspoons ground cardamom

¼ teaspoon ground cloves

⅛ teaspoon ground nutmeg

3 tablespoons distilled white vinegar

6 tablespoons vegetable oil

LAMB

5 to 6 pounds lamb shanks or other small bone-in lamb cut, about 8 pieces

Kosher salt

Banana leaves, thawed if frozen

SERVES 6 TO 8

One of the most iconic of all Omani dishes, *shuwa*, is typically reserved for celebrations like Eid al Adha and Eid al Fitr or weddings, and traditionally involves slathering a whole lamb, goat, or cow with oil and Omani spices, wrapping it in banana leaves, and lowering it into a pit filled with embers to slow-cook for a day. The process of making *shuwa* brings together families and entire villages who share the burden of digging the pit and hauling the meat out of it, as well as the pleasure of the luxurious meal that follows. The slow-roasted spices permeate to the bone, and the oil creates a crispy, charred crust on the outside of the meltingly tender meat. Our recipe is adapted for the oven for those of us without access to a smoker or cooking pit.

To make the spice paste, toast the cumin and coriander seeds in a skillet over medium-low heat until fragrant, about 2 minutes. Place in a blender or small food processor with the garlic cloves, red pepper flakes, salt, cinnamon, black pepper, cardamom, cloves, nutmeg, vinegar, oil, and 2 tablespoons water; pulse or purée until relatively smooth (there can still be some texture from the seeds). Transfer to a bowl or jar, cover with plastic wrap, and let sit overnight at room temperature.

The next day, remove the lamb from the refrigerator and allow the meat to rest at room temperature 1 hour. Preheat the oven to 350°F.

Generously season the lamb with salt; massage each piece with the spice paste, being sure to completely coat every surface but not slathering it on too thick (you'll want it to harden and dry a bit as it cooks). There should be little to no paste left over.

Continued

SHUWA (*continued*)

Wrap the lamb pieces separately in banana leaves, completely enclosing each and making little parcels. Line a roasting pan or 9 by 11-inch baking dish with a large whole banana leaf, letting it hang over both sides of the pan. Place the wrapped lamb parcels, seam side down, in the pan and tightly enclose with the overhanging banana leaf.

Roast until the lamb is cooked through and falling off the bone, 2½ to 3½ hours. Some of the spice rub should caramelize and form a bit of a crust.

Let rest 10 minutes. Remove the lamb from the banana leaves, discarding the leaves, and serve with steamed basmati rice.

CHAPTER 3

SAVORY PORRIDGES, STEWS, AND SOUPS

One wouldn't expect to find incredible warming winter stews, porridges, and soups in an arid country with average temperatures in the 80s and 90s, but the Omani canon of thick, hearty porridges and richly spiced soups is extensive. There are a number of different savory porridges, many which can be found in one form or another throughout the Arabian Gulf, but *arseeyah* is a purely Omani comfort food. *Arseeyah* is a rice and chicken version of a mashed wheat berry and meat porridge known as *harees* that's eaten throughout the GCC and South Asia. To prepare either dish, meat and rice or wheat are cooked for hours until the elements literally disintegrate into each other and can be mashed or blended into a creamy, smooth texture. The spicing is simple, often just cinnamon, salt, and black pepper with a drizzle of Omani Oil (page 243), a ghee infused with cumin and coriander seeds. Both comfortingly rich dishes are reminiscent to me of thick bowls of chicken and dumplings. The hearty combination of carbohydrate and protein is perfect for keeping full throughout the day, so it's no wonder these porridges are wildly popular during the holy month of Ramadan for *iftar*, the evening meal during which people break their fasts, and *suhoor,* the last meal eaten before sunrise.

The cream-of-wheat-textured dish *aseeda* seems to be in a category all its own. Dawn and I ate it in the far north near the Emirates in the town of Buraimi, and in the far southern city of Salalah, where I fell hard for the combination of this spongy, slightly sweet mixture of toasted flour and ghee and spicy *Lahm Kalia* (page 96), a dry-cooked, curried beef dish. Omanis will eat *aseeda* like this as a side with other savory dishes and also on its own for breakfast, dinner, or even dessert. Its light sweetness and tender texture are addictive.

One of my favorite dishes in Oman is *thareed* or *fattah*, which I liken to a savory bread pudding, and which has many variations. In the south near Yemen and in urban areas, like Muscat and Sohar, pillowy naan-like tandoor bread is used to soak up a meat and vegetable broth called *saloonat*. In the interior desert regions, paper-thin Omani bread is used for a much lighter dish. The Lawati people, descendants of Persian, Indian, and Omani traders, have their own variation of *thareed*, made with gnocchi-like fresh dough dumplings, which they call *dhokri*.

Bader Al Lawati took us to his family's home in the Al Ghubra neighborhood of Muscat, where his mother, Adila, demonstrated how to make the Lawati specialty. She rolled long ropes of dough, which she then carefully pinched off into bite-size dumplings, giving them a quick press with her fingers before slipping them into a pot of simmering tomato and lamb stew. As she rolled and pressed, she began to talk about her family's history in the rice and sugar trading business. The Lawati have always been a trading people, traditionally residing in the old seaside neighborhood of Mutrah, a series of winding alleyways and white stucco buildings with pastel doors built behind the souk and the beautiful, blue-domed Shia mosque. Over the years the seafarers intermarried with Iraqis, Persians, East Africans, and Indians from the ports along their trade routes, developing a creole language that combined Arabic, Farsi, Urdu, and Swahili. Many of the Lawati can trace their roots to Gujarat, but others insist their lineage traces back directly to Mutrah. Despite the cacophony of influences, or perhaps as a result of them, the foods of the Lawati people are subtle; like *dokri,* which is more reminiscent of a mild Italian stew than the dish of the same name found in India, which is heavily spiced and made with dal rather than lamb.

Lighter in texture but just as warming and rich are the Omani soups, like *shorbat harees,* a lamb broth punctuated by tender wheat berries, which is also popular during Ramadan as a lighter option for breaking the fast. Lentil soup is enlivened in the Sultanate with the addition of tart black limes and a sprinkle of cardamom, though every household has its own way with this simple soup. These Omani comfort foods are deliciously representative both of the indigenous Bedouin Arab culture, as with the traditional *arseeyah* and *harees* porridges, and of the diverse ways a basic dish, like *thareed,* can take on many forms across the Sultanate according to taste, tradition, and resources.

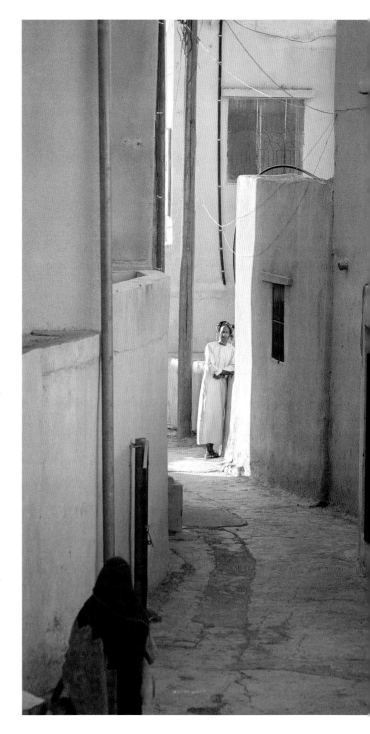

ARSEEYAH
(SAVORY CHICKEN AND RICE PORRIDGE)

2 cups long-grain white rice

1 pound boneless, skinless chicken, such as thighs, cut into 2-inch pieces

4 whole cardamom pods

1 cinnamon stick

¼ cup ghee or butter, melted, divided

2 tablespoons kosher salt

¼ teaspoon ground black pepper

Omani Oil (page 243), for garnish (optional)

SERVES 6 TO 8

Long-grain rice and chicken simmer for hours with cinnamon sticks and cardamom pods for this quintessential Omani comfort food. Thuraya's family cook, Shaymeena, shared her recipe with us. The chicken breaks down and the rice softens to the point that it can be mashed by hand into a smooth porridge, but, alternatively, you can use an immersion blender, depending on your preferred consistency. Though unfamiliar in terms of texture and cooking method in the West, this delicious, subtle dish is reminiscent of chicken and dumplings. It's traditionally served with *torshe*, a condiment whose preparation varies from a fruit vinegar–based sauce made in Jabal Akhdar to the Muscati version made using chicken livers, raisins, and tamarind, but we love *Arseeyah* served on its own with just a drizzle of ghee scented with cumin and coriander, called Omani Oil (page 243), or topped with melted butter.

Continued

ARSEEYAH (*continued*)

Soak the rice in a bowl, covered in water, 1 hour. Drain.

Bring the rice, 8 cups water, the chicken, cardamom, and the cinnamon to a boil in a large pot. Decrease the heat to low and cook, covered, about 1 hour.

Add 2 tablespoons of the ghee, the salt, and black pepper. Stir and continue cooking another 30 minutes to 1 hour, stirring often to prevent sticking and burning. If the mixture becomes too thick to stir or begins to stick, add a bit of hot water (up to ½ cup). The chicken will begin to break up into threads and the rice will be mushy when done.

Remove the cinnamon stick and cardamom pods with a fork. Taste and add more salt (up to 2 tablespoons), if desired.

As you would with mashed potatoes, cream the mixture using a large wooden spoon, potato masher, or immersion blender until the desired texture is reached, from perfectly smooth to slightly chunky depending on your preference. Drizzle with the remaining 2 tablespoons ghee or Omani Oil and serve warm.

MADROUBA

(MASHED CHICKEN AND RICE)

2 cups long-grain white rice

4 dried limes

3 medium red onions, minced

¼ cup ghee, plus ¼ cup for garnish

4 cloves garlic, minced

4 plum tomatoes, cored and minced

1¼ teaspoons ground turmeric

1 teaspoon ground cumin

1 teaspoon ground coriander

½ teaspoon ground ginger

¼ teaspoon ground cinnamon

¼ teaspoon ground black pepper

⅛ teaspoon ground cardamom, plus
    ½ teaspoon for garnish

⅛ teaspoon ground cloves

⅛ teaspoon cayenne

Pinch of nutmeg

1¼ pounds boneless, skinless
    chicken, such as breasts or thighs,
    cut into 3-inch pieces

2 tablespoons kosher salt

½ cup vegetable oil

2 small red onions, halved and
    thinly sliced

SERVES 6 TO 8

When our friend Thuraya began raving about the *madrouba*, a savory mash of rice and vegetables topped with chicken, that she had eaten at Omani chef Issa Al Lamki's restaurant in Muscat, we knew we had to go try it for ourselves. The Omani celebrity chef explained to us that the secret behind his superior, bright-flavored porridge was the use of fresh tomatoes instead of tomato paste, and a rich drizzle of his signature cardamom-infused ghee and crisp-fried onions to finish the dish. The complex combination of black limes, turmeric, cumin, cinnamon, and clove made this hearty dish one of our favorites, too.

Place the rice in a bowl and fill with water. Swirl with your hand to rinse, then drain. Repeat a few more times, until the water becomes clear. Cover the rice with clean water and soak 30 minutes. Drain when ready to use.

Remove the flesh of the dried limes by cracking the lime with the bottom of the handle of a heavy knife. Then cut the lime in half where pierced, pull out the thin, papery flesh, and discard the seeds and dried outer rind. (If the inside of the dried lime is dry and hollow or moldy, discard and use a new one.) This should yield about 4 teaspoons flesh.

Sauté the minced onions in ¼ cup of the ghee in a large Dutch oven or pot over medium-high heat until brown, 10 to 15 minutes. Add the garlic and tomatoes, cook a few minutes, then add the dried lime, turmeric, cumin, coriander, ginger, cinnamon, black pepper, ⅛ teaspoon of the cardamom, the cloves, cayenne, nutmeg, and chicken. Stir to mix well. Add 8 cups water and the salt, increase the heat to high, and boil until the chicken is cooked through, about 20 minutes.

Add the rice to the pot and bring back to a boil. Decrease the heat to low and cook, covered, 1½ to 2 hours, until the rice is mushy and begins to break down, being sure to stir frequently to prevent sticking, adding additional hot water if necessary.

Meanwhile, make the frizzled onions. Heat the oil in a medium skillet or saucepan over medium to medium-high heat, and fry the thinly sliced onions, in two batches if necessary, until deep golden brown, 5 to 8 minutes. Remove the onions using a slotted spoon and transfer to a paper towel–lined plate to drain.

When the rice is cooked through and mushy and the chicken has broken down into threads, whip and mash the mixture with a sturdy wooden spoon until it becomes smooth and porridge-like.

Melt the remaining ¼ cup ghee in a small skillet over medium-low heat. Stir in the remaining ½ teaspoon cardamom and let infuse until fragrant, about 2 minutes, then remove from the heat. To serve, garnish with the cardamom ghee and frizzled onions.

HAREES
(SAVORY WHEAT PORRIDGE)

2 cups shelled/pearled whole white wheat berries

1½ pounds bone-in chicken, such as thighs or breasts, skin removed

2 tablespoons kosher salt

1 teaspoon ground black pepper

2 cinnamon sticks

½ cup vegetable oil

2 small red onions, halved and thinly sliced

¼ cup Omani Oil (page 243), ghee, or butter, for serving

½ teaspoon ground cardamom (optional), for serving

SERVES 6 TO 8

This savory mash, which is beloved throughout the Gulf region, can be made using chicken or lamb, though if you use lamb, you will need to increase the cooking time to ensure the meat melts into the wheat berry mixture. The simple porridge is soul food in the Arabian Gulf and a favorite during the holy month of Ramadan. At its simplest, it is seasoned only with black pepper and cinnamon, though regional variations abound, like in the mountain villages of Jabal Akhdar, where they add ground ginger and red pepper flakes. We love ours topped with deep-fried frizzled onions and either a drizzle of traditional Omani Oil (page 243) or Muscat celebrity chef Issa Al Lamki's signature cardamom-infused ghee. Be sure to use pearled *harees* (shelled white wheat berries) for this recipe, as unpearled will not break down.

Soak the wheat berries in a bowl, covered in water, overnight. Drain when ready to use.

In a large Dutch oven or pot, bring 10 cups water to a boil and boil the chicken until the chicken is cooked through and the stock is flavorful, about 45 minutes. Remove the chicken from the stock and set aside.

Add the drained wheat berries to the stock and adjust the liquid level if necessary (the liquid should be 2 to 3 inches above the wheat berries; add up to 1 cup water if needed). Add the salt, pepper, and cinnamon sticks. Bring to a boil over high heat.

While the wheat berries are coming to a boil, shred the chicken, removing and discarding any fat and bones. Add the shredded chicken to the pot. Once boiling, turn down the heat to low, cover, and cook 3 hours, stirring frequently and adding 1 cup hot water about 1½ hours in, or when needed, to prevent burning. The wheat berries will begin to turn viscous after about an hour and the chicken will begin to break down into fine threads; when done, the wheat berries will be cooked through, with no bite, the chicken will be shredded, and the consistency will be that of a thick porridge.

When almost finished, make the frizzled onions. Heat the oil in a small skillet or saucepan over medium to medium-high heat and fry the onions, in two batches if necessary, until deep golden brown, 5 to 8 minutes. Remove the onions using a slotted spoon and transfer to a paper towel–lined plate to drain.

Remove the cinnamon sticks from the pot. Whip and mash the *harees* with a sturdy wooden spoon for more texture or use an immersion to purée until smooth.

Melt the Omani Oil in a small skillet over medium-low heat, or make cardamom-infused ghee: Melt plain ghee in a small skillet over medium-low heat then stir in the cardamom and let infuse until fragrant, about 2 minutes; remove from the heat.

Serve the *harees* drizzled with Omani Oil or the cardamom ghee and topped with the frizzled onions.

MADROUBA MALLEH

(SAVORY TURMERIC-SCENTED SALTFISH AND RICE PORRIDGE)

⅓ to ½ pound salt cod or salt pollock

2 cups long-grain white rice

4 or 5 dried limes

2 medium red onions, minced

½ cup ghee, plus more, melted, for serving

4 cloves garlic, minced

½ serrano chile, seeded and minced

3 plum tomatoes, cored and minced

2 teaspoons ground turmeric

¾ teaspoon ground coriander

¾ teaspoon ground cumin

¾ teaspoon ground ginger

¾ teaspoon ground black pepper

½ teaspoon red pepper flakes, plus more for garnish

¼ teaspoon cayenne

¼ teaspoon ground cinnamon

⅛ teaspoon ground cardamom

⅛ teaspoon ground cloves

⅛ teaspoon ground nutmeg

2 teaspoons kosher salt

½ cup vegetable oil

2 small red onions, halved and thinly sliced

Juice of 1 lime

SERVES 6 TO 8

Adnan Al Balushi and his wife, Souad Al Jabriya Aghsan Al Barakah, the owners of Aghsan Al Barakah Omani Foods restaurant in the northern suburb of Mabellah, taught us a seafood variation on chicken *madrouba* that can be found throughout the northern coastal regions of Muscat and Batinah. Saltfish is sautéed with onions and garlic before being added to spicy, turmeric-heavy rice in this flavorful porridge. Boiling and thoroughly rinsing the fish as well as using the highest-quality preserved fish you can find (which is only marginally more expensive than the cheap stuff) makes a big difference in the clean, fresh flavor of this dish.

Place the salt cod in a small saucepan and add enough water to cover; bring to a boil over high heat and cook 20 minutes. Drain the cod, return it to the saucepan, and repeat the process twice more. Transfer the cod to a bowl and let it cool. Flake the fish using a fork and set aside.

Rinse the rice a few times, until the water runs clear. Soak in clean water 15 to 30 minutes. Drain when ready to use.

Remove the flesh of the dried limes by cracking the lime with the bottom of the handle of a heavy knife. Then cut the lime in half where pierced, pull out the thin, papery flesh, and discard any seeds and the dried outer rind. (If the inside of the dried lime is dry and hollow or moldy, discard and use a new one.) Set aside.

Sauté the minced onions in the ghee in a heavy-bottom pot or Dutch oven over medium-high heat until the onions begin to brown, 10 to 15 minutes. Combine the garlic and chile in a small bowl and mash into a paste. Add the garlic-chile paste to the onions; stir and cook 2 minutes. Add the tomatoes and cook 5 minutes, stirring and mashing to break them up. Stir in the flaked fish, dried lime flesh, turmeric, coriander, cumin, ginger, black pepper, red pepper flakes, cayenne, cinnamon, cardamom, cloves, and nutmeg, and cook 5 minutes more.

Add 3 cups water, the drained rice, and salt; turn the heat to medium, bring to a boil, and boil 15 minutes. Decrease the heat to low and cook, covered, 50 minutes to 1 hour, adding hot water along the way as needed (anywhere from 3 to 4 cups total), stirring frequently to prevent sticking, until the rice begins to break down.

Meanwhile, make the frizzled onions. Heat the oil in a small skillet or saucepan over medium to medium-high heat, and fry the sliced onions, in two batches if necessary, until deep golden brown, 5 to 8 minutes. Remove the onions using a slotted spoon and transfer to a paper towel–lined plate to drain.

When the rice is cooked through and mushy, add the lime juice (use ½ lime if it's extra juicy, 1 to 2 tablespoons lime juice), stir well, then whip and mash with a sturdy wooden spoon until the rice becomes smooth and porridge-like.

To serve, drizzle with ghee, sprinkle with red pepper flakes, and top with the frizzled onions.

ASEEDA
(TOASTED FLOUR AND GHEE DUMPLING)

1½ cups unbleached all-purpose flour

1 cup plus 2 tablespoons sugar

Pinch of kosher salt

3 tablespoons ghee, plus more for serving

½ teaspoon ground cardamom

1 teaspoon rose water (optional)

SERVES 8 TO 10

This stick-to-your-ribs dome of toasted, cardamom-tinged flour and ghee is popular in the hinterlands of Buraimi in northern Oman and in the far southern province of Dhofar. A lightly sweet, giant dumpling of sorts, *aseeda* is delicious with hot tea or as an accompaniment to a spicy meat curry, like *Lahm Kalia* (page 96).

Toast the flour in a dry, medium Dutch oven over medium heat, stirring frequently, until it turns beige and has a nutty aroma, 15 to 20 minutes. Transfer the flour to a bowl.

Wipe the pot clean and add 3½ cups water, the sugar, and salt; turn the heat to medium-high and bring to a boil. Once the water boils, decrease the heat to medium and, very slowly, sift the toasted flour into the pot, adding a little at a time and whisking constantly to prevent small lumps from forming. When it becomes too thick to whisk, after about 5 minutes, decrease the heat to low. At this point, it will require a bit of arm power to stir. Cook about 10 more minutes, stirring constantly with a wooden spoon and adding a little hot water (a couple tablespoons at a time and up to ½ cup) if necessary, until the mixture begins to form a ball, pulling away from the pot. The *aseeda* will be dough-like and thick and will come together like a single, giant dumpling.

Stir in the ghee, cardamom, and rose water, if using, and cook 2 more minutes, stirring constantly. Remove and put on a plate or in a flat-bottomed bowl and rub the surface with more ghee as you mold it into a circular dome shape, smoothing over the top with the back of a spoon and making small indents on the surface; drizzle with more ghee. This is best eaten within an hour of cooking, as it will begin to congeal and dry out after that. Serve alongside spicy fried meat curry, *Lahm Kalia* (page 96), or with herbaceous Dhofari *Karak* (page 220).

THAREED
(BEEF AND FLATBREAD STEW)

Also called *fattah* in southern Oman and in Yemen, this recipe makes use of day-old Omani Bread (page 162) or tandoor flatbreads like naan to soak up the broth of a flavorful meat and vegetable medley. I order two or three pieces of takeout naan for this recipe, though frozen naan will work just as well. Use thin Omani Bread to make a lighter version of the dish.

1 pound boneless beef, such as chuck or round steak or roast, trimmed of fat and cut into 1½-inch cubes

1 cinnamon stick

3 whole cloves

2 medium red onions, minced

¼ cup vegetable oil

4 cloves garlic, minced

1 (2-inch) piece fresh ginger, peeled and minced

6 tablespoons tomato paste

2 tablespoons ground coriander

1 teaspoon ground cumin

1 teaspoon ground turmeric

½ teaspoon ground ginger

½ teaspoon ground cinnamon

¼ teaspoon cayenne

¼ teaspoon ground black pepper

¼ teaspoon ground cardamom

⅛ teaspoon ground cloves

1 medium or large russet potato, peeled and cut into 1½-inch cubes

2 medium carrots, peeled and cut into ¾-inch-thick coins

1 cup 1½-inch green bean pieces (about ¼ pound)

¼ green bell pepper, seeded and chopped

2 plum tomatoes, cored and minced

2 small zucchini, cut into 1½-inch half-moons

2 teaspoons kosher salt

1 chicken bouillon cube

2½ to 3 (9-inch) naan breads or day-old Omani Bread (page 162), torn into 2-inch pieces

¼ to ½ cup boiling water

SERVES 6 TO 8

Place 3 cups water, the beef, cinnamon stick, and whole cloves in a medium Dutch oven or saucepan. Bring to a boil and then decrease the heat to medium; cook, covered, until the meat is tender, 1 to 1¼ hours. Remove the meat, discard the whole spices, and reserve the broth and meat separately.

Sauté the onions in the oil in a large heavy pot over medium-high heat until they begin to brown, 8 to 10 minutes. Stir in the garlic and ginger and cook 1 to 2 minutes. Add the tomato paste, coriander, cumin, turmeric, ginger, cinnamon, cayenne, black pepper, cardamom, and ground cloves; stir well and cook 3 minutes. Add the potato, carrots, green beans, and bell pepper and cook, adding a splash of water if necessary, 5 more minutes.

Add the tomatoes, stir, and cook until they begin to break down, about 5 minutes. Pour in the reserved broth and cook, covered, over medium-high heat 20 to 25 minutes.

Add the zucchini, salt, bouillon cube, and reserved meat. Bring to a boil, then decrease the heat to medium; cook, covered, until all the vegetables and meat are tender, 12 to 15 minutes.

Turn off the heat. Add the naan pieces. Mix well and pour in the ¼ to ½ cup boiling water, depending on how saucy the curry is and how much naan is used. (It will look quite saucy, but the naan will quickly absorb all the liquid.) Stir, making sure the naan pieces are completely coated and submerged in any remaining liquid. Pat the top of the stew down gently with the back of a spoon, cover, and let sit 10 to 15 minutes before serving.

DHOKRI
(LAWATI LAMB AND DUMPLING STEW)

DOUGH

1½ cups unbleached all-purpose flour

2 tablespoons vegetable oil

1 teaspoon kosher salt

STEW

1 to 1¼ pounds lamb pieces, such as stew meat, or up to 2 pounds bone-in lamb

1 teaspoon plus 1 tablespoon kosher salt, divided

2 tablespoons vegetable oil

3 medium red onions, minced

4 cloves garlic, mashed into a paste

2½ teaspoons ground coriander

2 teaspoons ground cumin

½ teaspoon ground black pepper

½ teaspoon ground turmeric

½ teaspoon ground ginger

½ teaspoon ground cinnamon

¼ teaspoon ground cardamom

¼ teaspoon red pepper flakes

⅛ teaspoon ground cloves

⅛ teaspoon ground nutmeg

¼ cup tomato paste

2 plum tomatoes or medium tomatoes, cored and diced

Ghee, for serving (optional)

SERVES 4 TO 6

The Lawati people, whose creole heritage traces back to the traders of old Mutrah, have their own version of the Bedouin bread pudding, *thareed*, made with tender hand-rolled dumplings simmered in a mild tomato and lamb stew spiced with cumin, coriander, ginger, and nutmeg. Our friend Bader Al Lawati's mother taught us the traditional method of hand-forming gnocchi-like cylinders from a long rope of dough and gently pressing them into chewy, oval dumplings.

To make the dough, place the flour, oil, salt, and ½ cup water in a medium bowl and mix by hand until it just comes together. Knead the dough 2 to 3 minutes, until smooth and elastic; pat it into a ball, place in a bowl, and cover with a damp towel. Let rest 2 hours.

To make the stew, place the lamb, 1 teaspoon of the salt, and 4½ cups water in a medium saucepan and bring to a boil over high heat. Cover and simmer on low heat until the lamb is tender, 1 to 1½ hours. Strain and reserve the broth. If using bone-in lamb, shred the meat and discard the bones. Set the lamb aside.

In a large pot, heat the vegetable oil over medium heat. Sauté the onions until soft and brown, 8 to 10 minutes. Add the garlic paste, coriander, cumin, black pepper, turmeric, ginger, cinnamon, cardamom, red pepper flakes, cloves, and nutmeg. Stir and cook 1 minute. Add the tomato paste and tomatoes and cook 5 minutes, stirring occasionally. Add the reserved lamb meat, turn the heat to high, and cook, stirring, 3 minutes. Pour in the reserved broth (if it doesn't equal 4½ cups, add hot water to bring the liquid amount to 4½ cups) and add the remaining 1 tablespoon salt; bring to a boil and stir. Decrease the heat to medium-low and let simmer until slightly thickened, 10 to 15 minutes.

While simmering, divide the dough in half and stretch and roll each half into a long rope, about ¾ inch thick. Cut the dough into 1-inch pieces with a knife, like gnocchi. You can press each piece with two fingers to create small indentations, or simply drop the pieces as they are into the simmering broth one at a time, stirring to prevent sticking. Cover the pot, decrease the heat to low, and cook 35 to 40 minutes, stirring gently and frequently so the dumplings do not stick to each other or to the bottom of pot. The dumplings should be chewy but cooked through.

Add salt to taste and a spoonful of ghee for richness.

SHORBAT HAREES
(LAMB AND WHEAT BERRY SOUP)

½ cup shelled/pearled whole white wheat berries, lightly crushed in a mortar and pestle

2 tablespoons plus ½ cup vegetable oil, divided

2 medium red onions, halved

5 whole cardamom pods

1 cinnamon stick

1¼ teaspoons ground cumin

½ teaspoon ground black pepper, plus more for serving

⅛ teaspoon ground cloves

1 to 1½ pounds bone-in lamb, such as chops or shanks, roughly cut into large pieces

½ tablespoon kosher salt, plus more for serving

¼ teaspoon ground cinnamon, plus more for serving

1 beef bouillon cube

2 small red onions, thinly sliced

2 tablespoons finely minced fresh cilantro, for serving

MAKES 4 CUPS

Though traditionally a thick crushed wheat stew (a favorite *iftar* meal of Omani poet Nasra Al Adawu) we fell for chef Issa Al Lamki's lighter, modern version of this dish, in which supple wheat berries punctuate a salty, lamb-rich soup and add creaminess as they release their starch. A sprinkle of fried onions and fresh cilantro are the perfect finishing touch for this luscious soup.

Soak the wheat berries in water to cover at least 1 hour.

In a large stockpot or Dutch oven, heat 2 tablespoons of the oil over medium-high heat and fry the halved onions 5 minutes. Add the cardamom pods, cinnamon stick, cumin, black pepper, and cloves and fry 1 minute more. Add the lamb pieces and bones and brown, turning occasionally, 5 to 7 minutes. Pour in 9 cups water, add the salt, and bring to a boil; cook, uncovered, over medium-high heat 1 hour.

Remove the meat, whole spices, and onions with a sieve; discard the onions and spices. Shred the lamb into small pieces with a fork and return to the pot; discard the lamb bones.

Drain the wheat berries and add to the pot along with the ground cinnamon and the bouillon cube. Simmer over medium-low heat until the soup thickens slightly and the wheat berries are cooked but still have a little bite, 1¼ to 1½ hours, stirring occasionally and adding 2 to 3 cups hot water halfway through cooking, or as the wheat berries begin to absorb the liquid.

Meanwhile, make the frizzled onions. Heat the remaining ½ cup oil in a medium skillet or saucepan over medium to medium-high heat, and fry the thinly sliced onions, in two batches if necessary, until deep golden brown, 5 to 8 minutes. Remove the onions with a slotted spoon and transfer to a paper towel–lined plate to drain.

Serve the soup with a sprinkle of salt, pepper, and cinnamon, plus a pinch of minced cilantro and the frizzled onions.

OMANI LENTIL SOUP

2 dried limes

3 tablespoons ghee, plus more, melted, for serving

3 medium red onions, minced

3 cloves garlic, minced

1 (½-inch) piece fresh ginger, peeled and minced

3 plum tomatoes, cored and diced

2 tablespoons tomato paste

¾ teaspoon ground coriander

¾ teaspoon ground cumin

½ teaspoon ground turmeric

¼ teaspoon ground cinnamon

¼ teaspoon ground black pepper

¼ teaspoon ground cardamom, plus more for serving

⅛ teaspoon ground nutmeg

⅛ teaspoon ground cloves

2 teaspoons kosher salt, plus more for serving

1 cup red lentils, rinsed in water a few times

MAKES 8 CUPS

The warming flavors of the Sultanate—black lime, coriander, cumin, cardamom, and cinnamon, along with a pinch of nutmeg and clove and a final drizzle of melted ghee—make this simple lentil soup utterly distinctive and delicious.

Scrub the limes and soak them in water for a few minutes to soften the skin. Make a small hole in each by piercing with a paring knife.

Melt the ghee in a medium saucepan over medium-high heat. Sauté the onions in the ghee until they begin to brown, 10 to 12 minutes. Add the garlic and ginger, cook a few minutes, then add the tomatoes and cook a few minutes more. Stir in the tomato paste, dried limes, coriander, cumin, turmeric, cinnamon, black pepper, cardamom, nutmeg, and cloves; stir and cook 3 minutes.

Add 5½ cups water, the salt, and the lentils. Turn the heat to high and bring to a boil; decrease the heat to medium and simmer until the lentils are well cooked, about 20 minutes. Remove the dried limes and, in a blender or using an immersion blender, purée the soup until smooth. Serve drizzled with melted ghee, a pinch of ground cardamom, and more salt to taste.

CHAPTER 4

RICE: THE MAIN MEAL

Rice is the cornerstone of the most important meal of the day in Oman: *al gha'ada*, lunch served around two or three in the afternoon, when most Omanis are home from work and the heat of the day is beginning to wane. Many other foods can be eaten anytime, with breakfast and dinner dishes basically interchangeable, but rice, for many, is an essential element of the daily midday meal. Naturally, there is a wide variety of rice dishes in Oman, some with obvious connections to other places, like India-inspired biryanis, which are more mild in the Sultanate; and the Yemeni staple *mandi* (page 80), a saffron yellow rice dish infused with the drippings of chicken or roasting meat. Other rice dishes are rooted in the traditional cooking of the Arabian Gulf, like whole-spice-studded *kabuli* (page 71) topped with *chana dal* and fried onions, or tomato-enriched fried-rice-esque *maqboos* (page 74). If an elaborate rice dish isn't prepared at lunchtime, a dish of steamed basmati rice likely will be, served alongside everything from *paplou* seafood soup to saucy Omani curries called *marak*. And every region, every neighborhood, every household, has its own special version of these rice dishes that reflects the tastes of each individual family.

For some, like Thuraya, who likes to sleep late, lunch will be the first real meal of the day aside from Omani coffee and perhaps a few dates. Thuraya's uncle, Sayyid Jamshid bin Abdullah Al Said, was the last Sultan of Zanzibar before the revolution in 1964, and this heritage is reflected in her family's signature dish, Zanzibari Biryani (page 88). Part of the Omani empire since the late 1700s, the East African island was prized for its strategic position on the seafaring trade routes of Africa, India, Persia, and Oman, and no dish reflects this melee of influences quite as well as Thuraya's biryani, tinged with saffron and laced with rose water and fresh mint.

Rustic but just as delicious is our Muscati friend Ameer's Tuna *Kabuli* (page 77). Ameer learned to cook for himself while working for weeks at a time in the oil fields of Wusta, in the aptly named Rub'al Khali, the Empty Quarter, and his love for seafood and spice, and the lack of fresh seafood in the interior region, inspired the dish. Camping under the wide, black sky in the Wahiba Sands desert in Sharqiyah, about three hours south of Muscat, he watched closely as I struggled to dice tomatoes, onions, and bell pepper with a flimsy steak knife on a plastic plate set on the ground in front of me. I figured it was all going in the same pot, so I began hacking at the vegetables haphazardly. He frowned and took over, slowly, patiently cutting perfect little cubes. He tossed the onions and some finely sliced garlic into a deep pot set on a propane burner, where they sizzled in vegetable oil. He put basmati rice in a bowl to soak and handed me a spoon. I began to stir and after about a minute, I looked up at him. "Can I add the peppers and tomatoes now?"

"Not yet, keep stirring," he said, seriously.

Another minute passed.

"Now?"

He shook his head.

Two minutes later, he said, "Add them now."

I stirred the rest of the vegetables in and he added turmeric and a handful of other spices, followed by a few liberal shakes of crushed red pepper. As the spices bloomed, he opened a can of tuna. I grimaced. *Canned tuna?* I thought. He drained the fish and tossed it into the pot, mixing it with the meltingly soft vegetables and aromatic spices. Then he added the rice and covered it all with water before covering the pot with a lid.

Then we waited.

About ten minutes later, when the lid was removed, the smell of caramelized onions and garlic filled the cool desert air. He piled the rice and fish on plastic plates for everyone. The grains were perfectly tender and the fish had absorbed the flavors of the sautéed vegetables, eradicating any memory of the can it came out of. The lingering, spicy bite of the hot peppers warmed me from my tongue to my stomach. It was a simple dish that didn't require much of its cook aside from patience to transform into a deeply satisfying meal.

The variety of rice dishes in Oman is one thing, from the specialties of Salalah on the southernmost coast, where people like to layer rice with slow-cooked, pan-fried beef for *kalia kabuli* and steam basmati rice with thick chunks of seared kingfish for a specialty known as *sayadiyah*, to the simple steamed chicken and spiced rice *kabulis* of the northern border towns, but the sheer quantity of rice consumed in a single serving is astonishing in and of itself.

Dawn and I watched as young men picked at morsels of rice and camel meat from communal platters two feet in diameter at a roadside restaurant in the suburb of Mabellah until they'd consumed three or four cups each. I was taken aback at first when my dinner plate was mounded with rice, and disheartened when, after struggling to finish my portion, I was rewarded with another few scoops, so I came to love and prefer the Omani style of eating rice dishes, from one massive tray, on which everyone has their designated area in front of them. There is always enough, so no one worries about getting their share, or feels the need, spurred on by a deep sense of hospitality, to force more rice my way. We all have access to the whole, and everyone takes what they want. I make a little dent in my corner of the rice pile, and the pieces of meat that crown the grains are picked at delicately, choice pieces handed to fellow diners, or fed to one another in the ultimate act of dining intimacy.

It is this intimacy that is at the heart of the main meal of the day, when, despite the pressures of modern-day life and busy schedules, people still come together around a communal plate. These lunches reflect the Omani sense of tradition and family shared by all members of the incredibly diverse population.

BASIC BASMATI RICE

1 cup basmati rice

Pinch of kosher salt

MAKES 2 CUPS

Fragrant and flavorful, basmati rice retains the individual integrity of each grain and has a tender but firm texture when cooked properly. The key is rinsing off the excess starch and soaking before cooking to ensure the grains don't become mushy. Making proper rice is trickier than you might think, as Dawn and I found out. But these two methods consistently yield perfect, fluffy grains. Eaten throughout the country, basmati rice is the accompaniment of choice for the light, citrusy seafood-broth soup *Paplou* (page 107); rich Swahili Coconut Shrimp Curry (page 117); and even the Eid al Adha pit-roasted specialty, *Shuwa* (page 43).

Quick Boil Method

Place the rice in a bowl and fill with water. Swirl with your hand to rinse, then drain. Repeat a few more times, until the water becomes clear. Cover the rice with clean water and soak 15 minutes. Drain.

In a large saucepan, bring 6 to 8 cups water to a boil with a generous pinch of salt. Stir in the rice and boil rapidly, stirring occasionally, until the rice is cooked through, 8 to 10 minutes (check for doneness after 8 minutes). Turn off the heat and drain the rice using a large sieve or colander; let sit 1 minute. Return the drained rice to the saucepan, adjust the seasoning with salt to taste, cover, and let sit for a few minutes. Fluff the rice with a fork and serve.

Absorption Method

Place the rice in a bowl and fill with water. Swirl with your hand to rinse, then drain. Repeat a few more times, until the water becomes clear. Cover the rice with clean water and soak 30 minutes. Drain.

In a medium saucepan, bring 1¾ cups water to a boil with a generous pinch of salt. Stir in the rice and bring back to a boil. Turn the heat to the lowest possible setting, cover, sealing tightly with a lid, and cook 15 minutes. Turn off the heat (do not remove the lid) and let sit 5 minutes. Fluff the rice with a fork and serve.

RICE WITH RED LENTILS

1 cup basmati rice

2 teaspoons kosher salt, divided

½ cup red lentils, rinsed

SERVES 4

The most basic dish aside from plain, steamed white basmati rice, the addition of *masoor dal*, or red lentils, increases the protein of this side and adds a subtle, nutty flavor.

Place the rice in a bowl and fill with water. Swirl with your hand to rinse, then drain. Repeat a few more times, until the water becomes clear. Cover the rice with clean water and soak 15 minutes. Drain.

Bring the rice, 8 cups water, and 1 teaspoon of the salt to a boil in a large saucepan; once boiling, stir in the lentils and continue to boil rapidly, uncovered, 6 to 7 minutes, until the rice and lentils are just done (check after 6 minutes and watch closely, as this overcooks easily).

Drain immediately in a colander and rinse with a little water; transfer to a serving bowl and stir in the remaining 1 teaspoon salt while fluffing with a fork. Serve alongside curries, like Spicy Zanzibari Squid Curry (page 118), or with Coconut Creamed Spinach (page 129) for a light vegetarian meal.

CHICKEN KABULI
(BROTH-INFUSED RICE WITH CHICKEN AND LENTILS)

The most elemental and pervasive of the rice main dishes, chicken *kabuli* makes use of the flavorful broth of a boiled chicken, which is then finished with a quick shallow fry. The savory rice is topped with the fried chicken and *chana dal* or split yellow peas. Sometimes nuts or golden raisins are added as well—familial and regional variations abound. The challenge of this ubiquitous dish is making all the components separately and then layering them, which can be tricky timing-wise but is well worth it for the delicious, hearty dish in which these elements come together. It is great served with *Daqus* (page 238), a thin tomato-based Omani hot sauce popular in the north, or chunky, tangy tomato and garlic Omani Salsa (page 238).

CHICKEN

3 pounds bone-in chicken pieces (a combination of 6 thighs and 6 drumsticks works well), skin removed

2 tablespoons kosher salt

5 cloves garlic, smashed

5 whole cardamom pods

6 whole cloves

2 whole star anise

1 stick cinnamon

2 teaspoons ground coriander

1 teaspoon ground cumin

½ teaspoon cayenne

½ teaspoon ground black pepper

Vegetable oil, for frying

RICE

4 cups basmati rice

½ cup vegetable oil

1 large red onion, diced

2 tablespoons cumin seeds

1½ tablespoons ground cumin

1½ tablespoons ground coriander

1½ tablespoons kosher salt

4 or 5 bird's eye chiles

3 tablespoons ghee

YELLOW SPLIT PEAS

1½ cups yellow split peas, soaked in water 1 hour

3 tablespoons vegetable oil

1 large red onion, minced

¼ cup golden raisins, soaked in water 30 minutes and drained

½ teaspoon ground cardamom

1 teaspoon kosher salt

1 teaspoon ground cumin

½ teaspoon ground cinnamon

½ teaspoon ground turmeric

Pinch of saffron

Omani Salsa (page 238) or *Daqus* (page 238), for serving

SERVES 6 TO 8

Continued

Start by making the chicken broth. Place the chicken, salt, garlic, cardamom pods, cloves, star anise, cinnamon stick, coriander, cumin, cayenne, black pepper, and 6 cups water in a large pot, bring to a boil, and boil over high heat 40 to 45 minutes. Set aside to cool. When cool, remove the chicken and put on a plate to dry. Strain the remaining liquid through a fine-mesh sieve, discard the spices, and reserve the broth; set aside.

Meanwhile, to prepare the rice, place the rice in a bowl and fill with water. Swirl with your hand to rinse, then drain. Repeat a few more times, until the water becomes clear. Cover the rice with clean water and soak 15 minutes. Drain and set aside.

While the chicken is cooking and the rice is soaking, drain the yellow split peas and rinse. Bring a few cups of water to a boil in a small saucepan, add the split peas, and cook until tender, 25 to 35 minutes. Drain and set aside.

To cook the rice, heat ½ cup of vegetable oil in a large Dutch oven over high heat and sauté the onions about 6 minutes, until soft. Add the cumin seeds, sauté until fragrant, about 2 minutes, and add the drained rice; stir, then add the ground cumin, coriander, and salt. Continue to sauté, decreasing the heat to medium and stirring constantly to prevent burning, at least 10 minutes, until the rice is toasted and the onions are brown. Pour in the reserved chicken broth to just cover the rice, adding a little

CHICKEN KABULI (*continued*)

water if needed. Add the whole chiles. Increase the heat to bring the mixture to a boil. Cover, decrease the heat to medium-low, and cook until the rice is done, 10 to 12 minutes (check after 10 minutes). Turn off the heat, stir in the ghee, and adjust the seasoning with salt to taste. Keep warm until ready to serve.

While the rice is cooking, heat about 1½ inches of vegetable oil in a large skillet over medium-high heat. Pat the boiled chicken dry with a paper towel, and fry the chicken, flipping halfway through, until brown on both sides, 7 to 8 minutes total. Transfer to a paper towel–lined plate, adjust the seasoning with salt to taste, and set aside until ready to serve.

Meanwhile, finish the yellow split peas. Heat 3 tablespoons of vegetable oil in a medium skillet over medium-high heat and sauté the onion until it begins to soften and brown, 5 to 6 minutes. Add the drained raisins, cardamom, and reserved cooked yellow split peas; cook for a few minutes. Stir in the salt, cumin, cinnamon, and turmeric; cook for a few minutes more, stirring to prevent burning. Turn off the heat and stir in the saffron.

To assemble the *kabuli*, layer the rice on a large platter or serving tray, spoon the yellow split peas over the rice, and top with the fried chicken. Serve with Omani Salsa or *Daqus*.

MAQBOOS

(RED ONION AND TOMATO SPICED RICE)

1½ cups basmati rice

Pinch of kosher salt plus
   1½ teaspoons, divided

3 tablespoons ghee

2 small red onions, minced

4 cloves garlic, minced

2½ plum tomatoes, cored and
   minced

½ teaspoon ground cumin

½ teaspoon ground coriander

¼ teaspoon ground turmeric

⅛ teaspoon ground cardamom

⅛ teaspoon ground cloves

⅛ teaspoon ground cinnamon

⅛ teaspoon ground black pepper

1 chicken bouillon cube

SERVES 6

There are many versions of *maqboos*, a rice side that's flavored with tomatoes and spices. Our favorite is inspired by the one that celebrity chef Issa Al Lamki made for us. He uses fresh tomatoes in place of the more typically used tomato paste for a fresh-tasting rice dish that goes great with grilled or fried fish or chicken.

Place the rice in a bowl and fill with water. Swirl with your hand to rinse, then drain. Repeat a few more times, until the water becomes clear. Cover the rice with warm water and a pinch of salt. Soak 30 minutes, then drain.

Melt the ghee in a medium saucepan or pot over medium-high heat and sauté the onions until they begin to brown, 8 to 10 minutes. Add the garlic, stir and cook for a minute, then add the tomatoes and cook 5 minutes. Stir in the remaining 1½ teaspoons salt, the cumin, coriander, turmeric, cardamom, cloves, cinnamon, and black pepper; cook, stirring occasionally, until the tomatoes begin to break up and become pasty, 5 to 8 minutes.

Add 2½ cups water and the bouillon cube and increase the heat to bring to a boil. Add the drained rice to the pot; allow to come to a boil again. Decrease the heat to medium-low and cook, covered, until the rice is done, 7 to 9 minutes. Turn off the heat and let sit 5 to 10 minutes. Fluff the rice and serve.

TUNA KABULI
(SPICED TUNA AND VEGETABLE RICE)

2½ cups basmati rice

2 dried limes

¼ cup vegetable oil

1½ large red onions, minced

7 cloves garlic, minced

½ to 1 serrano chile, seeded and minced

½ green bell pepper, seeded and minced

2 plum tomatoes, cored and minced

1 tablespoon kosher salt

1 teaspoon ground coriander

½ teaspoon ground cumin

½ teaspoon red pepper flakes

⅛ teaspoon ground black pepper

⅛ teaspoon ground cinnamon

⅛ teaspoon ground cloves

⅛ teaspoon ground turmeric

2 (5-ounce) cans albacore tuna in water, drained

1 chicken bouillon cube

Fresh cilantro, chopped, for garnish

Lime wedges, for serving

SERVES 6 TO 8

This simple, inexpensive dish, which our friend Ameer Al Ghammari made while working in the oil fields of Wusta, is composed of basic pantry staples, including canned tuna, but yields flavorful, satisfying results. Ameer loves spicy food, as do I, but this recipe has been adjusted for a medium heat level. Increase or decrease the serrano chile and crushed red pepper to suit your taste.

Place the rice in a bowl and fill with water. Swirl with your hand to rinse, then drain. Repeat a few more times, until the water becomes clear. Cover the rice with clean water and soak 30 minutes. Drain.

Remove the flesh of the dried limes by first cracking the lime with the bottom of the handle of a heavy knife. Cut the lime in half where pierced, then pull out the thin, papery flesh and discard the seeds and dried outer rind. (If the inside of the dried lime is dry and hollow or moldy, discard and use a new one.)

Heat the oil in a large saucepan or pot over medium heat and sauté the onions until they begin to brown, 8 to 10 minutes. Add the garlic and both peppers, stir, and cook 5 minutes. Add the tomatoes, cooking and stirring for a few minutes until they begin to break down, then add the salt, coriander, cumin, red pepper flakes, black pepper, cinnamon, cloves, and turmeric. Stir to prevent the spices from burning and cook until fragrant, 1 to 2 minutes. Add the dried lime flesh and tuna; cook, stirring gently, 5 minutes more.

Add 3½ cups water, the bouillon cube, and the drained rice to the pot; increase the heat to bring to a boil. Decrease the heat to medium-low, cover, and cook until the rice is tender, about 10 minutes (check after 8 minutes). Turn off the heat and let sit, covered, 10 minutes. Remove the lid and fluff the rice with a fork. Garnish with the cilantro and serve with the lime wedges.

KALIA KABULI
(DHOFARI FRIED BLACK PEPPER BEEF WITH RICE)

2 cups basmati rice

1½ pounds fatty boneless beef, such as chuck, cut into 2-inch cubes

2½ teaspoons kosher salt, divided

⅓ cup yellow split peas

⅓ cup golden raisins

3 cloves garlic

1 serrano chile, seeded

1 (1½-inch) piece fresh ginger, peeled and sliced

Vegetable oil, as needed

¾ teaspoon ground cinnamon

¼ teaspoon ground black pepper

1 medium red onion, minced

1 bay leaf

½ cinnamon stick

2 whole cloves

4 whole cardamom pods

¼ teaspoon whole black peppercorns

¼ teaspoon fennel seeds

½ teaspoon cumin seeds

½ teaspoon coriander seeds

SERVES 6 TO 8

Popular in the meat-centric Dhofar region, where cows amble along the streets of the capital city, Salalah, and goats and sheep bay from the green hilltops that overlook the sea, this version of *kabuli* is layered with sweet, golden raisins, nutty *chana dal* or split yellow lentils, and tender cubes of beef that have been braised and browned. The black pepper kick is offset by hints of sweetness from the raisins and sautéed onion–studded rice.

Place the rice in a bowl and fill with water. Swirl with your hand to rinse, then drain. Repeat a few more times, until the water becomes clear. Cover the rice with clean water and soak 30 minutes. Drain.

Place the beef, ¾ cup water, and ½ teaspoon of the salt in a large Dutch oven or heavy pot and bring to a boil over high heat. Decrease the heat to medium-low, cover, and cook until tender, 40 to 45 minutes, checking every 10 minutes or so and adding a few tablespoons of water if needed to keep the meat covered.

In the meantime, bring several cups of water to a boil in a saucepan and boil the yellow split peas about 30 minutes, until cooked. Drain and set aside.

Soak the raisins in warm water 25 minutes; drain and set aside.

Make a paste of the garlic, chile, ginger, and 1 teaspoon of the salt in a mortar and pestle or small food processor, adding about 1 tablespoon water to make it smooth.

When the meat is tender and cooked and the water has completely evaporated, remove the lid and increase the heat to medium-high; allow the meat to fry and brown 5 to 10 minutes, adding a little vegetable oil if needed (if the meat isn't fatty enough). While frying, add the ground cinnamon and black pepper, plus the garlic-chile-ginger paste, and continue to brown, stirring occasionally, for a few minutes. Push the meat to one side of the pot and add the onion, adding a little vegetable oil if needed, and sauté the onion until it begins to soften, about 5 minutes, eventually mixing everything together.

Add the cooked yellow split peas and raisins, stir, then add the bay leaf, cinnamon stick, cloves, cardamom pods, peppercorns, and fennel, cumin, and coriander seeds, plus the remaining 1 teaspoon salt. Stir and cook until fragrant, 1 to 2 minutes.

Pour in 3 cups water and increase the heat to bring to a boil. Stir in the drained rice, allow the water to return to a boil, then decrease the heat to medium-low, cover, and cook until the rice is tender, about 10 minutes (check after 9 minutes). Turn off the heat and let sit, covered, 10 minutes. Remove the lid and fluff the rice with a fork, adjusting the seasoning with salt to taste. Remove the whole spices using a slotted spoon, if desired, and serve.

MANDI DJAJ
(YEMENI-STYLE ROASTED CHICKEN AND SAFFRON RICE)

CHICKEN

½ cup freshly squeezed lime juice

8 cloves garlic

2 teaspoons kosher salt

½ teaspoon ground black pepper

½ teaspoon red pepper flakes

¼ teaspoon ground turmeric

¼ teaspoon ground cumin

2 teaspoons vegetable oil

3 pounds chicken legs (thigh and drumstick), about 4 pieces, skin removed

RICE

2 cups basmati rice

2 tablespoons ghee

2 medium red onions, minced

6 whole cardamom pods, lightly crushed

5 whole cloves

3 small cinnamon sticks

1 tablespoon kosher salt

1½ teaspoons ground turmeric

¼ teaspoon ground black pepper

Pinch of saffron

Daqus (page 238) or Omani Salsa (page 238), for serving

SERVES 4 TO 6

Not quite *kabuli* or *maqboos*, *mandi* is a Yemeni dish of plump grains of rice, tinged yellow with turmeric, dotted with earthy, orange saffron, and flavored with the drippings of roast meat or chicken. *Mandi* is traditionally made by placing a large pot of seasoned rice in a hole over hot embers, topping the pot with a grate on which meat or chicken is placed, and covering the hole to allow the simmering rice to steam the meat and the dripping meat to flavor the rice. The dish is so incredibly popular in Oman, appearing on menus at roadside restaurants in dusty border towns in the north near the Emirates; in catering halls and Yemeni joints in the capital city of Muscat; and stuffed into silver takeout containers at stands lining the main drag of Salalah, that I felt it should be included in this book. We make our adapted version with chicken cooked directly in the saffron rice in a Dutch oven or baking dish, which makes for a simple, luscious, one-dish dinner.

Make a marinade for the chicken by puréeing the lime juice, garlic, salt, black pepper, red pepper flakes, turmeric, cumin, and oil in a blender or food processor until smooth. Place the chicken in a medium bowl, pour the marinade over, and mix well; cover with plastic wrap and chill 1 hour.

Preheat the oven to 375°F.

Place the rice in a bowl and fill with water. Swirl with your hand to rinse, then drain. Repeat a few more times, until the water becomes clear. Cover the rice with clean water and soak 30 minutes. Drain.

Heat the ghee in a large Dutch oven over medium-high heat and sauté the onions until brown, 12 to 15 minutes. Add the drained rice to the pot; cook, decreasing the heat to medium and stirring frequently to prevent burning, 4 to 5 minutes. Turn off the heat and stir in 3¼ cups water, the cardamom pods, cloves, cinnamon sticks, salt, turmeric, black pepper, and saffron. Alternatively, cook the onions and rice in a 12-inch skillet, then transfer to a 9 by 13-inch baking dish, stirring in the water and spices after transferring.

Remove the chicken legs from the bowl and shake off any excess marinade, then place on top of the rice mixture. Discard the remaining marinade. Cover the Dutch oven with aluminum foil to seal and cover tightly with the lid (wrap the pan twice with foil if using a baking dish). Bake 45 to 50 minutes.

Remove the lid and foil from the Dutch oven or baking dish and increase the oven temperature to 475°F. Cook until the chicken is brown, another 10 to 15 minutes.

Transfer the chicken to a plate and fluff the rice with a fork. To serve, scoop the rice onto a plate or platter and top with the chicken; serve with *Daqus* or Omani Salsa.

SAYADIYAH

(SALALAH-STYLE SEARED FISH IN RICE)

2 cups basmati rice

2 tablespoons ghee, plus more for serving

2 medium yellow onions, minced

5 cloves garlic, minced

1 (½-inch) piece fresh ginger, peeled and finely minced

1½ tablespoons kosher salt, plus more to season fish

6 whole cardamom pods, lightly crushed

4 whole cloves

6 whole black peppercorns

1 cinnamon stick

1½ to 2 pounds tuna, swordfish, or kingfish steaks, skin and bones removed, cut into thick 2-inch pieces

¼ teaspoon ground black pepper

2½ tablespoons vegetable oil

Coconut and Mint Yogurt Chutney (page 239), for serving (optional)

SERVES 4 TO 6

One major distinction that Omanis make when cooking rice is whether the protein is cooked on, in, or under the rice. In this classic southern Omani dish from the Dhofar province, thick steaks of kingfish, tuna, or swordfish are pan-fried before being cooked in the rice with cloves, cinnamon sticks, and black peppercorns. The fish, rice, and spices steam, infusing each grain with a subtle, deeply satisfying flavor. This recipe is inspired by a family favorite of Said Abdullah Al Hashli, whose auntie prides herself on making the best in Salalah. I love it with his Coconut and Mint Yogurt Chutney (page 239).

Place the rice in a bowl and fill with water. Swirl with your hand to rinse, then drain. Repeat a few more times, until the water becomes clear. Cover the rice with clean water and soak 30 minutes. Drain.

Heat the ghee in a medium Dutch oven or pot over medium-high heat and sauté the onions until they begin to brown, 8 to 10 minutes. Add the garlic and ginger, and cook 3 minutes. Then add 4¼ cups water, the salt, cardamom pods, cloves, peppercorns, and cinnamon stick. Increase the heat to high and boil 15 minutes.

Meanwhile, season the fish with a little salt and ground black pepper. Heat the vegetable oil in a wok or skillet over high heat and fry the fish until just brown, 4 to 5 minutes (the fish is fried for flavor and color and does not need to be cooked through).

Add the fish to the pot, stir, and add the drained rice. Bring to a rapid boil, then decrease the heat to medium-low and cook, covered, until the rice is done, 8 to 9 minutes (check after 7 minutes). Remove the whole spices using a slotted spoon, if desired, and fluff with a fork. Finish with a little ghee and salt and black pepper. Serve with Coconut and Mint Yogurt Chutney.

OMANI BIRYANIS

What makes a biryani a biryani, as opposed to any other rice dish, is the method: cooking the meat and spiced masala mixture separately from the fluffy basmati rice, then layering the elements and covering the pot to allow the mixture to steam briefly just before serving, ensuring the savory flavors are infused in every grain. A diverse range of spices and proteins are used in Omani biryanis, and though the resulting dishes are typically mild and quite different from those found in South Asia, the Omani cooks who have been making these rice dishes their entire lives, ironically, continue to insist they are Indian dishes, not Omani. One exception is the so-called Zanzibari biryani, which is tinged with saffron and mixed with torn fresh mint leaves and rose water. Though the dish was introduced to the elite, land-owning Omanis in Zanzibar by the 19th-century Indian traders who settled there, by the time the dish made its way to Muscat, the association with India had been replaced with that of East Africa.

OMANI LAMB BIRYANI
(LAYERED LAMB AND YOGURT MASALA RICE)

Omani lamb biryani is a dining-out favorite. Introduced by the large South Asian population, in the Sultanate the dish of layered spices, meat, and basmati rice takes on a distinctly local flavor with a mild, yogurt-enriched spice blend that's laced with saffron-infused rose water. The dish can be made with boneless lamb or chicken, though Omanis enjoy having the rice topped with bone-in pieces.

3 cups basmati rice

3 tablespoons ghee, divided

2 medium red onions, diced

5 cloves garlic, minced

1 (¾-inch) piece fresh ginger, peeled and finely minced

3 plum tomatoes, cored and minced

1 teaspoon ground cumin

1 teaspoon ground coriander

½ teaspoon ground ginger

½ teaspoon ground cinnamon

¼ teaspoon ground black pepper

¼ teaspoon ground cardamom

¼ teaspoon red pepper flakes

⅛ teaspoon ground cloves

⅛ teaspoon ground nutmeg

1 cup full-fat plain yogurt (preferably Greek)

1 dried lime, cut in half

2 to 2½ pounds lamb (bone-in or boneless; if using boneless, cut into 1½-inch pieces; if using bone-in, use 2½ pounds)

2 beef bouillon cubes

5 whole cardamom pods

5 whole cloves

5 whole black peppercorns

3 cinnamon sticks

1 tablespoon kosher salt

Pinch of saffron, soaked in 1 tablespoon rose water 5 minutes

Yogurt or Coconut and Mint Yogurt Chutney (page 239), for serving

SERVES 8

Place the rice in a bowl and fill with water. Swirl with your hand to rinse, then drain. Repeat a few more times, until the water becomes clear. Cover the rice with clean water and soak 30 minutes. Drain.

Melt 2 tablespoons of the ghee in a large Dutch oven or heavy pot over medium-high heat and sauté the onions until golden brown, 10 to 13 minutes. Add the garlic and fresh ginger, stir, and cook 1 minute, then add the tomatoes, cumin, coriander, ground ginger, ground cinnamon, black pepper, ground cardamom, red pepper flakes, ground cloves, and nutmeg. Cook, stirring often to prevent burning, until the tomatoes begin to break up, 3 to 5 minutes. Stir in 1 cup water, the yogurt, dried lime, lamb, and bouillon cubes; bring to a boil. Decrease the heat to medium and cook, covered slightly and stirring occasionally, 1½ hours. Remove the lid; if too much liquid remains (it should be saucy, but not too thin), increase the heat to reduce the sauce slightly, cooking on high 5 to 10 minutes more.

Meanwhile, place the drained rice, cardamom pods, whole cloves, peppercorns, cinnamon sticks, and salt in a large pot with 9 cups water and bring to a boil over high heat; boil 7 minutes, or until the rice is three-quarters cooked. Remove from the heat, drain in a large colander, rinse quickly with water, and drain again.

Melt the remaining 1 tablespoon ghee in a large Dutch oven or stockpot over low heat. Put half the partially cooked rice into the pot, spreading it to cover the bottom. Spread all the lamb mixture over the rice (if using bone-in lamb, carve the lamb off the bone before layering), and top with the remaining rice. Sprinkle the rose water and saffron mixture over the rice. Cover tightly with a lid and cook on the lowest heat possible about 25 minutes, or until the rice is cooked through.

To serve, stir gently to mix slightly and to distribute the sauce, pulling some lamb pieces to the top for presentation. Adjust the seasoning with salt to taste, and serve with yogurt or chutney.

SUR VEGETABLE BIRYANI
(SPICY LAYERED VEGETABLES AND RICE)

2 cups basmati rice

¼ cup vegetable oil

2 medium red onions, minced

4 cloves garlic, minced

2 plum tomatoes, cored and minced

2 tablespoons tomato paste

1½ teaspoons red pepper flakes

1 teaspoon kosher salt

1 teaspoon ground cumin

½ teaspoon ground cinnamon

½ teaspoon ground coriander

½ teaspoon ground black pepper

¼ teaspoon ground cloves

¼ teaspoon ground cardamom

¼ teaspoon ground nutmeg

1 bay leaf

1 chicken bouillon cube

1 serrano chile, seeded and minced

2 medium zucchini, cut into 1-inch rounds

2 carrots, cut into thin coins

1 medium to large russet potato, peeled and cut into 1½-inch cubes

1 small eggplant, cut into bite-size pieces

½ green bell pepper, minced

Plain yogurt, for serving

Chopped cucumber and tomato salad, for serving

Lime wedges, for serving

SERVES 6

This recipe comes from Wafa'a Al Shamakhi, who lives with her family in Sur. The city was, at one time, one of the most important trade ports connecting Oman and Zanzibar, and the city remains famous to this day for the production of *dhows*, traditional Arab trading vessels. This dish makes good use of produce and spices from Zanzibar and the subcontinent, using the vegetables in place of meat in the masala blend. It's delicious topped with Sur-style Fried Fish (page 108) and served with full-fat yogurt and a chopped salad. The healthy meal can easily be doubled or tripled to feed a crowd, which is a good thing for Wafa'a, as she has 14 children (*masha'Allah!*), a hungry husband, and throngs of extended family who love to stop by her villa at mealtime.

Place the rice in a bowl and fill with water. Swirl with your hand to rinse, then drain. Repeat a few more times, until the water becomes clear. Cover the rice with clean water and soak 15 minutes. Drain.

Heat the oil in a medium Dutch oven or pot over medium heat and sauté the onions until they begin to brown, about 10 minutes. Add the garlic, cook 1 minute, then add the tomatoes and tomato paste and continue cooking 5 minutes, stirring occasionally to break down the tomatoes. Add the red pepper flakes, salt, cumin, cinnamon, coriander, black pepper, cloves, cardamom, nutmeg, bay leaf, bouillon cube, chile, and vegetables. Decrease the heat to low, cover, and cook, stirring occasionally and adding a splash of water if necessary, until all the vegetables are tender and the sauce is dark in color, about 30 minutes. Remove the lid and increase the heat to medium-high, cooking until the sauce thickens, about 5 minutes.

Meanwhile, when the vegetables are almost done, cook the rice separately. In a large saucepan, bring 8 cups water to a boil with a generous pinch of salt. Stir in the rice and boil rapidly, stirring occasionally, until the rice is cooked through, 8 to 10 minutes (check for doneness after 8 minutes). Turn off the heat and drain the rice immediately in a large colander; rinse once and set aside to dry for a minute or two.

To assemble the biryani, create alternating layers of rice and the vegetable masala and mix gently just before serving. Adjust the seasoning with salt to taste. Serve with Sur-Style Fried Fish (page 108) and plain yogurt, as well as a chopped salad of cucumbers and tomatoes and lime wedges.

ZANZIBARI BIRYANI
(DOUBLE-COOKED CHICKEN IN ROSE WATER AND SPICE-INFUSED RICE)

Finished with rose water, fresh mint, and fried onions, this layered dish of rice, pan-fried chicken, and masala takes the longest of all the dishes in this chapter to make, but it also may be the most exotic of the rice dishes in Oman, and it has a real wow factor. It is labor-intensive, but worth the effort for the complex, unique flavors that come together in this Afro-Arabian dish from Oman's former East African stronghold. The broth from the boiled chicken is not used in this dish, so you can reserve it and use it as a base for a very flavorful chicken soup.

SPICE BLEND

2 teaspoons ground cumin

2 teaspoons ground coriander

2 teaspoons ground turmeric

1 teaspoon cayenne

1 teaspoon ground ginger

1 teaspoon ground cinnamon

½ teaspoon ground black pepper

½ teaspoon ground cloves

½ teaspoon ground cardamom

CHICKEN

3 pounds bone-in chicken pieces
(drumsticks and thighs), skin
removed

2 cloves garlic, mashed into a paste

1 (½-inch) piece fresh ginger, peeled
and finely minced or grated with a
Microplane

1 teaspoon kosher salt

¾ tablespoon ground cumin

½ teaspoon ground cinnamon

1 chicken bouillon cube

RICE

2½ cups basmati rice

1 serrano chile, split lengthwise

3 whole cardamom pods

1 cinnamon stick

1½ tablespoons kosher salt

1½ tablespoons vegetable oil

2 tablespoons minced fresh cilantro

1 tablespoon chopped fresh mint

ONION GARNISH

1 cup vegetable oil

1 medium red onion, halved and
very thinly sliced

SAUCE

1 plum tomato, cored and chopped

½ serrano chile, seeded

1 small to medium red onion, halved

⅓ cup packed fresh cilantro

½ teaspoon whole black
peppercorns

3 whole cloves

2 whole cardamom pods

1½ teaspoons cumin seeds

⅓ cup vegetable oil

1 small to medium red onion, finely
minced

½ green bell pepper, seeded and
finely chopped

6 cloves garlic, mashed into a paste

1 (2-inch) piece fresh ginger, peeled
and mashed into a paste

1 chicken bouillon cube

2 tablespoons ground coriander

1 teaspoon ground cinnamon

1 teaspoon kosher salt

1 teaspoon red pepper flakes

½ teaspoon ground turmeric

6 tablespoons tomato paste

ASSEMBLY

2 teaspoons rose water (with a few
threads of saffron soaked in it for
color; optional)

3 tablespoons ghee

SERVES 6 TO 8

Continued

To make the spice blend, combine the cumin, coriander, turmeric, cayenne, ginger, cinnamon, black pepper, cloves, and cardamom in a small bowl.

To prepare the chicken, place the chicken in a large pot with the garlic, ginger, salt, cumin, cinnamon, bouillon cube, 2 teaspoons of the spice blend, and water to cover (about 1 inch above the chicken, or 8 to 9 cups), and bring to a boil over medium-high heat. Cook, uncovered, until the chicken is cooked through, 40 to 45 minutes.

Meanwhile, prepare the rice. Place the rice in a bowl and fill with water. Swirl with your hand to rinse, then drain. Repeat a few more times, until the water becomes clear. Cover the rice with clean water and soak 30 minutes. Drain.

To make the frizzled onion garnish, heat 1 cup vegetable oil in a medium skillet or saucepan over medium to medium-high heat, and fry the thinly sliced onion, in two batches if necessary, until deep golden brown, 5 to 8 minutes. Remove the onions using a slotted spoon and transfer to a paper towel–lined plate to drain; set aside. Reserve the oil.

When the chicken is cooked through, transfer the chicken to a plate (reserve the broth for another use, if you like), remove and discard any skin, and set aside the chicken pieces to cool and dry.

To make the sauce, in a blender or food processor, purée the tomato, chile, halved onion, cilantro, peppercorns, cloves, cardamom pods, cumin seeds, and 2 tablespoons water into a smooth paste (adding a little more water if necessary).

Heat ⅓ cup vegetable oil in a large Dutch oven over medium-high heat and sauté the minced onion until brown, 9 to 12 minutes. Add the bell pepper, garlic, and ginger and cook, stirring, for a few minutes. Increase the heat to high and add the puréed paste, along with 1 tablespoon of the spice blend, the bouillon cube, coriander, cinnamon, salt, red pepper flakes, and turmeric, and cook a few more minutes. Stir in the tomato paste and cook 3 to 5 minutes, stirring and adding a little water at a time to prevent the sauce from burning, up to ⅓ cup total.

While the sauce is cooking, fry the chicken. Pat the cooked chicken dry and heat the reserved oil from the frizzled onions in a large skillet over medium-high heat. Fry the chicken pieces, flipping once, until brown on both sides, 3 to 4 minutes per side. Transfer to a paper towel–lined plate to drain.

Add the fried chicken to the pot of sauce and mix well to coat; cover, decrease the heat to low, and cook 10 to 15 minutes.

Meanwhile, cook the rice by placing 8 cups water, the drained rice, chile, cardamom pods, cinnamon stick, salt, and vegetable oil in a large pot and bringing it to a boil. Boil rapidly, uncovered, until the rice is just done, 6 to 9 minutes (check after 6 minutes, as it easily overcooks). Turn off the heat, drain the rice in a large colander, rinse once, shake to drain again, place in a large bowl, and stir in the cilantro and mint. Set aside.

Remove the pot of sauce from the heat and pour the chicken, sauce, and drippings into a bowl. Do not wash the pot.

To assemble the biryani, using the pot the sauce was cooked in, spread half the cooked rice to cover the bottom of the pot, sprinkle with 1 teaspoon of the rose water, spoon all the chicken and sauce over the rice, distributing it evenly, then top with the remaining rice. Sprinkle with the remaining 1 teaspoon rose water and dot with the ghee.

Tightly cover the pot, turn the heat to the lowest setting, and warm through, about 10 minutes. To serve, stir gently to mix just a little and distribute the sauce, pulling some chicken pieces to the top for presentation. Garnish with the frizzled onions.

CHAPTER 5

MEAT, SEAFOOD, AND
MARAK MAINS

The ethnic diversity in Oman is one of its most distinctive qualities. In addition to the families who trace their lineage to Gulf Arab tribes, there are Omanis whose ancestors came from Baluchistan, an area that spans modern-day Iran and Pakistan; ancient mountainous people know as Jabali, who have their own language; those who came from Zanzibar and the East African coast; and those whose ancestors were Shia traders from Mutrah who intermarried with Indians, Persians, Iraqis, and Africans, developing their own distinct creole language along the way. This mélange of influences is especially apparent in main dishes that are not rice-based like traditional Gulf Arab mains, but that might just as likely be served alongside bread, savory mashed green bananas, or the Zanzibari polenta called *ugali*.

Meat dishes like *lahm kalia*, which is similar to the slow-cooked, caramelized beef rendang curries of Southeast Asia, are delicious scooped up with sweet-savory *Aseeda* (page 56) or molasses-y Date Chapati (page 169). Rich Zanzibari Whole Fish in Coconut Sauce (page 104) is wonderful with plain white polenta, which they call *ugali* in East Africa. And the plethora of saucy Omani curries, called *marak*, which range from mild, coconut milk–enriched, creamy dishes to peppery, tomato-based *marak*, like kingfish curry laced with fennel seed from the coastal town of Sur, are served alongside everything from chapati to *ugali* to basmati rice with red lentils. This category of dishes, and the diverse ways they are enjoyed, reflects the global influences the ancient Arab seafarers brought back to Oman with them.

IT'S ALL *LAHM* TO ME

While traveling and cooking throughout Oman, we would always ask cooks what kind of meat they were using. The Arabic word for meat is *lahm,* which sounds awfully close to lamb, and even an Arabic word for lamb, *ghanim,* can sometimes mean goat. We spent a great deal of time scratching our heads and playing a kind of charades, with mooing and horns, desperately trying to figure out what to call for in our recipes, until we came to understand that meat is used rather interchangeably in Oman, based on what looks best at the butcher shop on a given day.

As in most of the world, meat is prized in Oman, and throughout the country it is an essential part of all celebratory meals, from pit-roasted *Shuwa* (page 43) to *Mishakik,* peppery beef skewers (page 26), to the stew-y, saucy meat dishes in this chapter. However, everyone we met during our travels pointed to the southern Omanis in Salalah in the Dhofar province as the biggest meat aficionados of all. "They have all kinds of meats there, and they love it too much!" our Muscati friend Sultan exclaimed.

We arrived in Salalah at the height of *khareef,* the season in August and September when misty rains blown in by Indian monsoons turn the hilltops around the coastal city emerald green.

Tourists from around the GCC flocked to the cool oasis, and people from surrounding Dhofari villages and Jabali mountain towns poured into the city to work at the festival and at pop-up roadside restaurants. Camels grazed in the misty hills and small herds of cows roamed the urban streets. Along the main thoroughfare, grillers charred spatchcocked chicken *madhbi* (page 37), simmered cubes of camel, and seared cuts of beef and goat alongside spirals of stuffed intestines. Between the takeout tents, rickety wooden shops were hung with curtains of drying beef and beef fat for the most popular Dhofari dish, called *ma'ajeen*, for which salted, air-dried strips of beef are cubed and fried in a pad of salted, dried beef fat over an open fire for a jerky-meets-cracklings snack that can be kept in a jar unrefrigerated for up to a month. This dish is so popular that it is almost always made and served at celebrations, like Eid, just like *shuwa* is in the rest of the country. These rows of restaurants dedicated to meaty meals, and *ma'ajeen*, the meatiest of snacks, have perhaps helped earn Dhofari residents their a reputation as the biggest meat lovers in Oman. Beef, goat, lamb, or even camel (if you can find it) are always fine substitutes for one another in our recipes, though you may need to adjust your cooking time to go a bit longer when using beef or camel, depending on the cut.

LAHM KALIA
(SLOW-COOKED CARAMELIZED BEEF)

1 to 1¼ pounds boneless beef, such as chuck or other marbled stew meat, cut into 2-inch pieces

4 whole cardamom pods

4 whole cloves

1 small cinnamon stick

1½ teaspoons ground coriander

1½ teaspoons ground cumin

½ teaspoon ground black pepper

½ teaspoon ground ginger

¼ teaspoon ground cardamom

¼ teaspoon cayenne

¼ teaspoon ground turmeric

1 teaspoon kosher salt

6 cloves garlic, smashed

1 large red onion, diced

¼ cup chopped fresh cilantro

SERVES 4

Cubes of lamb, beef, or camel simmer for hours with spices, onions, and garlic, until all that is left in the pot are dark, caramelized cubes of intensely flavorful meat in a slick of mahogany sauce. The method couldn't be easier: As with much of Omani cooking, it simply takes time. Our favorite recipe comes from one of Thuraya's family cooks, Shaymeena, who serves her beef *kalia* with Date Chapati (page 169), though it is also incredible paired with the lightly sweet flour-and-ghee dumpling *Aseeda* (page 56), as they do in the Dhofar province. If you want a spicier dish, a whole seeded serrano chile adds nice flavor, and if you find there seems to be too much liquid at the end of the cooking time, turn up the heat to evaporate it a bit more.

Combine the beef, cardamom pods, cloves, cinnamon stick, coriander, cumin, black pepper, ginger, ground cardamom, cayenne, turmeric, salt, garlic, onion, cilantro, and 2¼ cups water in a small Dutch oven or heavy saucepan. Bring to a boil and cook over medium to medium-high heat 30 minutes, adding water if necessary (up to 1 cup) and stirring occasionally. Decrease the heat to medium-low, and cook, covered, until the meat is tender, 1¼ to 1½ hours.

Remove the lid, stir, and turn the heat to high; cook, uncovered, 10 to 20 minutes more, depending on how much liquid remains, until nearly all the liquid has evaporated and only a thick glaze remains on the meat. Serve with subtly sweet *Aseeda* (page 56) mash or Date Chapati (page 169).

SWEET AND SPICY LAMB AND DATE STEW

1 teaspoon red pepper flakes

1 teaspoon ground turmeric

1 teaspoon ground ginger

1 teaspoon ground cinnamon

¾ teaspoon kosher salt

1 pound boneless lamb, such as shoulder or stew meat, cut into 1½-inch pieces

2 tablespoons vegetable oil

2 medium red onions, diced

3 cloves garlic, minced

4 cups Basic Omani Stock (page 234), or store-bought lamb or beef broth

2 tablespoons cornstarch

1 cup pitted dried dates (24 to 26 whole medium), roughly chopped

Cooked basmati rice, for serving

¼ cup sliced or slivered almonds, lightly toasted, for garnish

SERVES 4 TO 6

Though traditionally palm oil was the cooking oil of choice in Oman, in urban areas and the countryside alike, Omani vegetable oil has now become more common. Its use is promoted by companies like Oman Vegetable Oil & Derivatives that, much like the canned goods manufacturers of midcentury America, put out recipes like this one. Absolutely no one I know in Oman has ever heard of this dish, but it combines that ubiquitous Omani fruit, the date, with tender lamb for a sweet, savory, and slightly piquant sauce that, served over fluffy white rice and topped with a crunch of almonds, is one of the tastiest stews I've ever eaten.

Mix the red pepper flakes, turmeric, ginger, cinnamon, and salt in a large bowl. Toss the lamb in the spices and let sit 10 to 15 minutes.

Heat the oil in a medium Dutch oven or heavy saucepan over medium-high heat; cook the lamb until browned, 5 to 7 minutes, being sure to stir occasionally to prevent the spices from burning. Add the onions and garlic and cook until the onions begin to soften, 4 to 5 minutes. Slowly pour in the stock, scraping any brown bits from the bottom of the pot, and bring to a boil. Cover and simmer on low until the lamb is fall-apart tender, about 1½ hours.

In a small bowl, mix 2 tablespoons water with the cornstarch until dissolved. Uncover the pot and skim the fat from the surface, if necessary. Then stir in the cornstarch mixture and dates; cook, uncovered, until the stew is slightly thickened and the dates have softened, 20 to 25 minutes. Season with additional salt to taste; serve over basmati rice, sprinkled with the almonds.

BOUNTY OF THE SEA

Oman is blessed with nearly 1,300 miles of coastline, and the aquatic life is bountiful, with over 150 species of fish and crustaceans, from abalone in Salalah and lobster around the southern island of Masirah to tuna, hamour, grouper, and gigantic sweet prawns along the northern coast. Overfishing has depleted some of the stocks, so the government has put restrictions in place to protect this vital resource.

Seafood is extremely popular throughout Oman but is especially beloved far from the fertile coast in the mountains of Jabal Akhdar and in the deserts of the interior. In the mountain village of Al Hamra, residents have historically traded their precious, plentiful dates for fresh and dried fish from Muscat and Sohar. In the desert of Sharqiyah, the Bedouin likewise enjoy fresh tuna from places like Sur, Ashkharah, and Masirah Island. On the coasts, in the deserts, and in the mountains alike, dried salt cod called *malleh* and dried shark called *awal* are used in *kabuli* rice dishes and eaten as a kind of ceviche-like snack with lemon and onion.

Down in Salalah, I sat in the home of Saida, a former cook for His Majesty, with Salalah native Said Abdullah Al Hashli and some friends from Muscat. I asked Said why in this lush, coastal town I had encountered all manner of meat preparations but not a single seafood dish. "We have the cows and the goats, and so many meats, and we have the fish too. We eat fish, but it's an everyday kind of thing, so for festivals and celebrations, we prefer to make the meat," Said explained. "But you know something, if a really, really special guest comes to dinner, we will not serve him meat, we will serve him fish, because we want to show him that he is not a guest at all, but like our family."

After we left, our Muscati friend laughed and said, "We would rather die, literally rather die, than serve fish at a wedding or to an important guest." He paused, and added, "But we do love the fish. He's more healthy you know, and so tasty too."

MALLEH
(SALTFISH WITH CILANTRO AND LIME)

1 small to medium (about 2 ounces) salt cod or salt pollock fillet

¼ to ½ small red onion, quartered and thinly sliced

⅓ cup freshly squeezed lime juice

2 tablespoons chopped fresh cilantro

1 clove garlic, mashed into a paste

1 serrano chile, seeded and finely minced

Pinch of cayenne

Cooked basmati rice, for serving (optional)

SERVES 2 TO 4

This is a ceviche-like dish of salted white fish, like cod, or sometimes the dried baby shark called *awal*, that is soaked in lime with thinly sliced onion and cilantro. This dish has many variations, from a soupy mixture served in many restaurants to a drier version we ate from plastic containers on the beach. My favorite is moist and citrusy and can be eaten on its own or over the top of steamed basmati rice for a light dinner.

Place the salt fish in a small saucepan and fill with water until it covers the fish by at least 2 inches. Bring to a boil and boil 25 minutes, making sure not to break up the fish. Drain and rinse; return the fish to the saucepan and repeat this process one more time.

Drain the fish after the second boiling and rinse with cold water. Flake the fish with your hands (it will yield about 1 cup), making sure to remove any tiny bones. Place the flaked fish in a bowl and toss with the onion, lime juice, cilantro, garlic, chile, cayenne, and ¼ cup water; let sit at least 15 minutes. Adjust the amounts of lime juice, water, and chile to taste. Serve as a snack on its own or with cooked basmati rice.

SAMAKI WA KUPAKA
(WHOLE FISH IN COCONUT SAUCE)

This Zanzibari dish of roasted or grilled whole fish topped with a rich sauce of reduced coconut milk powder, oil, and chiles is simple to make. It is a delicious meal served with flatbread like Chapati (page 174) or polenta, called *ugali* in Zanzibar, and a simple Omani Vegetable Plate (page 136).

1 medium to medium-large (about 2 to 3 pounds) whole sea fish, such as sea bream, grouper, or red snapper, cleaned

1 lime or lemon, halved

FISH MARINADE

¼ cup freshly squeezed lime juice

2 cloves garlic

2 bird's eye chiles, stemmed

1 tablespoon vegetable oil

1 teaspoon kosher salt

½ teaspoon ground coriander

½ teaspoon ground turmeric

¼ teaspoon ground cinnamon

¼ teaspoon ground cumin

¼ teaspoon cayenne

SAUCE

6 tablespoons vegetable oil, divided

2 medium red onions, halved and thinly sliced

2 plum tomatoes, cored and minced

1 cup coconut milk powder

1 cup warm water

1 teaspoon tomato paste

2 tablespoons chopped fresh cilantro

1 bird's eye chile, stemmed

1 teaspoon kosher salt

1 teaspoon cornstarch

¼ teaspoon ground turmeric

2 tablespoons freshly squeezed lime juice

Lime wedges, for garnish

Cilantro sprigs, for garnish

SERVES 4 TO 6

Preheat the oven to 375°F. Line a baking dish or baking sheet with aluminum foil.

Clean the fish well by rubbing the cavity and body with the lime halves. Rinse and pat dry with a paper towel.

To make the marinade, in a blender or food processor, purée all the ingredients into a smooth paste.

Cut three ½-inch slashes in the skin of both sides of the fish and rub the marinade paste all over the body and into the slashes and cavity. Place the fish in the baking dish or on the baking sheet and let sit 20 minutes.

Roast the fish until cooked through, 30 to 45 minutes, depending on the size of the fish.

Meanwhile, to make the sauce, heat 4 tablespoons of the oil in a large skillet over medium-high heat and sauté the onions until they begin to brown, 8 to 10 minutes. Add the tomatoes and cook, stirring occasionally, another 5 minutes. Set aside for 5 minutes to cool.

In a small bowl, mix the coconut milk powder with the warm water until dissolved. Pour the coconut mixture into a blender or food processor and add the tomato paste, cilantro, chile, salt, cornstarch, turmeric, lime juice, and cooked onions and tomatoes. Purée until smooth.

Heat the remaining 2 tablespoons oil in the same skillet or pot over medium heat; add the sauce and cook, stirring often, until thickened, 10 to 15 minutes.

To serve, ladle a little sauce on a serving dish, place the roasted fish on the dish, and cover the fish, inside and out, with the sauce. Garnish with lime wedges and cilantro sprigs and serve with the remaining sauce on the side. This is great with Chapati (page 174) or *ugali*, a white polenta.

PAPLOU

(CITRUSY SEAFOOD SOUP WITH BASMATI RICE)

3 cloves garlic

1 (2-inch) piece fresh ginger, peeled and thinly sliced

¾ teaspoon ground turmeric, divided

1 teaspoon kosher salt

¼ cup chopped fresh cilantro, plus more for garnish

1 dried lime

¼ teaspoon ground black pepper

1 plum tomato, cored and diced

1 small or ½ medium red onion, diced

¼ cup freshly squeezed lime juice

⅛ teaspoon cayenne

1 pound tuna steaks, cut into 1½-inch pieces

Cooked basmati rice, for serving

Lime wedges, for garnish

SERVES 4

This light, citrusy soup is perhaps one of the healthiest dishes in the entire canon of Omani cooking. The origins of *paplou* are hotly debated, claimed by both Lawati Omanis, whose ancestors trace their roots to traders from the old Mutrah neighborhood and South Asia, and Baluchi Omanis with ties to Baluchistan in what is now eastern Iran and western Pakistan. The dish is one of the most popular in the coastal regions of Muscat and Batinah, beloved by nearly everyone. Variations abound, with some adding shellfish or *samak beed*, tuna roe, some versions spicy and others containing no chile at all, but the most common version of this dish is a simple but flavorful combination of black lime, onions, tomatoes, turmeric, chile, and fresh tuna. Served over a scoop of basmati rice, it is a wonderful summer supper.

In a small food processor or using a mortar and pestle, make a paste of the garlic, ginger, ¼ teaspoon of the turmeric, the salt, cilantro, and 1½ tablespoons water; set aside.

Scrub the dried lime and soak for a few minutes in water to soften the skin. Make a small hole by piercing it with a paring knife.

Bring 4½ cups water to a boil in a medium saucepan over medium-high heat; add the black pepper and the remaining ½ teaspoon turmeric and cook 2 minutes. Add the tomato, boil 5 minutes, then add the onion and cook 5 minutes more. Stir in the lime juice, garlic-ginger paste, cayenne, and dried lime; cover, decrease the heat to medium-low, and cook 15 minutes.

Remove the lime to avoid making the soup bitter. Add the tuna and gently stir; cover and simmer until the fish is cooked through, 10 to 15 minutes more. Serve over cooked basmati rice or Rice with Red Lentils (page 70), and garnish with chopped cilantro and lime wedges.

SAMAK MAQLI

(SUR-STYLE FRIED FISH)

1 small (about 1 pound) whole mild saltwater fish, such as branzino or porgy, cleaned, or 2 fish steaks

¼ cup freshly squeezed lime juice

2 cloves garlic, mashed into a paste

1 tablespoon ground cumin

1 tablespoon red pepper flakes

½ tablespoon ground turmeric

1 teaspoon kosher salt

Vegetable oil, for frying

SERVES 2

The spice blend for this fantastic pan-fried fish comes from home cook Wafa'a al Shamakhi, who lives in the historic port town of Sur. She roasts and blends her own spice rub for this basic fish fry, which is fantastic served atop her Vegetable Biryani (page 86). This spice blend and method work great with both small, whole fish and with steaks of firm-fleshed fish, like kingfish. The spice blend is easy to increase to accommodate the number of fish or steaks you want to make.

Wash the fish and pat dry with a paper towel.

Whisk the lime juice, garlic, cumin, red pepper flakes, turmeric, and salt together in a small bowl. Pour the marinade into a large resealable plastic bag, add the whole fish, seal, then shake and massage to coat the fish and cavity; let marinate 30 minutes in the refrigerator.

Heat about ½ inch of vegetable oil in a large nonstick skillet over medium to medium-high heat. Remove the fish from the marinade; discard the excess marinade. Fry the fish in the hot oil until crispy and cooked through, 4 to 7 minutes per side, depending on the size of the fish (2 to 3 minutes per side for steaks).

Serve with Sur Vegetable Biryani (page 86) or *Maqboos* (page 74).

RABEES

(CRISP-SAUTÉED SHARK WITH TURMERIC AND ONION)

2 pounds shark, bones and skin removed

2 cloves garlic

½ to 1 serrano chile, seeded

1 (1-inch) piece fresh ginger, peeled and sliced

1¼ teaspoons kosher salt, divided

2 tablespoons vegetable oil

1 large red onion, minced

1¼ teaspoons ground turmeric

1¼ teaspoons ground cumin

SERVES 4 TO 6

Unlike anything I've ever had before, *rabees* is a delicious sauté of shark, onions, turmeric, and hot chile, popular in the southern Dhofar province. The cooks at Bin Atiq restaurant in Salalah taught us the unusual method for making this dish. Boiling fresh shark and squeezing out the excess moisture with a cheesecloth before sautéing yields a deliciously crispy, flaked topping that is great served over steamed rice, as they do in Oman, or sprinkled on baked potatoes or pasta, or even mixed with mayo for an awesome alternative to a tuna sandwich. Shark is surprisingly inexpensive and most fishmongers carry it.

Place the shark in a pot, keeping the pieces as large as possible, and cover with cold water. Bring to a boil over high heat; cook 5 minutes. Turn off the heat and let sit 5 minutes. With a slotted spoon, transfer the shark pieces to a bowl. Let drain and cool in the bowl at least 1 hour; discard the liquid.

In a mortar and pestle or mini food processor, make a paste of the garlic, chile, ginger, and ¼ teaspoon of the salt, adding a sprinkling of water if necessary to smooth it out. Set aside.

When the shark has cooled, use your hands or wrap the fish in muslin or cheesecloth and squeeze out any excess water (the shark will be pliable and will become mushy and start to break up in your hands—this is normal). After squeezing as much moisture out as possible, flake the shark into small pieces, removing any skin or bones, and set aside.

In a medium or large skillet over medium heat, heat the oil and sauté the onion until it begins to soften and brown, 10 to 12 minutes. Add the garlic paste and cook 5 minutes; add the shark, turmeric, cumin, and the remaining 1 teaspoon salt, and continue to cook, mashing often to break up the shark and scraping the toasted bits off the bottom of the pan to prevent burning, but allowing for some browning. Do not add oil at any point. Cook until the shark is quite dry and breaks up into fine threads, 12 to 15 minutes.

Serve sprinkled over cooked basmati rice or another starchy base, like mashed potatoes, or over salads or in a sandwich.

OMANI MARAK (OMANI CURRY)

Saucy, spiced dishes in Oman are called *marak* or *saloonat* and are quite different from the curries found in India or Thailand. The flavor of Omani *marak* ranges from mild to only mildly piquant and features a distinctively Omani blend of spices. *Saloonat,* water boiled with vegetables, tomato paste, chicken, and Omani spices like cardamom, cloves, ginger, black pepper, and red chile, forms the mild base for quick rice dishes or a rustic variation of the savory bread stew *thareed,* and it is the most basic in this category of soupy dishes. But most *marak* are richer and more complex than basic *saloonat.*

Introduced to Zanzibar by traders from southern India, dishes like creamy Coconut Chicken Curry (page 114) and rich Coconut Shrimp Curry (page 117) prominently feature sweet milk from the coconuts that grow wild on the shores of Zanzibar; but once introduced to Oman, malty, deeply flavored coconut milk powder was swapped in for the fresh coconut milk. These dishes are enjoyed with both flatbreads, like chapati, and the traditional East African side, *ugali,* an unseasoned white polenta. Coastal seafood curries from places like the ship-building town of Sur and the small Dhofari fishing village of Mirbat feature tomato-based, black pepper–heavy sauces that are great counterpoints to sweet, local fish and squid or cuttlefish. These luscious, flavorful gravies are best eaten with bread, like pan-fried *Tawa* (page 182) or simple steamed basmati rice.

KUKU PAKA
(COCONUT CHICKEN CURRY)

¾ cup coconut milk powder, divided

2 large or 3 medium yellow onions, diced

3 tablespoons ghee

4 cloves garlic, minced

1 (2-inch) piece fresh ginger, peeled and finely minced

½ to 1 serrano chile, seeded and minced

1 teaspoon ground cumin

1 teaspoon ground coriander

1 teaspoon ground cinnamon

¼ teaspoon ground turmeric

4 whole cloves

1½ teaspoons kosher salt

1¼ cups warm water, divided

2 pounds bone-in chicken pieces, such as thighs and drumsticks (about 8 pieces), skin removed, or boneless, skinless chicken, cut into 1½-inch pieces

2 medium potatoes, such as Yukon Gold, peeled and cut into 1½-inch cubes

1 large carrot, cut into ½-inch coins (optional)

Handful of green beans, stemmed and cut into 1¼-inch pieces (optional)

SERVES 4 OR 6

A local adaptation of the Indian curries introduced by 19th-century South Asian traders, this Zanzibari favorite of chicken, potatoes, and sometimes vegetables simmered in a mixture of toasted coconut milk powder, ginger, chile, and subtle warm spices like cloves, cinnamon, and cumin is great with subtly sweet Date Chapati (page 169).

Place ½ cup of the coconut milk powder in a medium nonstick skillet. Turn the heat to medium-low and dry-toast, stirring frequently to prevent burning, until the powder becomes a very light shade of brown, 2 to 4 minutes. Remove from the heat and set aside.

In a medium Dutch oven or heavy saucepan, sauté the onions in the ghee until they begin to soften and brown, 10 to 12 minutes. Add the garlic, ginger, and chile, stir, and cook 5 minutes. Add the cumin, coriander, cinnamon, turmeric, and cloves, and fry for a minute to allow the spices to bloom, being sure to stir so they don't stick and burn. Add the toasted coconut powder, salt, and ½ cup of the warm water; stir and cook for a couple of minutes. Add the chicken and stir. Turn down the heat to medium-low and cook, uncovered, 5 minutes.

In a small bowl, stir the remaining ¼ cup coconut milk powder in the remaining ¾ cup warm water to dissolve. Add to the pot and increase the heat to medium-high to bring to a boil. Add the potatoes, decrease the heat to low, and cover; cook, stirring occasionally. After 30 minutes, add the carrots and green beans, if using; otherwise, cook for 40 to 45 minutes, until the curry has thickened slightly and the chicken and potatoes are cooked through. If the curry is still too thin after 45 minutes, turn the heat to medium-high and cook, uncovered, until slightly reduced, 5 to 10 minutes more. Serve alongside flatbread or basmati rice.

KAMBA WA NAZI
(SWAHILI COCONUT SHRIMP CURRY)

1½ to 2 pounds medium (41/50 count) fresh or frozen shelled shrimp, thawed if frozen, rinsed and drained

½ teaspoon ground black pepper

¼ teaspoon ground cardamom

½ teaspoon ground cinnamon, divided

4 to 6 cloves garlic, minced

1 (1-inch piece) fresh ginger, peeled and grated (about 1 tablespoon)

4 tablespoons freshly squeezed lime juice, divided

⅓ cup vegetable oil

2 medium red onions, minced

2 plum tomatoes, cored and minced

1 teaspoon tomato paste

⅔ cup coconut milk powder

1 cup warm water

1 teaspoon kosher salt

½ teaspoon ground coriander

¼ teaspoon ground cumin

¼ teaspoon ground turmeric

¼ teaspoon cayenne

2 tablespoons chopped fresh cilantro

1 or 2 serrano chiles, halved lengthwise and seeded, with stem attached

SERVES 4 TO 6

This fast, easy dish, introduced by Zanzibaris in Oman, is very popular in Muscat today. It utilizes an unusual technique in which the shrimp are tossed in a saucepan with garlic, lime juice, and ginger, without any water or oil, to slow-cook in their natural juices before being finished with a creamy, sweet-spicy coconut curry sauce.

Place the shrimp, black pepper, cardamom, ¼ teaspoon of the cinnamon, the garlic, ginger, and 2 tablespoons of the lime juice in a small saucepan and cook over medium or medium-low heat (do not add oil or water, as the shrimp will release quite a bit of liquid) until the liquid is almost gone, 20 to 25 minutes.

Heat the oil in a medium Dutch oven or heavy pot over medium heat and sauté the onions until they begin to brown, 12 to 15 minutes. Add the tomatoes and cook, stirring occasionally, until they begin to break down, 10 to 15 minutes; stir in the tomato paste and cook for a couple of minutes.

Mix the coconut milk powder with the warm water in a small bowl until dissolved. Add the coconut mixture to the pot, along with the salt, coriander, cumin, turmeric, cayenne, and the remaining ¼ teaspoon cinnamon and 2 tablespoons lime juice; stir and simmer for a few minutes. Add the shrimp and any drippings; cook, uncovered, over medium-low heat 10 minutes. Add the cilantro and split chile(s) and cook until fragrant, 3 to 5 more minutes. Serve with Savory Mashed Green Banana (page 130), Fried *Mandazi* bread (page 172), or steamed basmati rice.

SPICY ZANZIBARI SQUID CURRY

¼ cup vegetable oil

2 medium to large yellow onions, minced

1 small red onion, quartered

1 serrano chile, seeded

2 tablespoons plus 1 teaspoon freshly squeezed lime juice

½ teaspoon kosher salt

½ teaspoon ground coriander

½ teaspoon ground cumin

½ teaspoon ground ginger

½ teaspoon ground turmeric

¼ teaspoon cayenne

⅛ teaspoon ground cinnamon

⅛ teaspoon ground black pepper

⅛ teaspoon ground cardamom

Pinch of ground nutmeg

Pinch of ground cloves

3 tablespoons coconut milk powder

1 teaspoon cornstarch

¾ cup warm water

¾ pound cleaned squid, cut into ½-inch rings

SERVES 4

Despite the name, tart lime, rich coconut, sweet onion, and chile pepper harmonize in this dish, which is only slightly piquant. It can be made using squid or cubes of thicker cuttlefish, but in either case be careful not to overcook the seafood, and if using frozen, thaw before using. Many Swahili Omanis enjoy this dish served over *ugali*, a basic white polenta. It is also lovely over Rice with Red Lentils (page 70).

Heat the vegetable oil in a medium saucepan or pot over medium-high heat; sauté the yellow onions until slightly caramelized, 12 to 15 minutes.

Meanwhile, in a food processor or blender, purée the red onion, chile, lime juice, salt, coriander, cumin, ginger, turmeric, cayenne, cinnamon, black pepper, cardamom, nutmeg, cloves, and ½ cup water into a smooth sauce. Add the purée to the saucepan with the yellow onions and cook 5 minutes.

Mix the coconut milk powder and cornstarch with the warm water in a small bowl until dissolved. Add the slurry to the pan and decrease the heat to medium. Simmer 7 to 10 minutes, until slightly reduced. Stir in the squid and cook until just done, about 2 minutes. Serve with cooked basmati rice or *ugali*, plain white polenta.

MARAK SAMAK

(SUR-STYLE PEPPERY FISH STEAK TOMATO CURRY)

¼ cup ghee

2 medium red onions, minced

6 cloves garlic, mashed into a paste

2 tablespoons tomato paste

3 plum tomatoes, cored and minced

¼ green bell pepper, seeded and
  roughly chopped

1 serrano chile, halved lengthwise,
  seeded with stem attached

1 teaspoon kosher salt

1½ teaspoons ground cumin

¾ teaspoon ground black pepper

½ teaspoon ground cinnamon

¼ teaspoon cayenne

1½ pounds tuna or swordfish steaks,
  skin and bones removed, cut into
  1½- to 2-inch pieces

1 lime, halved

SERVES 4

In the ancient ship-building town of Sur, we met with Sulaf Al Rasbi in the quiet dining room of the Oman LNG (Liquefied Natural Gas) compound, where she works as the first professional female chef in town. She shared this recipe for a peppery tomato and tuna *marak* that is wonderful with with another Sur specialty, crisp *Muradef* (page 187) fennel bread, or with simple steamed basmati rice.

Melt the ghee in a medium pot or saucepan over medium heat. Sauté the onions until slightly caramelized, about 15 minutes. Add the garlic paste and cook for a few minutes, then stir in the tomato paste, tomatoes, bell pepper, and chile. Cook 15 minutes; then add the salt, cumin, black pepper, cinnamon, and cayenne. Stir and cook another minute or two.

Pour in 1 cup water and bring to a simmer. Add the fish and stir gently to mix, being careful not to break up any pieces. Simmer, uncovered, until the fish is cooked through, about 10 minutes.

Squeeze a lime half (or the whole lime if it's not particularly juicy) into the pot, stir gently, and remove from the heat. Cover and let sit 5 minutes before serving. Serve with basmati rice or flatbread, like *Muradef* (page 187).

MARAK HUBAR
(SPICY MIRBAT SQUID CURRY)

2 tablespoons vegetable oil

1 medium red onion, minced

3 cloves garlic, minced

2 plum tomatoes, cored and diced

1 tablespoon tomato paste

1 teaspoon kosher salt

1 teaspoon ground cumin

½ teaspoon ground ginger

¼ teaspoon ground turmeric

⅛ teaspoon cayenne

⅛ teaspoon ground black pepper

½ pound cleaned squid, cut into ½-inch rings

SERVES 4

In the small fishing village of Mirbat, just outside the city of Salalah in southern Oman, Said Naser Al Mamry runs Mina Seafood, a little restaurant overlooking the port where fishermen dock each morning. His menu is simple and appropriately seafood heavy, based around the catches that come in each day. He brought me a plate of cuttlefish, dressed in thick, burgundy-colored sauce studded with garlic and onions. I was surprised by the spicy kick of ground black pepper and cayenne at first bite; I had grown accustomed to the milder Omani spicing, and this was a pleasant change of pace. Here in the United States, we use squid in place of cuttlefish, as it is easier to come by and easier to work with. If you use cubes of cuttlefish, you will need to increase the cooking time to 20 to 40 minutes. The heat and texture of this squid dish stand up nicely to flaky squares of pan-fried *Tawa* bread (page 182).

In a medium skillet over medium-high heat, heat the oil and sauté the onion until it begins to brown and soften, 6 to 8 minutes. Stir in the garlic, cook 2 minutes, then add the tomatoes and cook until they begin to soften and break down, about 5 more minutes. Add the tomato paste, salt, cumin, ginger, turmeric, cayenne, and black pepper. Decrease the heat to medium and cook, stirring constantly, until the sauce becomes thick and somewhat pasty, 2 to 4 minutes more. Add the squid and cook until just done, about 2 minutes. Serve with a flatbread like *Tawa* bread (page 182).

CHAPTER 6

PRODUCE AND LEGUMES

It makes sense that in a country made up of 82 percent desert, the number of vegetarian dishes would be limited, the cuisine focused more on foods that keep for long journeys or sustain them, like the rice and meat that form the heart of the daily meal. But that's not to say produce and legumes aren't important in Oman. In the fertile mountains of Jabal Akhdar, people begin every meal with platters of the plentiful pomegranates, apricots, and nectarines that grow in their aptly named "Green Mountains." Down in Salalah, people sip fresh coconut water and eat baby bananas sold by roadside vendors. And dried dates, eaten day and night throughout the country, are perhaps the most important staple of the Omani diet (see page 137).

There are also a handful of key vegetable- and legume-based recipes that have been transformed and absorbed into the Omani culinary canon thanks to ancient connections with South Asia and East Africa. Indian dals trade the piquant heat of chiles for a distinctly Omani blend of warm, dried spices. Zanzibari staples like luscious, coconut-enriched *mohogo* (cassava), spinach, mashed bananas, and slow-cooked beans are made using flavorful dehydrated coconut milk powder and are enjoyed in Arab and Swahili homes and restaurants throughout Muscat.

So ordinary that it could be easily be overlooked, on every Omani table at every meal, you will find a plate of fresh, raw chopped tomatoes, cucumbers, onions, hot chiles, and a few shreds of cabbage or lettuce, without dressing or seasoning aside from salt and a wedge of lime. I have come to understand that their unadorned state is not a dismissal of this humble dish, but an acknowledgment of the vital, simple pleasure of fresh produce in an arid land.

MARAK DAL
(OMANI-SPICED RED LENTILS)

2 cups red lentils

2 large red onions, minced

6 cloves garlic, minced

3 plum tomatoes, cored and minced

1 serrano chile or small jalapeño, seeded and minced

1 teaspoon ground turmeric

½ teaspoon ground coriander, divided

¼ teaspoon ground cinnamon

¼ teaspoon ground ginger

¼ teaspoon ground black pepper

⅛ teaspoon ground cloves

⅛ teaspoon ground cardamom

⅛ teaspoon ground nutmeg

3 to 4 teaspoons kosher salt

2 tablespoons ghee, plus more for serving (optional)

½ teaspoon cumin seeds

1 medium to large russet potato, peeled and cut into ½-inch cubes

2 teaspoons tomato paste

2 dried limes

Fresh cilantro, for garnish

Lime wedges, for serving (optional)

SERVES 6

Every Omani household makes this Indian dish a little differently according to the tastes of the family and the origins of their cooks. This dal recipe was inspired by the distinctly Omani combination of heady spices like coriander, cinnamon, cloves, and ginger, and tart, dried black limes. We like to stir in lime juice and torn cilantro just before serving, but you can also serve with lime wedges and cilantro on the side as a garnish.

Soak the lentils in water 1 hour. Drain.

Place the lentils in a medium heavy saucepan or pot with 2½ cups water, about one-third of the chopped onions, half the garlic, the tomatoes, chile, turmeric, ¼ teaspoon of the coriander, the cinnamon, ginger, black pepper, cloves, cardamom, nutmeg, and salt. Bring to a boil, decrease the heat to low, and simmer, with the lid open slightly, 15 minutes.

Meanwhile, melt the ghee in a medium skillet over medium heat and sauté the remaining two-thirds of the onions until they begin to soften, 8 to 10 minutes. Stir in the cumin seeds and cook until fragrant, about 1 minute. Add the potatoes and the remaining half of the garlic and cook, stirring occasionally, until the onions and potatoes brown, 5 to 7 minutes. Add the remaining ¼ teaspoon coriander and the tomato paste; stir to coat.

Scrub the dried limes and soak in water for a few minutes to soften the skin. Make a small hole in the limes by piercing with a paring knife.

Add the potato and onion mixture to the lentils, along with the dried limes; stir and add more water as needed, ¼ to ½ cup. Simmer over low heat, stirring occasionally to prevent burning and with the lid slightly off, until the lentils and potatoes are tender, 20 to 25 minutes. Turn off the heat and let rest, covered, 10 minutes. Remove the dried limes and stir. Adjust the seasoning with salt to taste. Garnish with cilantro, and serve with lime wedges or melted ghee.

MCHICHA WA NAZI
(ZANZIBARI COCONUT CREAMED SPINACH)

3 tablespoons vegetable oil

2 medium red onions, minced

2 plum tomatoes, cored and minced

½ to 1 serrano chile, seeded and minced

2 (10-ounce) packages frozen spinach, thawed

1½ teaspoons ground cumin

1½ teaspoons kosher salt

½ cup coconut milk powder

⅓ cup warm water

SERVES 4 TO 6

This vegan Zanzibari dish, made with malty coconut milk powder, is the richest creamed spinach I've ever tasted. The luscious flavor develops in the last 10 minutes of cooking, so be sure to let it simmer for the full 30 to 35 minutes.

Heat the oil in a medium saucepan or pot over medium heat; sauté the onions until they begin to soften, 5 to 7 minutes. Add the tomatoes and chile and cook, stirring occasionally, 3 minutes.

Stir in ⅓ cup water, the spinach, cumin, and salt and bring to a simmer. Decrease the heat to low and cook, covered, until the tomatoes and onions are completely soft and the spinach is extra tender, 20 to 25 minutes.

In a small bowl, dissolve the coconut milk powder in the warm water. Stir the coconut milk mixture into the spinach and continue cooking, covered, on low heat until slightly thickened, about 10 minutes.

NDIZI MBICHI
(ZANZIBARI SAVORY MASHED GREEN BANANAS)

5 small to medium unripe green bananas (use completely green bananas; do not use plantains)

2 tablespoons vegetable oil

1 large yellow onion, minced

1 plum tomato, cored and minced

1 serrano chile, halved lengthwise and seeded, plus 1 thinly sliced, for garnish

1 teaspoon kosher salt

2 cups vegetable broth

¼ cup coconut milk powder

½ cup warm water

3 to 4 tablespoons freshly squeezed lime juice, plus more for serving

SERVES 4 TO 6

Deeply savory with bright hints of citrus and biting hot peppers, this starchy banana dish is a delicious, unusual, easy-to-make vegetarian main dish or side to serve along with other Zanzibari specialties like Coconut Shrimp Curry (page 117). Some cooks, like Hamida Badai, who shared her recipe with me, like to add boiled goat or lamb to theirs. You should use completely unripe (yellow) bananas—you'll know they are unripe when they are green and cannot be peeled by hand. You may have to ask at the supermarket if they have any in the back, as they typically do not put unripe fruit on the shelves.

Carefully remove the tough, fibrous banana peels with a paring knife. Cut the bananas into 2-inch pieces and soak in cold water until ready to use (this will prevent blackening).

Heat the oil in a medium saucepan or pot over medium-high heat and sauté the onions until they begin to soften and brown, 8 to 10 minutes. Add the tomato and cook, stirring occasionally, until it begins to break down, 4 to 5 minutes.

Drain the bananas and add to the pot, along with the chile halves and salt. Pour in the broth, decrease the heat to medium, and simmer, covered, until the bananas begin to soften, 15 to 20 minutes.

In a small bowl, mix the coconut milk powder with the warm water until dissolved. Add the coconut mixture to the bananas, as well as half the lime juice. Cook, covered, on low until the bananas are cooked through and tender, another 15 minutes.

Remove the lid and stir in the remaining half of the lime juice; adjust the seasoning with salt to taste. With a wooden spoon, gently mash some of the bananas, leaving about half the pieces whole. Continue cooking, uncovered, on medium-high heat until slightly thickened, about 10 minutes. Garnish with the thinly sliced chiles and finish with lime juice to taste.

MAHARAGWE YA NAZI

(ZANZIBARI SLOW-COOKED COCONUT BEANS)

1 (16-ounce) bag dried light red
   kidney beans

¼ cup vegetable oil

3 small to medium red onions, diced

½ green bell pepper, seeded and
   chopped

4 cloves garlic, minced

4 plum tomatoes, cored and diced

¼ cup tomato paste

1 teaspoon ground coriander

1 teaspoon ground cumin

1 chicken bouillon cube

⅓ cup coconut milk powder

¾ cup warm water

2 Scotch bonnet chiles

2 teaspoons kosher salt

MAKES ABOUT 6 CUPS

Inexpensive and easy to make, these chile-and-coconut-laced beans
are traditionally eaten for breakfast in Zanzibar. We found that the
coconut flavor intensifies as it sits, so it's even tastier the day after
cooking. I love to eat these savory beans with slightly sweet Fried
Mandazi bread (page 172). Be sure to use light red kidney beans as
the dark have a different flavor.

Soak the kidney beans in water overnight. Drain when ready to use.

Heat the oil in a large saucepan or stockpot over medium-high heat
and cook the onions, stirring occasionally, 5 minutes; add the bell
pepper and cook until it begins to soften, about 5 more minutes.
Add the garlic and tomatoes, cook 5 minutes, then stir in the tomato
paste, coriander, and cumin and cook 2 minutes more. Pour in 6 cups
water and add the bouillon cube and beans; increase the heat to high
to bring to a boil. Decrease the heat to medium or medium-low and
cook, covered and stirring occasionally, until the beans are very tender,
2½ to 3 hours.

In a small bowl, mix the coconut milk powder with the warm water until
dissolved. Add to the beans, along with the chiles and salt, and cook,
covered, 10 to 15 more minutes (adjust the heat to make sure the chiles
don't burst). Let sit, covered, at least 10 minutes (the beans taste better
the longer you wait) before serving. Adjust the seasoning with salt to
taste and serve with cooked basmati rice or sweet Fried *Mandazi* bread
(page 172).

DANGO
(CHILE-LIME CHICKPEAS)

1 (16-ounce) bag dried chickpeas

¼ cup ghee

4 to 6 cloves garlic, finely minced

2 teaspoons kosher salt

¼ teaspoon ground black pepper, plus more for serving

⅓ cup freshly squeezed lime juice

¼ teaspoon cayenne, plus more for serving

Lime wedges, for serving

SERVES 6 TO 8

Served throughout the GCC, this simple soupy dish of chickpeas in a slightly piquant lime broth with small, round red chiles from Africa is a favorite snack or breakfast and is served at many of the roadside tea shops. We make ours with ground cayenne, which is much more accessible and lends the same red chile flavor. Use dried chickpeas, not canned, as the flavor and texture will be far better, and the legume is the star of this dish.

Soak the chickpeas in water overnight, or up to 12 hours. Drain when ready to use.

Heat the ghee in a large saucepan or stockpot over medium heat; sauté the garlic until fragrant and just starting to brown, about 2 minutes. Add the drained chickpeas and 6 cups water; turn the heat to high and bring to a boil. Stir in the salt and black pepper and decrease the heat to low. Simmer the chickpeas, covered, until cooked through and tender, 1¾ to 2 hours.

Remove the lid and stir in the lime juice and cayenne; adjust the seasoning with salt to taste. Ladle into bowls with a little liquid and serve with lime wedges and a sprinkling of black pepper and cayenne.

THE OMANI VEGETABLE PLATE

1 large cucumber, sliced

1 or 2 ripe tomatoes, sliced

½ to 1 sweet red onion, sliced

3 to 5 bird's eye or serrano chiles

Shredded cabbage or lettuce

1 or 2 limes, cut into wedges

Salt, for serving

SERVES 4 TO 6

Though it's perhaps too simple to warrant a recipe, I felt compelled to honor this staple of the Omani table. No matter what ethnicity, whether at home or at a restaurant, at lunch and dinner you will always find a plate piled with crisp cucumber slices, juicy cut tomato, rings of red onion, hot chiles, and, often, shreds of cabbage or lettuce served alongside the hearty Omani mains.

Arrange the vegetables and lime wedges artfully on a plate and serve with salt.

DIVINE DATES

Majlis is the Arabic word for outer receiving rooms, typically built in the front of a home or sometimes as a communal hall in the middle of a small village, where neighbors can sit and pass the hours catching up and guests are welcome anytime, day or night. There are always steaming carafes of Omani coffee at the ready along with a bowl of intensely sweet dried dates: the ultimate symbol of Omani hospitality and the perfect sugary foil for the black coffee.

The exact origin of the date, cultivated since prehistoric times, is unknown, but the earliest signs of its harvest can be traced to the Middle East, specifically to the dry Gulf region, where the fruit remains an indispensable cornerstone of the diet. With 70 percent sugar by weight, ample protein, some fat, and a few essential vitamins, *tamir*, dried dates, have long sustained the nomadic people of Arabia, who at times subsisted on camel milk and the dried fruit alone. Consumed as snacks throughout the day, fiber-rich dates continue to be essential to the Omani diet to balance out the staple meals built around rich meat, bread, and rice dishes.

More than mere sustenance, dates are seen as a divine gift, and with good reason: The fronds are used for fuel and woven into everything from brooms to thatched roofs to baskets and mats. As a food, the fruit can be eaten out of hand, pressed for syrup, baked into cakes as a sweetener, and, in places where date palms are plentiful, like the small mountain village of Al Hamra, the fruit is soaked in water and lime and squeezed into a refreshing juice. Their religious significance in Islam is celebrated throughout the Muslim world, especially during Ramadan, when the Prophet Mohammed was said to have broken his daily fast with three or five dates. Many Muslims like to follow suit, considering it the healthiest and most pious way to begin their *iftar*, the first meal eaten after sundown during the holy month.

Once dried, this amazing fruit can withstand the heat of a desert trek or the chill of a mountaintop winter snowstorm, remaining delicious and at the ready to be savored or offered to a hungry guest, making it the perfect food to represent a people for whom every meal, no matter how humble, is a celebration of the daily gifts of life.

BETWEEN MEALS

Dawn and I began our north-to-south Omani home-cooking road trip in Dubai in the United Arab Emirates, our first destination the border town of Buraimi. A maze of checkpoints broke up the flat tundra strewn with low brush, and as we crossed the border, I began to see the familiar Omani architecture of low, flat-roofed buildings and the royal crest waving on flags atop government buildings. As we drove, sand rippled across the pavement like swimming eels.

Then it began to rain.

The rain in the desert, where the air is thick with dust and sand, is slow. That afternoon, it fell in thick, unhurried drops before rolling up the windshield. Our friends, Ameer and Sultan, started to grin, pulling out their cell phones to take pictures. Desert dwellers passionately love the rain. And it doesn't rain often, maybe a dozen times a year. By odd chance, it always seemed to rain at least once when I was there.

It is as though the thick, slow rain in Oman keeps the same steady pace as the Omani people, who savor its appearance, every time it comes, for as long or short as it lasts. As with so many things, they seem to have perfected the art of taking life as it comes, the good and bad, with an utter confidence that it is all part of life and God's plan. *Dunia*, as they say, "That's the life." It made me wonder if someone like me, from a hurried, competitive land where destiny is thought to be of our own making, could

learn how to live more slowly, more in the present, like they do.

Ameer's cell phone rang. *"Salam Alaikum, kef hallek?"* he murmured. It was Maryam, the woman we were going to cook with at the Buraimi Women's Association. He said a few more words, then turned the car back toward the sea and the ancient port city of Sohar. "The rain, it flooded the road of their village, so she told us to come back tomorrow," he said.

My stomach grumbled as he pulled off the highway to stop at the Ahlain! gas station. He jumped out and returned with bottles of water and bags of Chips Oman, a tangy, sweet-spicy chili-flavored potato chip that's a favorite snack in the Sultanate. He drove up to the adjacent tea shop and honked the horn twice. An Indian man ambled out to take our order.

"Araba karak chai, wa khubz ragag ma'a beed wa jibnee," he ordered. The man returned with steaming cups of milky, sweet tea and paper plates of thin Omani bread folded around a smear of creamy white cheese and egg.

I savored the warming, thick tea as I tore off bites of soft bread oozing with salty cheese. Warm and dry and satiated until our next meal, I leaned back in my seat and let the sounds of classic Arabian Gulf music—the whine of the stringed oud and the wail of the *khaleeji* singer—playing softly on the radio wash over me. I watched the desert sky streak pink and gray and white. I lived in that moment, knowing it would just be one of many peaceful, satisfied times to come on our long journey south. That moment, like a sustaining snack between great meals, was brief and perfect.

Throughout our drives, I had many wonderful bites between meals. I learned that tea and cheese-smeared *Khubz Ragag* (page 162) is about the best breakfast you can ask for, but it also makes for a wonderful pick-me-up anytime day or night, whether at the base of the towering mountains of Jabal Akhdar or along the bustling byways of Muscat. I learned that each visit to the Mutrah souk meant brown paper bags of *Sambusa* (page 148) and *Kachori* (page 147), fried snacks that made their way to the Sultanate via Zanzibar. In the far southern city of Salalah, I found that the local, cracker-like *Kak* bread (page 184), studded with nigella seeds and scented with cardamom, was the perfect accompaniment to a hot cup of Dhofari *Karak* (page 220), rich with sweetened condensed milk, cardamom, and herbaceous wild thyme. And at every home we entered along our thousand-mile trek, coffee and dates always awaited us.

Except for the meat and rice of the midday meal, all else was interchangeable, as with *Balaleet* (page 197), the sweet vermicelli and salty egg dish so loved in Buraimi and the Emirates. Desserts like Dhofari *Karas* (page 208), fresh noodles simmered in sweet, cinnamon-laced coconut milk, are also enjoyed for breakfast. And the thick, gelatinous Omani *Halwa* (page 210), a dessert of sugar and ghee flavored with saffron or sometimes dates, was offered with coffee just before or after the main meal of the day, or at night, or in the afternoon, or served any time a sweet, a satisfying bite was in order to get us through to the next stop.

CHAPTER 7

SAVORY BITES

Late one Friday night, Dawn and I arrived at chef Issa Al Lamki's mother's house in the suburban neighborhood of Al Khoud. We sat in the front room on overstuffed sofas, the sweet smell of frankincense wafting around us. Fresh juices were passed and the large space began to fill with brothers, sisters, in-laws, children, and a new baby until the cavernous home echoed with the sounds of happy voices. Issa's mother, wrapped in brightly colored purples and greens that contrasted beautifully with her dark skin, sat quietly, smiling over her brood of children and grandchildren. I asked Issa if he had cooked everything. He laughed, shaking his head. "Not in this house. Here, my mother is the head chef, but I made a few things. Let's go eat."

He led us out of the sitting area and into an adjacent dining room where, laid out on a plastic sheet covering the Persian rug, were all manner of savories: *Mishakik* beef skewers (page 26); a dried fish and mango salad of Issa's own creation; *Musanif Djaj* (page 152), a double-fried circle of dough stuffed with spiced, shredded chicken and caramelized onions; and

the trinity of fried Zanzibari snacks: tuna croquettes (page 144), chile-spiked potato puffs (page 147), and chicken and beef *sambusas* (page 148). Though *kachori* are found in India, in Oman they are associated with Zanzibar, where 19th-century Indian traders settled and swapped recipes with the local population. Zanzibaris and Arab Omani traders then brought these foods to Muscat with them, and the association stuck. Lubna, Issa's sister, turned to me: "This is so exciting for us. We usually only eat like this during Ramadan to break our fast."

Typically these fried delicacies are found at stands in the souk or at tea and coffee shops along the roadsides, so beyond *iftar* dinners during Ramadan, or a casual gathering, most snacking is done outside the home. I had only ever enjoyed these treats at places like Zanzibar Island restaurant and the tea shops in the Mutrah souk. So that night, eating fresh, homemade versions of these delectable fried foods, surrounded by the roaring din of this joyous family, made for the best midnight snack I'd ever had.

KATLESI ZA SAMAKI
(TUNA CROQUETTES)

2 medium to large russet potatoes, peeled and cut into 1-inch pieces

1 teaspoon kosher salt, plus a pinch, divided

2 tablespoons minced fresh cilantro

1 tablespoon freshly squeezed lime juice

½ teaspoon ground black pepper

¼ teaspoon cayenne

¼ teaspoon ground cumin

2 large egg whites

2 (5-ounce) cans tuna in water, drained and squeezed dry

1 (1 to 1½-inch) piece fresh ginger, peeled and mashed into a paste or grated on a Microplane

3 cloves garlic, mashed into a paste

1 serrano chile, seeded and minced

Vegetable oil, for frying

2 large eggs, beaten

3 cups unseasoned breadcrumbs

Lime wedges, for serving

Hot sauce or Omani Mango Chutney (page 242), for serving (optional)

MAKES 16 TO 20
CROQUETTES

This tasty blend of mashed potato, canned tuna, hot chiles, and lime costs almost nothing to make. Once breaded, they can be deep-fried or shallow-fried, but be sure not to refrigerate the mixture before cooking, as this affects the flavor of the potato. Serve with mild Omani Mango Chutney (page 242), if you like.

Bring a pot of water to a boil, add the potatoes and a pinch of salt, and boil until cooked through and tender, about 15 minutes. Drain and transfer the potatoes to a large bowl; mash until smooth. Stir in the cilantro, lime juice, black pepper, cayenne, cumin, egg whites, tuna, ginger, garlic, chile, and the remaining 1 teaspoon salt; mix well. Divide the mixture into 16 to 20 fish stick–shaped croquettes, about 3 inches long and ¾ inch thick, and place on a baking sheet. Let sit 30 minutes.

Heat 2 inches of oil in a medium pot over medium-high heat until a deep-fry thermometer reads 350°F. Place the beaten eggs and breadcrumbs in separate shallow bowls. Dip each croquette into the eggs and then roll in the breadcrumbs; fry until golden and crisp, 2 to 4 minutes. Alternatively, bread the croquettes and then shallow-fry in a little oil in a skillet over medium-high heat 3 to 5 minutes. Remove with a slotted spoon and drain on paper towels. Season with more salt if needed; serve with lime wedges and hot sauce or Omani Mango Chutney.

KACHORI
(FRIED POTATO-CHILE PUFFS)

2 large russet potatoes, peeled and cut into 1-inch pieces

2 tablespoons minced fresh cilantro

2 cloves garlic, mashed into a paste

½ to 1 serrano chile, seeded and minced

1 tablespoon freshly squeezed lime juice

2 teaspoons kosher salt, divided, plus more as needed

¾ cup gram flour (chickpea flour)

½ teaspoon ground cumin

½ teaspoon ground turmeric

Vegetable oil, for frying

MAKES 1 DOZEN PUFFS

Similar to the *kachori* found in India, in Oman this battered and fried potato puff is associated with Zanzibar, where it was introduced by the 19th-century Indian traders who settled there. Though they are fried and seem like they should be super-crispy, *kachori* often come out on the softer side, the coating there to hold together the fluffy seasoned potato, but not always to lend a big crunch. Our recipe was developed to try to maximize the crunch, but it takes some practice to achieve the desired texture. Despite the flecks of hot chile pepper, these puffs are relatively mild, so they pair well with a chutney or hot sauce.

Bring a large pot of water to a boil and boil the potatoes until cooked through and tender, about 15 minutes. Drain and transfer the potatoes to a medium bowl; mash until smooth and let cool slightly. Stir in the cilantro, garlic, chile, lime juice, and 1 teaspoon of the salt. Roll the potato mixture into about a dozen balls slightly smaller than golf balls.

Make a batter by whisking the flour, cumin, turmeric, remaining 1 teaspoon salt, and ¾ cup water until smooth and slightly thick. (Add a sprinkle of water if it becomes too thick, as it thickens as it sits.)

Heat about 2 inches of oil in a wok or medium saucepan over medium or medium-high heat until a deep-fry thermometer reads 325°F. Working in batches, dip the potato balls in the batter and carefully drop into the hot oil; fry until golden and crispy, 2 to 4 minutes. Remove with a slotted spoon and drain on paper towels; season with more salt, if desired. Serve with hot sauce, ketchup, or a fruit chutney.

SAMBUSA

(FRIED TRIANGLE PASTRIES STUFFED WITH GROUND CHICKEN)

FILLING

1 tablespoon vegetable oil

3 scallions, chopped

1 small red onion, minced

3 cloves garlic, minced

1 (½-inch) piece fresh ginger, peeled and grated or finely minced

1 serrano chile, seeded and minced

1 pound ground chicken

2 tablespoons minced fresh cilantro

1¼ teaspoons ground cumin

1 teaspoon kosher salt

½ teaspoon ground black pepper

1 tablespoon unbleached all-purpose flour

25 frozen or refrigerated 6-inch square samosa or spring roll pastry wrappers (not rice wrappers), thawed if frozen

Vegetable oil, for frying

MAKES 25 PASTRIES

Most intriguing and exemplary of the complex web of culture and trade throughout the Indian Ocean is the mystery of the *sambusa*, a triangular fried pastry stuffed with various fillings from cabbage to ground beef to the spiced chicken-and-onion mixture called for here. Despite its strong association with India, where it is called samosa, the *sambusa* originated in the Middle East, with versions found in ancient Mesopotamian and Palestinian cookery. It traveled through Central Asia to South Asia via the trade routes in the 13th century, but in Muscat today, people do not associate this popular snack with their close Middle Eastern neighbors and longtime trade partners in Iraq, or even with India, but instead consider it a Zanzibari snack. How did this happen? Did the fried treats come to Zanzibar from Egypt with the Saharan trade caravans? Did 19th-century Indian traders introduce them to East Africa? No matter the route they took, the fact remains that these fried snacks took the long way to get from their ancient birthplace in central Arabia, circumnavigating the trade routes of the east, before being reintroduced to Oman by the traders of Zanzibar. They are wonderful with fruit chutney or with spicy Dhofari Coconut-Eggplant Chutney (page 241).

To make the filling, heat the oil in a medium skillet over medium-high heat and sauté the scallions and onions until they begin to soften and brown, 5 to 8 minutes. Add the garlic, ginger, and chile, stir, and cook for a few minutes. Add the chicken, cilantro, cumin, salt, and black pepper. Cook, stirring frequently to crumble the chicken, until cooked and browned, about 5 minutes. Taste and adjust the seasoning with salt and pepper; set aside to cool.

Continued

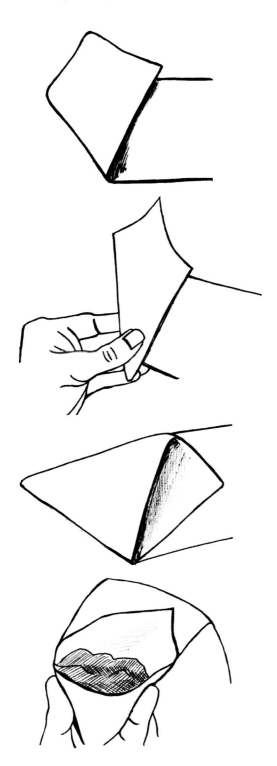

Mix 3 tablespoons water with the flour in a small bowl to make a kind of pastry glue. Cut each square pastry wrapper in half and put the 2 pieces together to form a rectangular strip, overlapping by ½ inch. Paste the overlapping pieces together with the pastry glue, creating long rectangles. Working with one wrapper strip at a time, make a cone at the bottom by lifting the bottom right corner closest to you up and over to the left so the point of the corner sticks out ½ inch over the left edge, then fold it back on itself to form a pocket. Spoon 1½ to 2 tablespoons of the chicken filling into the cone and then fold the filled cone, as you would a flag, in on itself, until the entire wrapper is folded, creating a sealed triangle. Use a little pastry glue to seal the triangle closed. Transfer the *sambusas* to a baking sheet and cover with a damp towel until ready to fry.

Heat 2 inches of oil in a wok or medium saucepan over medium to medium-high heat until a deep-fry thermometer reads about 325°F. Drop in several *sambusas* at a time and fry, flipping as necessary, until golden and crispy, 4 to 6 minutes. Transfer with a slotted spoon to a baking sheet lined with paper towels to drain. Serve with Omani Mango Chutney (page 242).

MUSANIF DJAJ
(TWICE-FRIED CHICKEN DUMPLINGS)

FILLING

½ pound boneless, skinless chicken breast, cut into 1-inch pieces

1 tablespoon finely minced garlic

1 tablespoon finely minced fresh ginger

2 tablespoons freshly squeezed lime juice, divided

1 tablespoon vegetable oil

2 medium red onions, minced

1½ teaspoons kosher salt

¼ teaspoon ground cinnamon

¼ teaspoon ground black pepper

1 serrano chile, seeded and minced

2 tablespoons minced fresh cilantro

BATTER

2½ cups unbleached all-purpose flour

2 large eggs

½ teaspoon kosher salt

2 tablespoons vegetable oil, plus more for frying

MAKES ABOUT
30 DUMPLINGS

Using a simple, pancake-like batter, these dumplings require a two-step frying process to hold their shape while staying thin and crispy. And though they can be deep-fried or shallow-fried, we prefer the slightly chewier texture of the shallow-fried version. The steps involved are well worth the effort, as these crisp, chewy patties, stuffed with sweet charred onions and shredded chicken, are one of the most satisfying and singular of all Omani snacks.

To make the filling, in a medium saucepan, bring 2 cups water to a boil and cook the chicken, garlic, ginger, and 1 tablespoon of the lime juice, covered, over medium heat 45 minutes. Drain the chicken mixture and discard the liquid. When the chicken is cool enough to handle, finely chop the chicken, garlic, and ginger.

Heat the oil in a medium skillet over medium-high heat and sauté the onions until they begin to soften and brown, 8 to 10 minutes. Turn off the heat; stir in the salt, cinnamon, black pepper, chile, cilantro, remaining 1 tablespoon lime juice, and the chopped chicken mixture. Let cool.

To make the batter, a few minutes before you are ready to assemble the dumplings, whisk the flour, eggs, salt, 2¼ cups water, and the vegetable oil together to make a thin, pancake-like batter, adding a little more water in order to achieve this consistency if the mixture is too thick.

To form the *musanif*, heat a large nonstick skillet over medium-high heat. Spoon 1 tablespoon batter into the pan and spread it out, using a circular motion, into a thin pancake about 2½ inches wide. Put 1 tablespoon of the filling in the middle and spread to flatten, then drizzle about 1 teaspoon batter over the filling. Cook until set, 1 to 2 minutes, then flip and press down with a spatula to flatten; cook for another minute or two, trimming any excess with the tip of spatula to keep the circular shape, if desired. Place on a baking sheet until ready to fry. Repeat until the batter and filling are gone, putting several in the skillet at once and rubbing the pan lightly with oil as needed to prevent sticking and burning.

Heat ½ to 1 inch of oil in the same skillet over medium-high heat until a deep-fry thermometer reads about 350°F. Fry the *musanif*, flipping once, until golden brown and crisp, 4 to 6 minutes. Drain on paper towels and serve with hot sauce or a chutney, if you like.

AL HAMRA MUSANIF LAHM
(PAN-SEARED MEAT DUMPLINGS)

DOUGH

4½ cups unbleached all-purpose flour

1 teaspoon kosher salt

FILLING

2 medium red onions, minced

2 tablespoons ghee, plus ¼ cup, melted, for oiling hands and for frying

1 pound boneless beef steak, such as shoulder or chuck, cut into ½-inch pieces

1 teaspoon kosher salt

1 teaspoon ground cumin

½ teaspoon ground coriander

½ teaspoon ground cinnamon

½ teaspoon ground ginger

¼ teaspoon ground black pepper

¼ teaspoon ground cloves

⅛ teaspoon ground cardamom

⅛ teaspoon ground nutmeg

⅛ teaspoon ground turmeric

MAKES 25 TO 30
DUMPLINGS

In the mountain town of Al Hamra, near the ancient trading city of Nizwa, women from the Al Abry tribe taught me how to make a popular village snack of pan-fried dumplings stuffed with Omani-spiced meat. Unlike the twice-fried dish of the same name popular in Muscat, this rustic dough is formed and stuffed in the hand and simply griddle-charred before being drizzled with rich ghee.

First, make a loose, elastic dough by whisking the flour and salt in a bowl and slowly adding 2 cups water while stirring to form a dough. Using your hand, knead the dough in the bowl using a slapping and grabbing motion until it comes together and is smooth, 1 to 2 minutes (the dough will be a little sticky and loose). Cover with plastic wrap and set aside at room temperature 30 minutes.

To make the filling, in a medium saucepan, sauté the onions in 2 tablespoons of the ghee over medium heat until they begin to brown, 8 to 10 minutes. Add the meat, salt, cumin, coriander, cinnamon, ginger, black pepper, cloves, cardamom, nutmeg, turmeric, and ½ cup water. Simmer over medium heat, slightly covered and stirring occasionally to prevent burning, until the meat is tender and most of the liquid has evaporated, about 30 minutes. Let the filling cool 10 minutes.

To make the dumplings, rub a little melted ghee in the palm of your hand to make working with the dough easy and to prevent it from sticking to your hands. Pinch off a piece of dough slightly smaller than the size of an egg, or about 1½ tablespoons, then pat and flatten it into an oval shape in the palm of your hand. Put about 2 teaspoons of the filling in the center, fold the dough over and seal, then pat into a flat circle, like a hockey puck, about ½ inch thick (it is fine if pieces of the meat poke through the dough in some places—it doesn't need to be perfectly enclosed). Place on a greased baking sheet and repeat, oiling your hand with ghee each time, until the dough and filling are used up.

Melt 1 to 2 teaspoons of ghee in a large cast-iron skillet over medium to medium-high heat. Cook the *musanif*, about 3 at a time, until the dough is cooked through and browned with a few charred spots, 2 to 3 minutes per side. Add more ghee to the pan between batches. Serve on their own or with hot sauce, if you like.

CUCUMBERS WITH SALT AND LIME

2 seedless Persian cucumbers,
  cut into coins

Salt

1 lime, cut into wedges

SERVES 2 TO 4

At humble restaurants and the odd hotel dive bar in Muscat, a bowl of sliced cucumbers will be offered, along with lime wedges and salt. The simple combination is a wonderfully refreshing between-meal snack.

Sprinkle the cucumbers with a pinch of salt and a squeeze of lime juice just before serving. Serve with wedges of lime and a salt shaker on the table.

CHILI, LIME, AND GHEE CORN CUPS

3 medium to large ears of corn, shucked and washed

2 to 3 tablespoons ghee or butter, melted

4 teaspoons freshly squeezed lime juice

1 teaspoon kosher salt

¼ teaspoon cayenne

MAKES 4 (½-CUP) SERVINGS

Similar to Mexican *esquites*, this citrusy steamed corn snack is found in cities throughout the Sultanate, but it is especially popular in the southern city of Salalah during *khareef*, the peak tourist season, when the cool winds of the Indian monsoons draw visitors from around the region. Paper or Styrofoam cups of freshly steamed corn, doused with a healthy dollop of margarine (we prefer ours with ghee or butter), a splash of lime, a pinch of salt, and a shake of cayenne, are hawked along with fresh mango slices, french fries, and ice cream from carts lining the perimeter of the Salalah souk and from pushcarts at the *wadis* (dry riverbeds) and the waterfalls in the surrounding hills.

Bring an inch of water to a boil in a large pot fitted with a steamer basket. Steam the corn until just cooked, 5 to 10 minutes, depending on the freshness of the corn. Remove and, using tongs or a towel to hold the ears, cut the corn off the cobs and place in a medium bowl.

Stir in the ghee, lime juice, salt, and cayenne while the corn is still hot. Adjust the amounts of everything to taste. Serve hot, in disposable cups, if you like.

CHILI-SPICED POTATO CHIPS

5 or 6 small russet potatoes, peeled and sliced 1/16 inch thick using a mandoline

¼ cup distilled white vinegar

1 to 2 green scallion tops

Zest of 1 lime

1 tablespoon sweet paprika

1 tablespoon kosher salt, plus more as needed

½ teaspoon cayenne

½ tablespoon sugar

½ teaspoon granulated garlic or garlic powder

¼ teaspoon black lime powder

Canola oil, for frying

SERVES 6 TO 8

When driving through the Sultanate, at least a few times an hour, we would hear: "*Nahnoo buhiboo Chips Oman! Buhiboo Chips Omaaaaaan! Chips Oman!*" ("We love Chips Oman! Love Chips Omaaaan! Chips Oman!") It was the maddeningly catchy theme song of the beloved tart, mildly spicy chili-flavored potato chips that have been made in the Al Wadi Al Kabir neighborhood of Muscat since 1989. This recipe is inspired by the ubiquitous chips that are eaten by the bagful, crumbled into *khubz ragag* with cheese and egg (page 162), and sprinkled over bread and Puck cheese spread for "Chips Oman sandwiches." Use small potatoes, sliced super-thin, to achieve the classic wavy shape and super-crisp texture of these chips.

As the potatoes are sliced, place them in a bowl of cold water to prevent browning. When finished, drain the potatoes and cover with fresh cold water and the vinegar; mix and let soak until ready to fry.

To make homemade dried scallions, thinly slice the green scallion tops, spread out the bits between two paper towels, and microwave on high 3 minutes. To make dried lime zest, do the same, but microwave 1 to 2 minutes. Set aside.

Pulse the paprika, salt, cayenne, sugar, garlic, lime powder, ½ teaspoon of the dried scallions, and ½ tablespoon of the lime zest in a spice grinder and transfer to a large bowl; set aside.

Drain the potatoes and use a salad spinner to dry them, working in small batches. Alternatively, spread them out in a single layer on paper towels to dry.

Heat about 2 inches of oil in a medium saucepan or pot over medium to medium-high heat until a deep-fry thermometer reads 300° to 325°F. Working in batches, fry the potatoes until golden and crisp, 3 to 6 minutes, adjusting the heat as necessary. Using a slotted spoon, transfer to a baking sheet lined with paper towels to drain briefly, then place all the chips in the bowl with the spices and toss to combine.

CHAPTER 8

OMANI BREADS

It is amazing that in a rice-centric country like Oman, there is such a vast array of breads to be found. Nearly all of them are skillet cooked on the stovetop, usually in a generous amount of ghee or oil, like the flaky chapati variations and delicate Omani crêpes (page 178) popular in Muscat and Zanzibari specialties like sesame bread and the slightly sweet fried triangles called *Mandazi* (page 172). The southern Dhofar region has by far the widest range of breads, including a dense, doughnut-like variation of airy *mandazi*, called *mucuscus*; squares of thick, fried *Tawa* bread (page 182); oil-blistered *Khubz Lahooh* (page 178) crêpes; and cardamom laced, cracker-like *kak* bread (page 184). Some of these breads are served alongside curries for dinner, but the majority are most popular eaten as breakfast or as a snack with tea. Only paper-thin *Khubz Ragag* Omani bread (page 162) will be found served alongside the traditional midday meal of rice.

KHUBZ RAGAG
(OMANI BREAD)

4 cups unbleached all-purpose flour

1 teaspoon kosher salt

MAKES 6 TO 20 PIECES, DEPENDING ON SKILL AND WASTED DOUGH!

This paper-thin bread, a simple mixture of flour and water with a pinch of salt, smeared on a sizzling-hot pan and chipped free with a pastry knife, or a paint chipper as they use in Oman, takes some practice to get down, but it is a fun and easy bread once you get the hang of it. It can be eaten with any of the rice dishes for an extra crunch or crumbled and used in place of thick tandoor bread for a lighter version of *Thareed* (page 58). It is essential for making the delicious Omani breakfast *Ragag Ma Beed Wa Jibne* (page 166).

Place the flour, salt, and 2 cups water in a large bowl and mix well with your hands, squeezing out any lumps in the dough, until smooth. This will take up to 15 minutes and the dough will be somewhat sticky. Cover with a damp kitchen towel and let rest 30 minutes or up to several hours.

Prepare to make the bread by having paper towels ready for wiping off excess dough, a bowl of warm water, a trash bowl, and a paint chipper or pastry cutter (a paint chipper is ideal, as its long handle keeps your knuckles away from the heat of the pan).

Heat a flat circular cast-iron griddle, a heavy metal crêpe pan, a cast-iron pizza pan, or another skillet with low or no sides over medium to medium-high heat. (To test if the pan is ready, sprinkle with water. If ready, it will sizzle and evaporate immediately.)

Continued

Cooking Method 1

Pinch off about a golf ball–size piece of dough and place it on the hot surface.

Working quickly, use your paint chipper or pastry cutter and apply a little pressure to smear a thin layer of the dough in a circular motion, making a circle to cover the surface of the pan.

Scoop off any excess dough and put it back in the dough bowl. In a few seconds, steam will rise from the surface of the dough and the edges will brown; using firm pressure, scrape off excess dough on the surface of the crisping bread with the chipper or cutter. Don't worry if you scrape a little hole in the dough; it doesn't have to be perfect. However, if the dough all peels off the pan, then the pan is not hot enough. Discard the excess dough scraps into the trash bowl.

Working around the edges and moving to the center of the circle, use the chipper or cutter to peel the crisp bread off the pan.

Transfer the bread to a plate and repeat until all the dough is used.

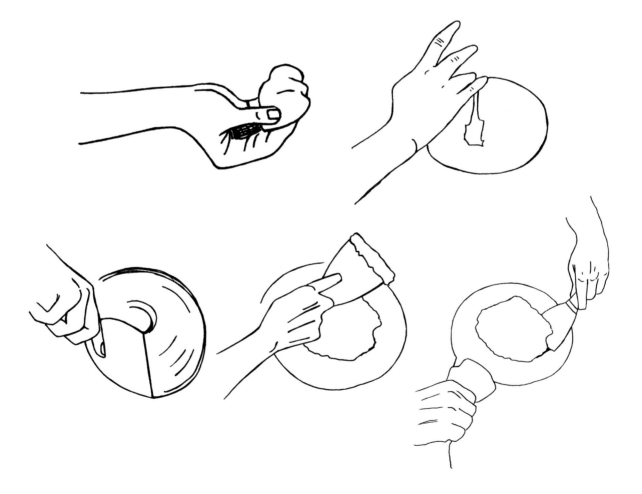

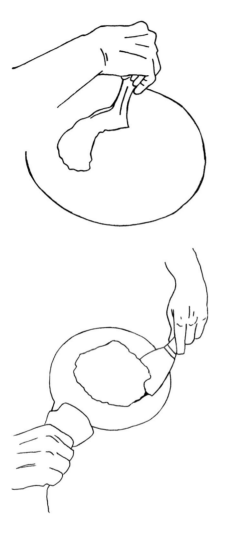

Cooking Method 2

Grab about a softball-size handful of dough and, working quickly, swiftly touch the dough ball to the hot surface of the pan, creating overlapping dots until you have a pan-size circle of crisping bread. Immediately use your paint chipper or pastry cutter to slide under the edge of the crisp dough, working around the edges and moving toward the center to peel the bread off the pan.

Transfer the bread to a plate and repeat until all the dough is used.

RAGAG MA BEED WA JIBNE

(OMANI BREAD WITH EGG AND CHEESE)

4 cups unbleached all-purpose flour

1 teaspoon kosher salt

4 or 5 eggs, beaten, plus more as needed

1 small container Puck cheese or other soft, spreadable white cheese, such as cream cheese

MAKES ABOUT 5 BREADS

As the thin round of Omani bread dough crisps, a quick smear of Puck cheese or cream cheese and a cracked whole or whipped egg give the brittle bread just enough moisture to become pliable enough to fold into the signature half-moon shape. The process moves quickly, and it can be tricky to get the toppings on crisping bread before it begins to burn, so we whisk our eggs before getting started to buy us a bit more time. Eaten alongside any of the sweet *karak* milk teas, it is one of Dawn's and my favorite breakfast meals.

Place the flour, salt, and 2 cups water in a large bowl and mix well using your hands, squeezing out any lumps in the dough, until smooth. This will take up to 15 minutes and the dough will be somewhat sticky. Cover with a damp kitchen towel and let rest 30 minutes or up to several hours.

Prepare to make the bread, as the process is quick. Set a bowl with the beaten eggs and a shaker of salt near the cooking area (we like to add a few shakes of salt to our uncooked egg mixture as well as to the cooked bread, tasting the first stuffed flatbread and adjusting our seasoning accordingly). Make sure you have a spoon in your cheese container, paper towels to wipe off excess dough, a bowl of warm water, a trash bowl, and a paint chipper or pastry cutter (a paint chipper is ideal, as its long handle keeps your knuckles away from the heat of the pan). The whole cooking process should take about a minute from start to finish.

Heat a flat circular cast-iron griddle, a heavy metal crêpe pan, a cast-iron pizza pan, or another skillet with low or no sides over medium to medium-high heat. (To test if the pan is ready, sprinkle with water. If ready, it will sizzle and evaporate immediately.)

Continued

RAGAG MA BEED WA JIBNE (*continued*)

Pinch off about a golf ball–size piece of dough and place it on the hot surface. Working quickly, use your paint chipper or pastry cutter and a little pressure to smear a thin layer of the dough in a circular motion to make a circle covering the surface of the pan. (See these steps illustrated on pages 164–165.)

Then, quickly drop about 1 tablespoon of the cheese on the bread and top with about ¼ cup of the beaten egg, enough to mostly cover the bread. Smear both over the surface of the bread with a fork, leaving about a 1-inch border between the filling and the edge of the round. Let cook for a few seconds and then scrape under one side, working from the outer edge, to fold in half.

Remove the half-moon from the pan, transfer to a plate, cut it into 3 pieces, and serve immediately.

Repeat until all the dough is used, beating more eggs if you run out.

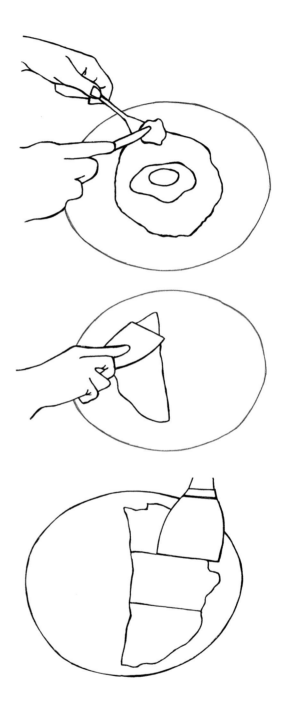

MALDOUF
(DATE CHAPATI)

½ cup packed, pitted dried dates
(7 to 15, depending on size)

1 cup boiling water

2¼ cups unbleached all-purpose
flour, plus more for dusting and
rolling

1 teaspoon kosher salt

1 large egg, at room temperature

¼ cup ghee, melted, plus more
for brushing and frying (at least
another ⅓ cup)

MAKES 10 TO 12 BREADS

This distinctly Omani variation of South Asian chapati bread yields a deeply flavorful, flaky bread with a subtle molasses sweetness that complements spicier dishes like *Lahm Kalia* (page 96). This is best made using high-quality dates, such as Medjool.

Place the dates in a small bowl and cover with the boiling water; soak until softened, at least 1 hour. Mash by hand, then purée with the soaking liquid in a blender or using an immersion blender. Strain over a bowl through a fine-mesh sieve, using a wooden spoon to firmly mash and press the date pulp to extract as much liquid as possible. Scrape the date pulp on the underside of the sieve into the bowl; discard the date pulp in the sieve and set aside the date purée liquid.

Whisk the flour and salt in a large bowl. Stir in the egg and the ghee and mix with a wooden spoon until a crumbly dough forms. Slowly add the date purée, a little at a time, and begin mixing with your hands (add about ⅔ cup of the date purée in total) until the dough comes together; knead the dough until smooth and elastic, 2 to 4 minutes. Divide the dough into 10 to 12 golf ball–size balls and briefly knead each ball in one hand until smooth and crease-free. Place in a shallow baking dish or bowl and cover with a damp kitchen towel; let rest at room temperature 1 hour.

Continued

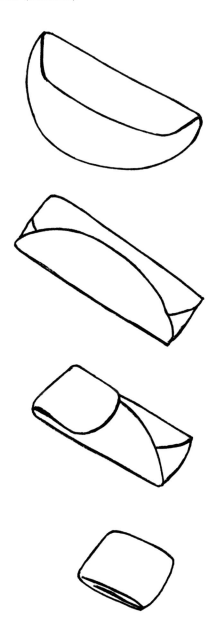

On a lightly floured surface, using a rolling pin dusted with flour, roll each ball of dough into a thin circle, 8 to 10 inches wide. Brush the surface with melted ghee; fold up the bottom edge about 2 inches from the top, then fold the dough down from the top over the folded half so the dough just touches the bottom edge. You should now have a long, thin rectangle. Brush the surface again with a little ghee and fold each side in, one on top of the other, to make a square. Roll the square dough out, turning several times, to make a large, thin piece about 8 inches square. Brush the surface again with plenty of ghee.

Heat a medium or large cast-iron skillet over medium heat and fry the chapati, ghee side down first, for 45 seconds to 1 minute per side (if it doesn't puff up, the pan isn't hot enough), brushing the top with plenty of ghee before flipping to make sure both sides brown evenly.

Transfer to a plate, sprinkle with more salt, if desired, and serve with a curry like *Lahm Kalia* (page 96).

FRIED MANDAZI
(SWEET CARDAMOM ZANZIBARI FRIED BREAD)

1 (¼-ounce) packet active dry yeast

½ cup warm water (100° to 110°F)

1¾ cups unbleached all-purpose flour, plus more for rolling

⅓ cup sugar

3 tablespoons dried milk powder

1 teaspoon baking powder

1 teaspoon ground cardamom

½ teaspoon kosher salt

3 tablespoons vegetable oil, plus more for frying

MAKES 20 BREADS

This Zanzibari specialty also has a baked variation and, in the south, a denser version called *mucuscus*, but the airy, fried version is by far the most popular. The moment when the doughy triangle hits the oil and begins to puff is pure magic, and the subtle sweetness of the tender bread is lovely with tea or used to scoop up saucy, savory dishes like Coconut Creamed Spinach (page 129) or Slow-Cooked Coconut Beans (page 133).

Combine the yeast and warm water in a small bowl; mix well and let sit until foamy, about 10 minutes (if it doesn't foam at all, the yeast might be dead and you may want to discard it and repeat this step with a new packet of yeast).

Whisk the flour, sugar, milk powder, baking powder, cardamom, and salt in a medium bowl. Stir the yeast mixture and the oil into the dry ingredients by hand until the dough comes together, adding a sprinkling of flour if the dough is too wet and sticks to your hands.

Sprinkle some flour on a work surface and continue to knead the dough until it becomes smooth and elastic, 4 to 6 minutes. Pat it into a ball, put back in the same bowl, and cover with plastic wrap; let sit in a warm place to rise slightly (it will not double in size), a minimum of 1 hour and no more than 3 hours.

Remove the dough from the bowl and knead on a lightly floured surface a few more times, until smooth and pliable. Divide into 5 balls. Knead each ball by squeezing it in your hand a few times before rolling it out into a disk about 8 inches wide and ⅛ inch thick, using a floured rolling pin on a lightly floured surface, and turning the dough every few rolls. Using a knife, cut each circle of dough into 4-inch triangular quarters.

Heat 2 to 3 inches of oil in a wok or pot over medium-high heat until a deep-fry thermometer reads 350°F. Carefully drop the *mandazi* triangles in the oil, a couple at a time, and fry, ladling oil over the cooking *mandazi* with a large spoon and flipping once after the *mandazi* puffs, for a total of 30 seconds to 1 minute, until light golden brown. Remove using a slotted spoon and drain on a paper towel–lined plate.

Serve warm alongside a *karak* tea (page 218) as a snack or as an accompaniment to a coconut-simmered vegetable dish.

CHAPATI
(PAN-FRIED FLATBREAD)

2 cups unbleached all-purpose flour

1 teaspoon kosher salt

2 tablespoons vegetable oil

⅔ cup warm water, plus more as needed

⅓ to ½ cup ghee, melted, for rolling and cooking

MAKES 6 BREADS

This flaky pan-fried South Asian bread has become ubiquitous on dinner tables throughout the Sultanate and can be found at all the casual, Indian-run restaurants; it is an essential accompaniment to Omani curries, called *maraks* (see pages 121–122). When making a batch, crack an egg over the frying bread after it has been flipped once for a quick, delicious breakfast (see the variation).

In a large bowl, mix the flour, salt, vegetable oil, and warm water by hand to form a dough, adding a sprinkle more water if the dough is too dry and crumbly and doesn't begin to come together after a minute or so. Knead until the dough becomes smooth and elastic, 5 to 8 minutes. Cover with a damp kitchen towel and set aside to rest 30 minutes.

Knead the dough again for a few minutes and divide into 6 balls. On a lightly floured surface, roll a dough ball into a large thin circle, 8 to 10 inches wide, dusting with flour as needed. Brush the surface with about 1 teaspoon of the ghee. Roll the dough on itself into a cylinder and pinch the ends together. Repeat with each ball of dough.

Pick up a cylindrical piece of dough and create a long rope by holding the ends and twisting the dough in the air like a jump rope, being careful to move your hands to hold it where it's strongest (not at the very tips as it stretches out, but a bit in toward the middle of the dough rope) so it doesn't break. When the dough is 20 to 24 inches long, place it on a flat surface and wind it into a tight coil, pinching or tucking the ends in. Press down to flatten and put in a baking dish covered with a damp cloth to prevent drying out while preparing the others.

Heat a skillet over medium heat. Roll each coiled round of dough back out into an 8-inch circle. Place in the dry skillet and cook until it begins to puff, 1 to 2 minutes. Lift up the chapati, add about 1 teaspoon of the ghee to the pan, and flip. Cook for 45 seconds to 1 minute. Brush the first side with more ghee, flip, then cook 1 more minute, pressing down with a spatula. The total cooking time should be 3½ to 4 minutes.

Variation: CHAPATI WITH EGG

1 or 2 large eggs, beaten with a pinch of salt and ground black pepper

After cooking the chapati on one side, flip as directed, adding more ghee, and pour the beaten egg over the top, letting it go underneath the dough to firm up and begin to cook; flip again after about 30 seconds and cook until done, another 30 seconds or so.

MKATE WA UFUTA

(ZANZIBARI SESAME BREAD)

3½ cups unbleached all-purpose flour

1 (¼-ounce) packet active dry yeast

1½ teaspoons kosher salt

1 cup plus 2 tablespoons coconut milk

1 large egg

⅓ to ½ cup vegetable oil

3 to 4 tablespoons sesame seeds

MAKES 6 BREADS

I learned about this dense, chewy bread, griddled with untoasted sesame seeds that develop their signature nutty flavor as the bread cooks, from Raiya Al Sukairy, an instructor at the National Hospitality Institute in Ruwi. She fondly remembers the pleasant smell of toasting sesame filling the streets of Zanzibar each night during Ramadan when she was a girl growing up there. I love the comforting aroma that lingers in the kitchen after making this seeded bread almost as much as I love the crunch and flavor.

Whisk together the flour, yeast, and salt in a large bowl; stir in the coconut milk and egg until combined and knead with quite a bit of strength until the dough is smooth, 5 to 7 minutes. Cover the bowl with a damp kitchen towel and leave in a warm place to rise a little, at least 30 minutes.

Divide the dough into 6 balls. Pat each ball of dough into a round shape between the palms of your hands to form a thick circle about 6½ inches wide and ½ to 1 inch thick. Rub one side generously with oil and sprinkle some of the sesame seeds on top.

Heat a large cast-iron skillet over medium-high heat; cook each bread, sesame side down, 1½ to 2 minutes. Allow it to puff, and then rub the surface of the bread with plenty more oil and sprinkle with more sesame seeds and a little salt before flipping. Flip and cook until browned in spots and done in the middle, 1 to 2 minutes more.

KHUBZ LAHOOH
(CRISP-FRIED DHOFARI CRÊPES)

3 large eggs

¾ cup sugar

1¼ teaspoons kosher salt

3 cups unbleached all-purpose flour

About ½ cup vegetable oil

MAKES 9 OR 10 (12-INCH) BREADS

Every year during *khareef*, or monsoon season, women from around the southern Dhofar province come to the city of Salalah to make stacks of this crispy crêpe variation at the Salalah Festival, which draws tourist from around the country and the region. The key to the distinctive texture of this bread is a generous glug of oil poured under the cooking dough, where it bubbles and essentially crisp-fries the outer layer of the crêpe while preserving the tender, interior chew. These luscious, lightly sweet breads make a hearty snack or breakfast alongside Dhofari *Karak* (page 220), but are also delicious as a counterpoint to savory or spicy foods.

In a large bowl, whisk together the eggs, sugar, and 3 cups water. Add the salt and slowly whisk in the flour until a smooth, thin batter forms.

Heat a 12-inch nonstick skillet over medium-high heat. Brush with a little oil. Pour ½ cup of the batter in the pan, and, working quickly, swirl the pan to evenly spread the batter, as you would with a crêpe. Cook until golden and set at the edges, 30 to 45 seconds. Flip the bread with a spatula and quickly lift up one edge to pour about a tablespoon of oil into the skillet, shaking and distributing it under the bread and allowing it to bubble and fry. Cook until there are some nice brown spots on the bread, about 1½ minutes, then flip and fry the other side again, without adding additional oil, until slightly crisper, about 1½ minutes more.

Repeat with the remaining batter, wiping the pan clean between crêpes.

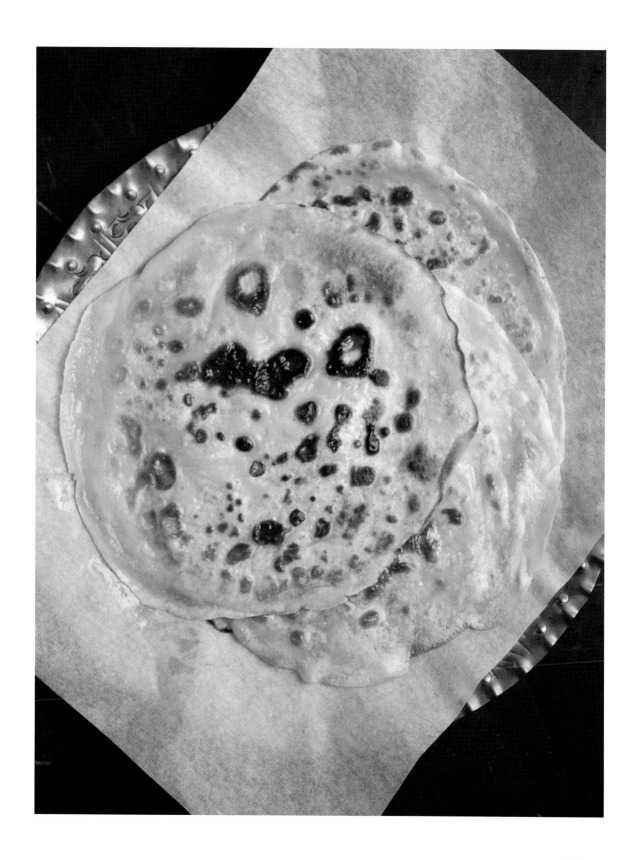

KHUBZ MAHALLAH
(CRÊPES WITH DATE SYRUP)

2 cups unbleached all-purpose flour

2 tablespoons sugar

2 tablespoons dried milk powder

1 teaspoon kosher salt

2 tablespoons vegetable oil, plus more for cooking

Date syrup or date molasses, for serving (optional)

MAKES ABOUT 1 DOZEN BREADS

Noora Al Balushi, our dear friend Miad's mother, taught me this simple recipe for Omani-style crêpes finished with a drizzle of rich date syrup, which can be purchased at any Middle Eastern shop and at most health food stores. They are served as a dessert, snack, or breakfast dish in Oman, and I find them to be perfect for a leisurely weekend breakfast in place of pancakes.

Whisk together the flour, sugar, milk powder, and salt in a medium bowl. Slowly add 2½ cups water and mix to form a thin batter, then whisk in the oil. Let rest 15 minutes.

Heat a large nonstick skillet over medium or medium-high heat; drizzle in a little oil and pour about ⅓ cup batter into the pan, quickly tilting the pan and moving it in a circle to distribute the batter evenly. Cook until the crêpe browns and puffs on one side, 1 to 2 minutes. Flip and, lifting the edge closest to you with a spatula, drizzle a little more oil under the crêpe, shake to distribute, and cook 1 to 1½ minutes more. Flip again if needed and cook the other side 15 to 30 seconds more. Transfer to a plate and drizzle with date syrup. Repeat with the remaining batter, wiping the pan clean between crêpes as needed.

KHUBZ AL TAWA
(DHOFARI PAN-FRIED FLATBREAD)

4 cups unbleached bread flour, plus more for rolling

1 tablespoon kosher salt

½ cup melted ghee, melted, plus more for brushing and frying (at least another ½ cup)

MAKES 5 LARGE BREADS

I learned about this large, square fried bread, a thicker version of chapati with greater heft and more substantial chewy layers, from Rasmiya Naseeb, an entrepreneurial Dhofari woman who sells her bread and other Dhofari specialties from a catering hall she opened on the corner of a quiet residential Salalah street. She recommends it for breakfast, along with a strong cup of chai, or with a *marak* for dinner.

In a large bowl, whisk together the flour and salt. Add 1½ cups water and the ghee and mix by hand, adding a little more water (1 to 2 teaspoons) if needed to form a dough. Knead the dough until smooth, about 15 minutes.

Divide the dough into 5 balls. Place in a bowl or baking dish and cover with a damp kitchen towel; let rest at least 30 minutes.

On a lightly floured surface using a lightly floured rolling pin, roll each dough ball out into a large rectangle as thin as possible (at least 8 by 12 inches). Brush the surface with ghee, fold one-third of the dough onto itself lengthwise, and fold the remaining one-third over the top. Brush the surface with ghee again and fold the top down, then the bottom up, to make a square.

Let the dough pieces rest again 10 to 15 minutes. On a lightly floured surface using a lightly floured rolling pin, roll each dough piece back out into a large, thin square, about 10 inches wide and long. Brush the surface with plenty of ghee (about 1 tablespoon).

Heat a large cast-iron skillet over medium-high heat; cook the bread, ghee side down, until brown in spots, 4 to 5 minutes. Brush the top with plenty more ghee (about 1 tablespoon), flip, and cook 4 to 5 minutes more, until browned and cooked through. The bread should be thin, flaky, and chewy. Sprinkle with salt, if desired, and serve with *Marak Hubar* (page 122), a spicy squid dish from the village of Mirbat.

KAK
(NIGELLA SEED AND CARDAMOM CRISPBREAD)

1 (¼-ounce) packet active dry yeast

3 tablespoons plus ¼ teaspoon sugar, divided

¼ cup warm water (100° to 110°F), plus more as needed

2 cups unbleached all-purpose flour, plus more for rolling

1½ teaspoons ground cardamom

1 teaspoon nigella seeds

1 teaspoon kosher salt

¼ cup ghee, softened

MAKES 8 (8-INCH) CRACKERS

When Omani tourists travel to Salalah, one of the favorite items to bring back to their respective home cities is *kak* bread. Pressed on a clay mold and cooked in a tandoor oven, these crisp, cracker-like rounds are flavored with nigella and ground cardamom, with just a pinch of sugar added to bring out the flavors. It is wonderful with coffee or sweet milk tea.

Dissolve the yeast and ¼ teaspoon of the sugar in the warm water. Let sit until foamy, about 10 minutes.

Whisk together the flour, cardamom, nigella seeds, salt, and remaining 3 tablespoons sugar in a large bowl. Stir in the ghee with a wooden spoon and add the yeast mixture. Begin mixing by hand until a firm dough forms, adding a little water at a time if needed (up to 4 tablespoons), and knead until smooth, 5 to 6 minutes. Cover with a damp kitchen towel and let rest 1 hour.

Preheat the oven to 400°F and line a baking sheet with parchment paper.

Knead the dough briefly to bring it together, then divide it into 8 balls. On a lightly floured surface using a lightly floured rolling pin, roll out each ball into an 8-inch circle about ⅛ inch thick. Using the tines of a fork, gently poke holes in each dough disk, forming the pattern of a circle around the edge, like a border, with an X in the middle.

Bake in batches on the parchment-lined baking sheet, turning the pan halfway through cooking, until light brown and crispy, 11 to 13 minutes. Let cool, and serve as a snack with Dhofari *Karak* (page 220) or Special *Karak* tea (page 218).

MURADEF
(SUR FENNEL "STEP" BREAD)

5 cups unbleached all-purpose flour

1 teaspoon kosher salt

1 teaspoon fennel seeds, coarsely crushed in a mortar and pestle

1 large egg

¼ cup date syrup

¼ to ½ cup vegetable oil

MAKES ABOUT 20 BREADS

In the famous coastal ship building city of Sur, Wafa'a Al Shamaki taught me how to fold the dough for this fennel-laced flatbread into a layered triangle before searing it on a pan, so that when the fragrant anise-and-date-scented bread was finished, it could be gently pulled apart like a paper doll into the thin layers, or "steps," for which it is named. This is delicious eaten with Sur-Style Peppery Fish Steak Tomato Curry (page 121).

Whisk together the flour, salt, and fennel seeds in a large bowl. Add the egg, date syrup, and 1¼ cups water (adding a sprinkle more if necessary), mixing until a dry-ish dough forms; knead with strength until smooth, 7 to 8 minutes. Cover with a damp kitchen towel and let rest at least 30 minutes.

Rub your hands liberally with vegetable oil, pinch an egg-size ball of dough off, and roll it in your hands to make a ball. Using a rolling pin, roll it out into a large thin circle, 8 to 10 inches. Brush the surface of the dough with a little oil. Fold the circle in half, rub with more oil, then fold in half again to make a triangle. Roll the triangle out until thin, keeping its shape as much as possible, until it is about 8 inches long at its longest point. Set aside on a baking sheet until ready to cook. Repeat with the remaining dough.

Heat a large cast-iron skillet or other heavy skillet over medium-low to medium heat and sprinkle with a little oil; cook the bread about 1½ minutes, then flip, oiling a little if necessary, and cook until brown in spots and cooked through, about 1½ minutes more. Repeat with all the dough pieces. Eat as a snack on its own or serve alongside a curry, like *Marak Samak* (page 121).

HASSAN BIN YOUSAF ALI TRADING STORE
الحلوى العمانية
OMANI SWEET
C.R: 2/3128
GSM: 92119
Top-up
Hayyak
here
EXIT

CHAPTER 9

OMANI SWEETS

Omanis have a definite sweet tooth, and their national dessert, Omani *Halwa* (page 210), a long-cooked mixture of sugar and ghee, thickened with cornstarch and colored with saffron, is proof positive of that. They take their sweets with black Omani coffee or unsweetened tea, and the sugar in these treats balances out the bitterness of the beverages much like a date would. Besides the famous Omani *halwa*, which is almost always purchased rather than made at home, the most popular dessert, from Buraimi to Dalkut, are *Luqaimat* (page 192), fried rounds of dough topped with honey, date syrup, or a cardamom-saffron simple syrup, depending on the region and the household. They range from perfect orbs dressed in a light sugary coating flecked with saffron, as are the ones at our friend Thuraya Al Said's gracious home, to rustic fried patties drizzled with thick, homemade date syrup or honey, like the Bedouins in Bediyah make, using nothing but a pot of oil and a knife for flipping the fried treats. At the takeout stands in Sur, *luqaimat* are topped with a sprinkle of sesame seeds, and in Zanzibar, formerly part of the Sultanate, they go by the name *kaimati*, but every version shares the same crisp crust and soft interior, perfect for absorbing whatever syrup they are soaked in for intense bursts of sweetness.

Not all Omani desserts are so sugary. Zanzibari pumpkin (page 213) or plantains in coconut cream (page 195) are only lightly sweet, and some of my favorite desserts contain almost no additional sugar at all, taking advantage of the natural sugars in that prized Omani fruit, the date, from luscious date pudding (page 202) and cake (page 207) to simple date and toasted sesame seed cookies (page 190). Some desserts, also eaten for breakfast, verge on the savory, like the noodle dishes *Karas* (page 208), which is spiked with cumin and simmered in coconut milk; *Saweeyah bil Haleeb* (page 205) that's cooked in rose water–scented milk; and *Balaleet* (page 197), sweet vermicelli tossed with salted egg that's popular in Northern Oman and throughout the Gulf region. Thanks to the leisurely pace of meals in Oman, even after the heartiest of mains, a long chat and a few cups of strong Omani coffee will ensure there is always room for a sweet finish.

DATE AND SESAME BISCUITS

1 (13-ounce) package baking dates, or about 2 cups packed high-quality whole dried dates

15 rectangular semisweet tea biscuits (or 30 small square ones), or about ½ package of the Turkish brand Ülker

½ cup sesame seeds, lightly toasted

MAKES 30 COOKIES

By using premade, semisweet biscuits, as they do in Oman, and date paste (available at Middle Eastern shops, health food stores, and many supermarkets) instead of squeezing dried dates by hand, these nutty, sweet, chewy cookies are one of the easiest desserts to whip up. They are best eaten within a few hours of making them, as the biscuits tend to soften.

If using whole dates, pit and remove any outer tough papery skin, then mash into a paste between your fingers.

Break the rectangular tea biscuits in half. Cover the biscuit halves with date paste by mashing about 1 teaspoon date paste between your fingers into a thin layer, and wrapping and pressing it around the biscuit to even out into a square.

Roll the cookies in the sesame seeds, pressing gently to adhere. Serve with coffee or tea.

LUQAIMAT
(CHEWY FRIED DOUGH IN SAFFRON SYRUP)

DOUGH

1 tablespoon active dry yeast

2 tablespoons warm water (100° to 110°F)

1½ cups unbleached all-purpose flour

¼ cup plain full-fat Greek yogurt

¼ teaspoon kosher salt

¾ cup cold water

SYRUP

1 cup sugar

¼ teaspoon ground cardamom

Pinch of saffron (15 to 20 threads)

Vegetable oil, for frying, plus more for oiling spoon

Sesame seeds, lightly toasted, for sprinkling (optional)

MAKES ABOUT 2 DOZEN PIECES

Popular throughout Oman and even in Zanzibar, formerly part of the Sultanate, these springy Omani doughnuts can be drizzled with honey, date syrup, or the appropriately elegant saffron-and-cardamom-infused simple syrup that is the favorite of our friend Thuraya, a member of the royal family.

To make the dough, dissolve the yeast in the warm water and let sit until foamy, about 10 minutes.

Mix the flour, yogurt, salt, and yeast mixture together, then slowly add the cold water to form a wet, loose, sticky dough, mixing with your hands for a few minutes. Cover with plastic wrap and let rest 2½ to 3 hours at room temperature.

When the dough is almost ready, make the syrup by simmering the sugar with ½ cup water in a small saucepan over medium heat about 5 minutes. Remove from the heat and stir in the cardamom and saffron and let sit until the dough is ready. Gently reheat the syrup if it gets cold and too thick.

Heat about 2 inches of oil in a medium saucepan over medium-high heat (a wok also works really well) until a deep-fry thermometer reads 350° to 360°F.

Continued

LUQAIMAT *(continued)*

Mix the dough with one hand, pulling and stretching to kind of knead it; it will be very sticky but elastic at this point. Using an oiled hand, pull a handful of the dough and squeeze a small ball of dough (about 1 tablespoon) out between your thumb and index finger by making a fist. Use an oiled spoon to scoop the ball of dough from between your fingers and drop it into the hot oil. Fry several doughnuts at a time, letting them puff a little before moving the balls around, then continually ladle oil over the top of the frying dough with a metal spoon. Fry until brown, crunchy, and cooked through, 5 to 8 minutes, adjusting the temperature as necessary. Remove with a slotted spoon and transfer to a paper towel–lined baking sheet to drain.

Place all the doughnuts on a plate or in a shallow serving dish; drizzle with the prepared syrup, rolling to coat each ball, and sprinkle with sesame seeds. *Luqaimat* are best eaten within a few hours of making, though they will keep for up to 2 days in an airtight container at room temperature.

NDIZI MBIVU
(SWEET PLANTAINS IN COCONUT CREAM)

½ cup coconut milk powder

1½ cups warm water

2 tablespoons sugar

2 teaspoons cornstarch

¼ teaspoon ground cardamom

3 very ripe, blackened sweet plantains

SERVES 6

For this recipe, from Omani chef Issa Al Lamki's sister Lubna, ultraripe plantains are simmered in coconut milk for a subtle dessert that tastes great garnished with strawberries or raspberries when they are in season.

In a small bowl, whisk the coconut milk powder in the warm water until dissolved. Whisk in the sugar, cornstarch, and cardamom.

Cut off the ends of the plantains, carefully peel, and cut each in half lengthwise. Scoop out the black center with a small spoon and cut each half in half crosswise to make shorter pieces. Place the plantains in a medium saucepan or deep skillet and pour the coconut mixture over them; gently mix, turn the heat to medium-high, and bring to a boil. Decrease the heat and simmer, covered, over low heat until the coconut milk has thickened slightly and the plantains are tender, 30 to 35 minutes, depending on the thickness of the plantains. If the sauce is too thin, remove the lid and increase the heat to medium-high, cooking until it thickens (keeping in mind that the sauce will also thicken as it cools). Serve warm or cold.

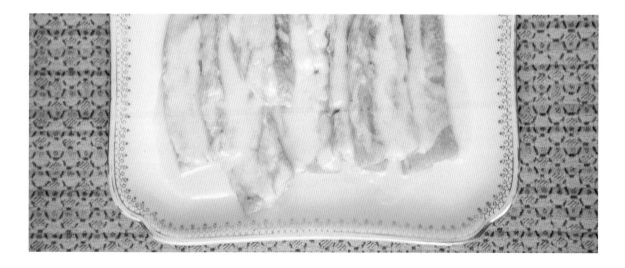

BALALEET
(SWEET VERMICELLI WITH SALTY EGG)

6 tablespoons vegetable oil, divided

2 cups Middle Eastern–style dried vermicelli (short broken pieces, or use Goya broken angel hair pasta)

4 cups boiling water

3 large eggs, beaten

½ teaspoon kosher salt

½ cup sugar

¼ teaspoon ground cardamom

SERVES 4 TO 6

This dish of sweetened vermicelli noodles tossed with salty egg is a classic throughout the Gulf and is popular in northern Omani border towns like Buraimi. The sweet and salty combination is typically eaten for dinner or dessert, but I enjoy it best as a breakfast dish.

Heat 3 tablespoons of the oil in a large deep skillet over medium-high heat; add the vermicelli and fry, stirring occasionally to prevent burning, until half of the pasta is golden brown, 4 to 5 minutes. Add the boiling water to the pan until it covers the pasta by about ½ inch and simmer until al dente, 3½ to 5 minutes, being sure to check for doneness after 3 minutes. (If using broken angel hair pasta, it might need to cook slightly longer.) Drain immediately.

Wipe the skillet clean and heat the remaining 3 tablespoons oil over medium heat. Pour in the eggs and salt, let cook until just set, 20 to 30 seconds, and then scramble into extra-large curds. Cook the eggs for about 1 minute, making sure not to let them brown. Add the drained vermicelli, sugar, and cardamom. Mix well and cook over medium-high heat to remove any excess water or oil, 2 to 4 minutes. Let sit a few minutes and serve warm (though it also tastes quite good cold).

QASHAT BIL NARGIL
(COCONUT COOKIES)

½ cup dried milk powder

1½ cups unsweetened shredded coconut

¾ cup sugar

MAKES ABOUT 25 COOKIES

The Al Saqri family in Jabal Akhdar whipped up this brittle-like coconut cookie just before we sat down to lunch, adding shreds of unsweetened coconut to a simple syrup and spreading it on a smooth marble surface to harden. By the time lunch was finished, the crumbly, sweet treats were ready to be cut and enjoyed with our coffee. Don't worry if your cookies don't completely harden; the first day they retain some chew.

Lightly oil a baking sheet or line it with parchment paper.

Mix the milk powder and coconut in a bowl.

Place the sugar and ½ cup water in a medium saucepan. Turn the heat to medium-high and cook, stirring occasionally (it will begin to simmer), until slightly thickened, about 12 minutes. A candy thermometer should read 220°F, or to test if ready, use a spoon to drip a little of the sugar syrup into a glass of cold water. If the syrup is ready, it will coagulate into a ball or thread; if it's not ready, it will dissolve like oil. Remove from the heat and quickly mix in the dry ingredients until evenly coated.

Transfer the mixture to the prepared baking sheet and flatten it out slightly. Using a rolling pin, roll it into a 9 by 11-inch rectangle about ¼ to ½ inch thick (you can cover it with a piece of parchment paper, if you have it, to ensure the mixture doesn't stick to your rolling pin). Let set until cool, at least 1 hour or up to 8 hours, and then cut into 2½-inch diamond-shaped pieces. Store at room temperature, wrapped in aluminum foil. They will retain some chew for the first day or two and then harden into a crunchier confection. They are best eaten within a week.

DAFTAR KAJI
(LAWATI CRISP FRIED DOUGH WITH SUGAR)

1 cup plus 2 tablespoons unbleached all-purpose flour, plus more for dusting and rolling

¼ teaspoon kosher salt

6 tablespoons cold water, divided

2 tablespoons vegetable oil, plus more for frying

¼ cup coarse sugar

Ground cinnamon (optional)

MAKES 8 TO 10 PIECES

Adila Al Lawati, whose ancestors trace their roots to the old Mutrah neighborhood of Muscat by way of northern India, taught us this classic Lawati dessert of fried dough pressed in sugar (and sometimes cinnamon). It is a wonderful, crispy snack alongside a light infused cinnamon tea (page 226) or creamy *karak* (page 218).

Whisk the flour and salt together; add 2 tablespoons of the cold water and the oil and begin working the dough with your hands. Add the remaining 4 tablespoons cold water slowly and knead the dough until it becomes smooth and elastic, about 5 minutes. Pat into a ball, place in a deep bowl, cover with a kitchen towel, and let rest 2 hours.

Divide the dough into 8 to 10 small balls. On a lightly floured surface, roll out each ball of dough with a floured rolling pin into a very thin circle about 5 inches wide.

Sprinkle the sugar onto a plate, mix in a little cinnamon, if you like, and set aside.

Heat about ½ inch of oil in a medium skillet over high heat until a deep-fry thermometer reads about 400°F. Working in batches, drop a dough disk in the oil and immediately begin pressing down with a spatula, as the dough will begin to puff. Fry, continuing to press down on any air bubbles with a spatula all over the disk; flip when golden to dark brown and do the same on the other side, cooking about 30 seconds per side. Transfer to a paper towel–lined plate to drain for 30 seconds. Press the hot fried dough in the sugar on both sides to coat. *Daftar Kaji* are best eaten the day they are made, though the extra-crispy leftovers are nice with coffee the next day.

ROYAL STICKY DATE PUDDING

CAKE

¾ cup packed dried pitted dates, chopped (18 to 20 medium dates)

1 teaspoon baking soda

1¼ cups boiling water

1½ cups unbleached all-purpose flour, plus more for dusting pan

1 teaspoon baking powder

¼ teaspoon kosher salt

½ cup (1 stick) unsalted butter, softened, plus more for greasing pan

¾ cup packed light brown sugar

1 large egg

1 teaspoon vanilla extract

STICKY DATE SAUCE

¾ cup (1½ sticks) unsalted butter

¾ cup heavy cream

⅓ cup plus 2 tablespoons date syrup or date molasses

½ cup lightly packed light brown sugar

SERVES 12

Dawn and I attended a royal wedding at the opulent Al Bustan Palace hotel in Muscat, and amid the sparkling gowns and pink and white centerpieces, the showstopper dessert wasn't the equally flashy tiered wedding cake, but a dense date pudding. The Al Bustan recipe is a closely guarded secret of the chef, so inspired by cravings and the sight of our glittering ball gowns hanging in the closet, Dawn developed this delicious approximation.

To make the cake, place the chopped dates in a small bowl and toss with the baking soda. Pour the boiling water over, stir, and set aside until the dates soften and cool, about 1 hour. Using an immersion blender or blender, purée until smooth.

Preheat the oven to 350°F. Grease and flour a 7 by 11-inch cake pan. In a small bowl, whisk together the flour, baking powder, and salt.

In a large bowl using an electric mixer on medium speed, cream the butter and brown sugar, stirring for a few minutes, until light and fluffy. Mix in the egg and vanilla. Alternate stirring in the date purée and sifting in the dry ingredients, mixing well until the batter is smooth. Pour the batter into the greased pan and bake 30 to 35 minutes, until a toothpick inserted in the center comes out clean. Let cool on a rack. Poke deep holes all over the top with a fork or chopstick to ensure the date sauce will soak in.

To make the sticky date sauce, place the butter, cream, syrup, and brown sugar in a small saucepan and turn the heat to medium. Simmer until the sauce darkens and thickens, 5 to 7 minutes (it will continue to thicken as it cools).

Pour the warm sauce over the top of the cake, allowing it to seep into the cake. Let sit at least 5 minutes before serving.

SAWEEYAH BIL HALEEB
(VERMICELLI IN ROSE WATER–CARDAMOM MILK)

1 cup Middle Eastern–style dried
vermicelli (short broken pieces, or
use Goya broken angel hair pasta)

4 cups milk

⅓ to ½ cup sugar

1 teaspoon ground cardamom

¼ teaspoon rose water

Finely chopped toasted pistachios
or almonds, for garnish (optional)

SERVES 6 TO 8

This delicate dessert of tender noodles simmered in a subtly sweet
milk infused with rose water and cardamom is South Asian in origin
but is now popular in Oman, especially in the diverse capital city of
Muscat. It is delicious served warm or cold.

Bring several cups of water to a boil in a medium saucepan and cook
the vermicelli until al dente, 2 to 3 minutes, checking after 2 minutes to
ensure the pasta doesn't overcook. Drain immediately, and rinse quickly
in cold water.

Bring the milk to a simmer in a medium saucepan over medium-high
heat. Add the sugar and simmer gently 6 to 7 minutes, whisking so
the milk doesn't burn. Whisk in the cardamom and rose water, let cook
1 minute, then stir in the vermicelli and turn off the heat. Serve warm
or cold and garnish with nuts.

SAMAR'S DATE CAKE

1½ cups packed large Medjool
    dates, pitted (about 25 large), plus
    more for garnish

1 teaspoon baking soda

1½ cups boiling water

1 cup unbleached all-purpose flour

1 teaspoon baking powder

½ teaspoon kosher salt

4 tablespoons (½ stick) butter,
    softened, plus more for greasing
    pan

¾ cup lightly packed brown sugar

2 large eggs

¼ cup coarsely chopped walnuts
    (optional)

Date syrup, for serving

MAKES 1 BUNDT CAKE

Muscat baker and former café owner Samar Al Khusaibi loves taking international recipes and using local flavors and ingredients to give them her own twist, as with this moist Bundt cake sweetened with dried dates.

In a small bowl, toss the dates with the baking soda and pour the boiling water over; let sit until the dates have softened and cooled, about 1 hour. Drain, discarding the liquid, and purée the dates in a blender or food processor until smooth (this should yield about 1¼ cups).

Preheat the oven to 325°F. Grease a 9 or 10-inch Bundt pan.

Whisk the flour, baking powder, and salt together in a small bowl.

Cream the butter and brown sugar together in a large bowl using an electric mixer on medium speed until fluffy, 3 to 5 minutes. Stir in the eggs, then sift in the dry ingredients. Fold in the date purée.

Sprinkle the walnuts in the bottom of the Bundt pan. Spoon the batter evenly into the pan. Bake until cooked through but still moist, about 30 minutes.

Let cool slightly, and then invert onto a plate. Drizzle the warm cake with date syrup and garnish by filling the center with plump dates.

KARAS

(FRESH PASTA SIMMERED IN COCONUT CREAM)

DOUGH

2 cups unbleached all-purpose flour

¾ cup warm water

SAUCE

2 tablespoons ghee

½ medium yellow onion, finely minced

1 (25.5-ounce) can coconut milk (about 3 cups)

5 tablespoons sugar

Heaping ½ teaspoon ground cardamom

Heaping ½ teaspoon ground cinnamon

Heaping ½ teaspoon ground cumin

⅛ teaspoon kosher salt

SERVES 6

This startling combination of fresh pasta left to dry overnight, sautéed onion, cumin, and sweet coconut milk comes together for a warming, creamy, utterly delicious dessert that also is a great alternative to oatmeal on a cold winter morning.

To make the dough, mix the flour and water to form a firm pasta dough. Knead a few minutes and let rest 10 minutes. Using quite a lot of strength and a rolling pin, roll the dough into a rectangle, as thin as possible, covering almost the entire surface of an inverted 12 by 16½-inch baking sheet. Leave to harden overnight (some spots in the middle may stay a little soft; this is normal). The next morning, cut the pasta dough into 2 to 3-inch triangles; set aside.

To make the sauce, heat the ghee in a medium saucepan over medium-low heat and sauté the onion until soft, being sure not to brown and stirring occasionally, 6 to 8 minutes. Pour in the coconut milk and bring to a boil. Whisk in the sugar, cardamom, cinnamon, cumin, and salt and simmer 2 to 3 minutes.

Add the pasta, a triangle at a time, stirring to prevent sticking. Cook, stirring often to prevent sticking to the bottom, about 15 minutes. Pour in ¾ cup water (adding more if necessary), stir, and continue cooking until the dough is cooked through and chewy and the sauce has thickened, about 5 minutes more. Remove from the heat and adjust the seasoning with salt to taste. Serve immediately, as *karas* begins to thicken rather quickly.

HOMEMADE OMANI HALWA

½ cup cornstarch

¾ cup ghee or vegetable oil

1 teaspoon ground cardamom

3 cups sugar (white for "yellow" halwa or light or dark brown sugar for "red" halwa), packed if using brown

Pinch of saffron

2 teaspoons rose water

2 tablespoons sesame seeds, lightly toasted

Slivered almonds or cashews, toasted, for garnish

MAKES ABOUT 3 CUPS

Most of my Omani friends looked at me with abject horror, or simply laughed, when I told them I was going to attempt to make Omani *halwa* at home. Typically made in massive batches by rows of men stirring simmering sugar and ghee in brass pots at places like the Omani Halwa Factory in Barka, this is not a dessert typically made at home. But we have no Omani *halwa* factories in New York, so I set about stirring and simmering until I figured out this small-batch variation on the bulk dessert recipe. It takes an hour of concentration, watching the sugar mixture and stirring, but it is a fun challenge if you are so inclined, and it is truly one of the most classic and singular Omani flavors. Serve with Omani Coffee (page 216).

Make a slurry by whisking together the cornstarch and ½ cup water until dissolved. Set aside.

Melt the ghee in a small bowl in the microwave; stir in the cardamom. Set aside.

Place the sugar and 3 cups water in a large deep heavy pot or Dutch oven; turn the heat to high and bring to a boil, letting the sugar dissolve without stirring, 6 to 7 minutes.

Whisk the cornstarch slurry again and slowly pour it into the pot, stirring constantly with a long wooden spoon (the mixture will begin to thicken immediately); add the saffron.

Decrease the heat to medium and continue to cook, stirring constantly, until the *halwa* starts to become gelatinous and pull away from the pot (it will start jelling), 15 to 20 minutes. If the sugar starts to sputter and splash you, turn down the heat a bit.

Slowly pour the ghee into the pot, about 1 tablespoon at a time, stirring constantly so that the ghee is incorporated into the sugar mixture before adding more. Continue to do this until all the ghee has been added and incorporated into the mixture. This should take 12 to 15 minutes.

Decrease the heat to medium-low and continue to stir until the mixture begins to solidify into an amoeba-like blob, 5 to 7 minutes. Stir in the rose water and sesame seeds. Cook 3 minutes more. Remove from the heat and carefully pour into a shallow heatproof glass bowl or baking dish, smoothing out the top with the back of the spoon. Garnish with nuts.

After the *halwa* cools a little, pour off any excess oil or ghee that has pooled on the surface (especially if you used ghee, as it will begin to resolidify). Eat, a teaspoon at a time, with Omani Coffee (page 216).

BOGA LA NAZI
(SWEET PUMPKIN WITH CARDAMOM AND COCONUT CREAM)

2 pounds kabocha squash (about half a large squash) or other smooth pumpkin/squash variety, seeded, peeled, and cut into 1½ to 2-inch pieces

½ cup whole milk

3 tablespoons plus 1 teaspoon sugar

4 teaspoons coconut milk powder

1 teaspoon cornstarch

¼ to ½ teaspoon kosher salt

⅛ teaspoon ground cardamom

SERVES 4 TO 6

This light Zanzibari dessert, laced with coconut milk and cardamom, works best with creamy-smooth, sweet-fleshed Japanese kabocha squash. (Butternut squash is not ideal because it lends a grainier texture.) The flavors are especially nice in the early fall as the weather begins to cool and squash come into season.

Place the pumpkin in a medium saucepan with 1 cup water and boil, covered, over medium heat 15 minutes. Meanwhile, whisk the milk, sugar, coconut milk powder, cornstarch, salt, and cardamom in a small bowl.

Decrease the heat to low and add the milk mixture to the pot; stir gently to avoid mashing the squash. Cook, uncovered, until the mixture thickens, 5 to 10 minutes. Serve warm in small bowls.

CHAPTER 10

BEVERAGES

Unlike in North Africa and the Near East, where tea is the hot beverage of choice, in the Gulf the traditional offering is Arabic coffee, made with lightly roasted green beans ground with cardamom and sometimes finished with rose water. Introduced to Yemen in the 16th century from Ethiopia, coffee was then brought to Mecca. From there it quickly spread throughout the Islamic world. Omani coffee remains an important part of the fabric of daily life, on offer day and night in the *majlis* or receiving room where male friends and neighbors meet and talk, and in almost every Omani office and home where it is served black with dried dates on the side to lend their sweetness.

But that's not to say tea isn't consumed as well. Over the past decade, *karak shay* tea shops, introduced by the South Asian population, have cropped up in towns throughout the Sultanate, serving creamy, spiced teas sweetened with condensed milk. A homemade version of ground ginger and cardamom-spiced *karak*, introduced by the condensed milk industry, became so ubiquitous that it is now referred to as "Omani breakfast tea," and fancy versions of the sweet milk tea, like opulent saffron *karak*, have emerged as well. There is also an entire canon of tea-free teas: hot infusions that make use of fresh ginger, cinnamon bark, and the fantastic bitter-sour digestive dried black lime.

Alcohol is not served with meals in this Muslim country, so in addition to soft drinks and bottles of Vitmo, a carbonated beverage flavored with spiced grape, raspberry, and currant juices, fresh juice cocktails are usually offered. Omanis tend to enjoy sweeter beverages than we do in the West, so feel free to decrease the amount of sweetener by half for any of the beverages in this chapter, from the *karaks* to the juices.

KAHWA AL OMANI
(OMANI COFFEE)

1½ teaspoons rose water

½ teaspoon ground cardamom

1 tablespoon finely ground Arabic coffee

5 whole cardamom pods, crushed

SERVES 8 TO 10

Omani coffee is made with lightly roasted beans, and some Omanis even roast their own green beans at home before grinding them with whole cardamom pods. The resulting brew is light, almost tea-colored, and is traditionally poured into *fenjans*, short, handle-free coffee cups, from a *dallah*, a curvaceous coffee urn with a long arched spout. Though these days, the coffee is more commonly poured from an insulated thermos, it is still poured using only the left hand, as a sign of respect and honor for the guest, and the small *fenjans* are filled only half to three-quarters full to ensure the coffee remains hot and to allow the host more opportunities to serve his or her guest in this traditional act of hospitality. Rather than being sweetened with sugar, the bitter coffee is served alongside dates or with *halwa* for sweetness, though some people told me that when entertaining guests, it is traditional for only the women take their coffee with sweets, while men will take theirs black unless they are alone with family.

Place the rose water and cardamom in a serving vessel, such as a 1-liter *dallah*, thermos, or pitcher. Set aside.

Bring 3 cups water, the coffee, and cardamom pods to a boil over medium-high heat in a small saucepan; boil 1 minute and turn off the heat.

Slowly pour the coffee into the serving vessel, leaving as many of the grounds behind as possible. Cover and let steep with the cardamom and rose water for 10 minutes, then serve in small cups.

SPECIAL KARAK
(SPICED SWEET MILK TEA)

6 to 8 whole cardamom pods, lightly crushed

2 whole cloves

½ large or 1 small cinnamon stick

2 thin slices fresh ginger, bruised

½ cup sweetened condensed milk

3 black tea bags, or 1½ tablespoons loose black tea

¼ teaspoon ground cardamom

SERVES 5 OR 6

Introduced by the large South Asian immigrant population in Oman, this spiced tea, enriched with sweetened condensed milk, is a staple of roadside tea shops and is especially popular as an accompaniment to *Ragag Ma Beed Wa Jibne*, Omani bread stuffed with cheese and egg (page 166).

Toast the cardamom pods, cloves, and cinnamon stick in a small dry skillet over medium-high heat until fragrant, 1 to 2 minutes.

In a small saucepan, combine 2½ cups water, the ginger, and toasted spices. Bring to a boil, then lower the heat and simmer until the mixture is fragrant, about 2 minutes. Stir in the milk, bring back to a simmer, then add the tea bags and simmer for another minute. Turn off the heat, stir in the ground cardamom, and steep 2 to 3 minutes. Strain and serve in small glasses.

SAFFRON KARAK
(SAFFRON SWEET MILK TEA)

¼ teaspoon saffron

2 cups warm water

4 whole cardamom pods, lightly crushed

4 to 5 tablespoons sweetened condensed milk

2 black tea bags, or 1 tablespoon loose black tea

MAKES 4 (½-CUP) SERVINGS

Our friend Miad Al Balushi is easily one of the most glamorous women I've ever met: She matches the detailing on her stylish, flowing abayas to her designer heels, sports well-chosen, glittering accessories, and always has her makeup perfectly done. So it couldn't be more appropriate that this luxurious drink, sweet and rich and tinged yellow by the world's most expensive spice, is one of her favorites.

Soak the saffron in the warm water 10 minutes.

In a small saucepan, bring the saffron water to a simmer with the cardamom pods. Stir in the condensed milk, simmer 2 minutes, then add the tea bags; continue simmering until the tea is a creamy brown-yellow color, 2 to 3 minutes more. Turn off the heat and let steep 1 minute. Remove the tea bags, strain if desired, and serve in small glasses.

DHOFARI KARAK
(CARDAMOM-THYME SWEET MILK TEA)

6 tablespoons sweetened condensed milk

3 teaspoons dried za'atar, wild thyme (good-quality, large-leaf Middle Eastern variety, not za'atar spice blend)

¾ teaspoon ground cardamom, plus more for garnish (optional)

3 black tea bags, or heaping 1 tablespoon loose black tea

SERVES 4 TO 6

In Dhofar, the southernmost region of Oman, this milky *karak* is spiked with ground cardamom and wild fresh thyme. The herbaceous tea pairs wonderfully with lightly sweet, cracker-like Dhofari *Kak* bread (page 184).

Bring 3 cups water to a boil in a small saucepan. Whisk in the condensed milk, then the za'atar and cardamom. Add the tea bags and simmer on medium-high heat 3 minutes. Turn off the heat and steep 2 to 3 minutes more. Strain and serve, garnishing with a pinch more cardamom, if desired.

"RED" MINT TEA

¼ cup sugar

1 cup packed fresh mint leaves, plus more for serving

2 black tea bags, or 1 tablespoon loose black tea

SERVES 4

When tea is offered in Oman, this is what you are likely to be served: a simple black tea simmered with fresh mint, which is best with a healthy dose of sugar mixed in. The "red" in the name differentiates it from the creamy "white" breakfast teas.

Bring 4 cups water to a boil in a medium saucepan; stir in the sugar and mint and simmer 5 minutes. Add the tea bags and turn off the heat; cover and let steep 5 minutes. Strain, adjust the amount of sugar to taste, and serve in glasses with a few torn mint leaves in each cup.

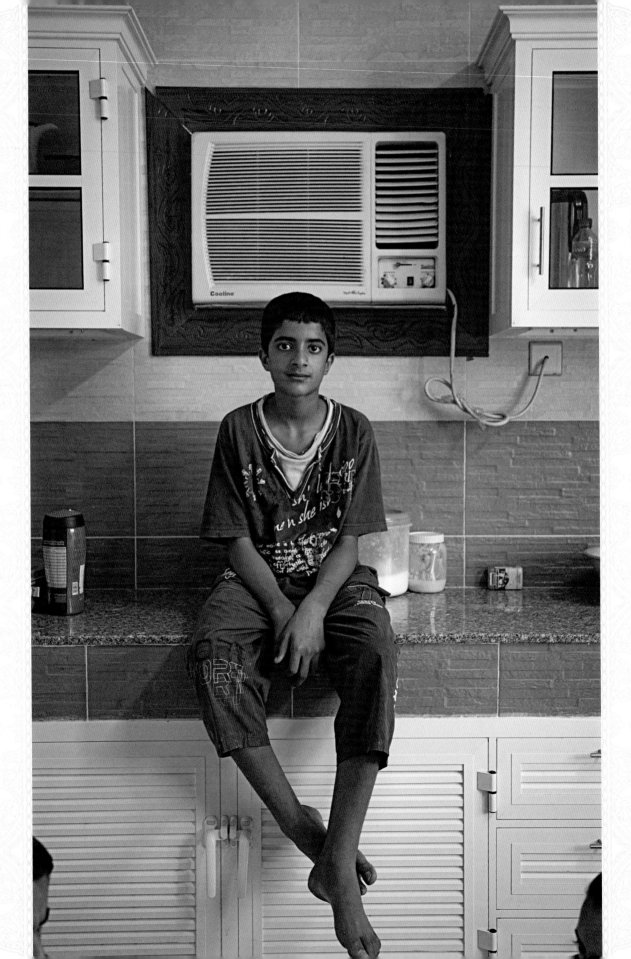

KARAK "GHASSAN"
(GINGER-CARDAMOM OMANI BREAKFAST TEA)

1 teaspoon ground cardamom

½ teaspoon ground ginger

¼ cup sugar

3 black tea bags, or 1½ tablespoons loose black tea

¾ cup evaporated milk

MAKES 6 TO 8 (½-CUP) SERVINGS

At the Al Shamakhi family's home, Ghassan, one of matriarch Wafa'a's fourteen children, taught me this recipe for Omani breakfast tea, popularized by evaporated milk companies in Oman. It makes use of basic pantry ingredients: ground ginger, Lipton tea, sugar, and evaporated milk.

Place the cardamom and ginger in a serving vessel, such as a 1-liter *dallah*, thermos, or pitcher.

Bring 3 cups water, the sugar, and tea bags to a boil in a small saucepan over high heat; boil 2 to 3 minutes. Stir in the evaporated milk; bring to a boil again. Turn off the heat and strain as you pour into the serving vessel, whisking as you pour. Serve in small glasses.

BLACK LIME TEA

6 dried limes, scrubbed

Sugar (optional)

SERVES 4 TO 6

The dried limes known as *limoo Omani*, or black limes, range in color from brown to black, and either can be used. Breaking the orbs and simmering the pieces in water allows the tang of the gummy black flesh and bitterness of the skin to be fully released in this intensely tart digestive. The funkiness of this tea is polarizing, but after a sip or two, it becomes quite addictive, and it really does wonders to settle an upset stomach after a big meal. You can add sugar, but I think it tastes best black. Omani limes can be found at most Middle Eastern markets or ordered online.

Carefully cut the dried limes in half and discard any seeds. Roughly chop the dried limes into pieces. Place in a medium saucepan with 4 cups water and bring to a boil over high heat. Decrease the heat to low and simmer until the flavor is earthy and tart, 15 to 20 minutes (the tea becomes more bitter the longer you let it simmer). Strain the tea into glasses and sweeten to taste with sugar, if desired.

CINNAMON BARK TEA

4 cinnamon sticks

Sugar

SERVES 4

I first tried this delicate, warming tea at Kargeen Caffe, a wonderful restaurant and *sheesha* bar in Muscat. Despite being in the Arabian Gulf, I was immediately transported by one sip of this tea to a cozy fireside during the winter holidays in America.

Bring 4 cups water and the cinnamon sticks to a boil in a small saucepan; simmer 15 minutes. Pour into glasses, placing a cinnamon stick in each glass, and sweeten with sugar to taste.

FRESH GINGER TEA

1 (3½-inch) piece fresh ginger,
  peeled, thinly sliced, and bruised
  (about ¼ cup total)

Sugar

Fresh mint leaves, for garnish
  (optional)

SERVES 2 TO 4

Fresh ginger is simmered in water until it turns a light golden color
for this spicy tea, which is a favorite home remedy for common colds
in Oman. A few torn mint leaves balance the sharp bite of the ginger.

Place 4 cups water and the ginger in a medium saucepan and bring to
a boil; simmer until the ginger has softened and the tea turns a light
brown color, about 30 minutes. Strain the tea into glasses and sweeten
with sugar to taste. Garnish with mint leaves.

Served in lieu of wine with lunch and dinner, fresh juice and juice cocktails are also served at the cafés overlooking the sea in the posh Al Qurum neighborhood of Muscat, where friends meet for mocktails and *sheesha*. One of the most popular juices is sweet-tart Tamarind Juice (see below), which is a nice counterpoint to heavy rice and meat mains. Citrus and mint blends make wonderful afternoon refreshments along with more subtly sweet, floral hibiscus juice. One of the most interesting drinks might be the so-called "Date-Lime Refreshment" that the woman at Bait al Safa in the mountain village of Al Hamra taught me: Pounds of dried dates are put in cheesecloth bags hung from the rafters to soak in lime and water before being squeezed into pitchers and served as a sweet-tart drink that lives up to its name.

TAMARIND JUICE

½ cup packed seedless tamarind paste

2 cups boiling water

5 cups cold water

⅔ cup sugar

SERVES 6 TO 8

Break up the tamarind paste into pieces and place in a medium bowl; pour the boiling water over the paste and let soak until the tamarind softens, breaks up, and cools, about 1½ hours.

Using a masher, break up the paste and pulp in the water as much as possible. Using a fine-mesh sieve, strain the tamarind concentrate over a large bowl or into a pitcher, a little at a time, using a wooden spoon to firmly mash and press the pulp to extract as much liquid as possible, occasionally scraping the pulp on the underside of the sieve into the bowl. This will take a few minutes and yield about 1½ cups tamarind liquid. Discard the mashed fibrous pulp in the sieve.

Combine the tamarind liquid, cold water, and sugar, and whisk to dissolve the sugar. Pour into glasses over ice.

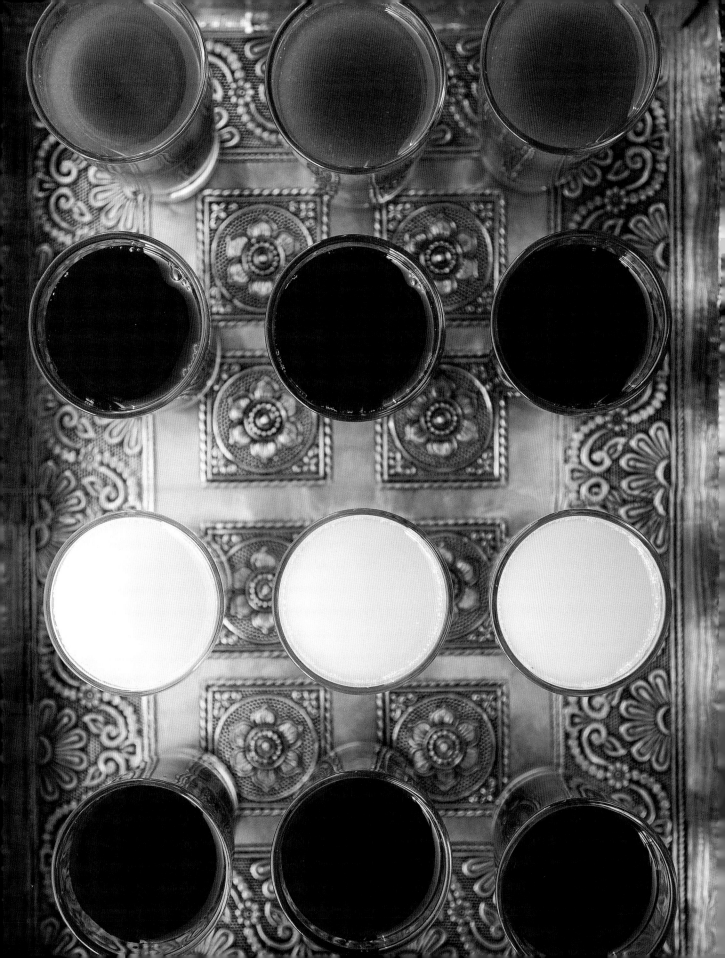

HIBISCUS JUICE

¾ cup sugar, plus more as needed

2 cups loosely packed dried
hibiscus flowers

SERVES 8 TO 10

Bring 8 cups water and the sugar
to a boil in a medium saucepan.
Remove the pan from the heat
and add the hibiscus flowers. Let
steep, uncovered, 2 to 4 hours.

Strain the liquid and transfer to
a pitcher. Adjust the amounts of
sugar or water to taste, if desired.
Chill and serve over ice.

LEMON-GINGER-MINT JUICE

1¾ cups cold water

6 tablespoons freshly squeezed
lime juice

3 tablespoons freshly squeezed
lemon juice

1 (1-inch) piece fresh ginger, peeled
and thinly sliced

2 tablespoons packed fresh mint
leaves

3 to 4 tablespoons sugar

SERVES 2 TO 4

Place the cold water, lime juice,
lemon juice, ginger, mint, and
sugar in a blender and stir to
dissolve the sugar. Purée until
completely smooth. Adjust the
amounts of sugar and water to
taste, and strain through a fine-
mesh sieve into small glasses
with ice.

AD DAKHILIYAH DATE-LIME REFRESHMENT

2 cups boiling water

1 cup packed pitted dried dates (about 12 large high-quality Medjools or 30 medium to small dates)

⅓ cup freshly squeezed lime juice

¼ cup cold water

SERVES 4

Pour the boiling water over the dates in a medium bowl; cover with plastic wrap and let the dates soak until cool and soft, at least 3 hours or up to overnight.

Mash the dates by hand in the water, squeezing each date to break it up as much as possible. Strain the liquid through a fine-mesh sieve over a bowl, a little at a time, mashing and scraping the date pulp firmly with a wooden spoon to extract as much juice as possible. This should take a few minutes. Scrape the pulp from the underside of the sieve into the bowl, and discard any date pulp in the sieve. Stir in the lime juice and cold water, adding more water to taste, if desired. Serve chilled or over ice.

CHAPTER 11

OMANI PANTRY BASICS
AND CONDIMENTS

Most cooks in Oman, like many of us in the United States, enjoy the convenience of picking up premade staples and condiments, buying their bags of dried limes, Omani spice blends, and jars of ghee at hypermarkets, where these items are as ubiquitous as garlic salt and apple butter are in the West. Though we too can purchase specialty Omani ingredients online or substitute store-bought stock for homemade, this section offers the option of making your own Omani cookery staples—great not only for the recipes in this book, but also for adding a subtle, exotic twist to the foods in your own repertoire. Here you will also find recipes for Omani condiments, from traditional tomato and garlic hot sauces to coconut and eggplant chutney to a spicy mayo, all of which help to enliven Omani rice dishes, grilled meats, and fried snacks.

BASIC OMANI STOCK

8 whole cardamom pods, lightly crushed

5 whole cloves

1 cinnamon stick

1 teaspoon cumin seeds

1 teaspoon coriander seeds

½ teaspoon whole black peppercorns

2 teaspoons kosher salt

2 medium yellow or red onions, halved

6 cloves garlic, smashed

3 thin slices fresh ginger, peeled and bruised

1 pound beef or lamb bones

MAKES ABOUT 5 CUPS

Homemade Omani-spiced stock is simple to make and really pays off in depth of flavor in dishes like Lawati Lamb and Dumpling Stew (page 60) or any broth-based soup, from French onion to split pea. Stored in the refrigerator, the stock should be used within 2 to 3 days. It will keep in the freezer for up to 6 months.

In a large dry stockpot, toast the cardamom pods, cloves, cinnamon stick, cumin and coriander seeds, and peppercorns over medium heat until fragrant, 1 to 2 minutes. Pour in 8 cups water and the salt, increase the heat to high, and bring to a boil. Add the onions, garlic, and ginger and boil 5 minutes. Add the meat bones and bring to a boil again; decrease the heat to medium-low or low and simmer with the lid partially off 2 hours.

Remove the bones with a slotted spoon, strain the liquid through a sieve or cheesecloth, and discard the solids. Store the broth in the refrigerator and use within 2 to 3 days, or freeze up to 6 months.

LIMOO OMANI
(DRIED BLACK LIMES)

¼ cup salt

5 limes, preferably thin-skinned Mexican variety

MAKES 5 LIMES

Using small, thin-skinned limes like the ones grown in Mexico, you can dry your own supply of *limoo Omani*, though it can take quite a bit longer in humid climates than in the arid kitchens of Oman, where it only takes a week or two. Dawn and I took to leaving our limes in the fruit bowl instead of the vegetable crisper, and rather than tossing them out when they began wilting, we let them sit and shrivel. Within a month (or a few months in the winter), we had bowls of the dark, hollow-sounding orbs, which we tossed into our Omani Lentils (page 126) and boiled into musky, tart teas (page 224). Once dry, the limes keep for up to 2 years.

Bring 4 cups water and the salt to a boil in a medium saucepan over high heat.

Drop the limes into the boiling water and blanch over high heat 3 to 5 minutes, until they become slightly lighter green and you can faintly smell lime.

Prepare an ice bath. Remove the limes with a slotted spoon or strainer and place in the ice bath to chill until fully cool, 5 to 10 minutes.

Dry the limes completely with a towel, then place them in a dry, well-ventilated place to air-dry 1 to 12 weeks, depending on the humidity level where you live.

Alternatively, when you buy limes, wash them and keep them in your fruit bowl instead of in the vegetable crisper, and if they go unused, they will eventually become black limes. How long this will take depends on the climate. The limes in my fruit bowl in Oman began to harden after only a week and were ready within two, but in New York in the damp fall and winter, it can take months. In either case, this "leave-and-wait" method is a great way to salvage languishing limes from ending up in the trash.

In addition to the bottle of mild, vinegary hot sauce found on almost every Omani table, rice dishes are typically served with either a small bowl of chunky tomato, chile, and garlic Omani salsa or, in the southern Dhofar province near Yemen and in the north near the border of the United Arab Emirates, a thin tomato and garlic hot sauce called *daqus*. The tartness of the tomato and slight bite of the chile perk up the hearty meat and rice mains of the midday meal with their fresh flavors.

OMANI SALSA

2 plum tomatoes, cored and halved

¼ to ½ serrano chile, seeded, depending on taste

2 tablespoons roughly chopped fresh cilantro

1 clove garlic

½ teaspoon kosher salt

MAKES ABOUT 1 CUP

Place all the ingredients in a blender; pulse to purée into a coarse salsa. Adjust the seasoning with salt and additional chile to taste. Keep refrigerated and use within a day or two for the best flavor.

DAQUS

(KHALEEJI TOMATO-GARLIC HOT SAUCE)

4 ripe plum or small tomatoes, halved

2 cloves garlic, finely minced

½ teaspoon kosher salt

¼ teaspoon cayenne

MAKES 1¼ CUPS

Using an immersion blender or blender, purée the tomatoes until smooth. Using a fine-mesh sieve, strain into a saucepan. Use a wooden spoon to firmly mash and press the tomato pulp to extract as much liquid as possible; scrape the pulp on the underside of the sieve into the pan and discard the pulp in the sieve.

Add the garlic, salt, and cayenne to the saucepan; bring to a simmer over medium heat. Decrease the heat to low, and cook, uncovered, 20 minutes, stirring occasionally. Let cool completely, and adjust the seasoning with salt to taste before serving. Keep refrigerated and use within a day or two for the best flavor.

SPICY MAYO

½ cup mayonnaise

2 tablespoons Sriracha, plus more as needed

¼ teaspoon garlic salt, or ⅛ teaspoon granulated garlic

⅛ to ¼ teaspoon ground cumin

⅛ teaspoon cayenne

Pinch of red pepper flakes

MAKES ⅔ CUP

In urban Muscat, we fell in love with a squeeze-bottle chili mayo we would buy from LuLu Hypermarket to dress our beachside kebab sandwiches (pages 29–30), and because it can't be found in America, we developed our own simple approximation of it.

Mix all the ingredients together in a small bowl. Add more garlic salt or Sriracha to taste. Keep refrigerated and use within 3 days.

COCONUT AND MINT YOGURT CHUTNEY

½ cup plus 2 tablespoons unsweetened shredded coconut

2 tablespoons coconut milk powder

½ cup warm water, plus more as needed

1 cup plain full-fat Greek yogurt

2 cloves garlic

1 serrano chile, seeded

20 fresh mint leaves

2 tablespoons chopped fresh parsley

½ teaspoon kosher salt

MAKES ABOUT 2 CUPS

In the southern city of Salalah, there are a myriad of chutneys made daily to accompany grilled meats, fried breads, and signature Dhofari rice dishes like seared tuna *Sayadiyah* (page 83). Salalah native Said Abdullah Al Hashli shared his aunt's recipe for a yogurt-based coconut and mint chutney that she serves with her *sayadiyah*, but which we also love with Omani Lamb Biryani (page 84). Store in the refrigerator and use within 3 to 5 days.

Mix the coconut and coconut milk powder with the warm water and let sit 5 minutes.

Using a blender or immersion blender, purée the coconut mixture with the yogurt, garlic, chile, mint, parsley, and salt until smooth, adding 1 to 2 tablespoons more water, if needed. Transfer to a bowl and cover with plastic wrap; let sit in the refrigerator overnight before serving.

From top left: Spicy Mayo (orange color, page 239), Omani Salsa (page 238), Coconut and Mint Yogurt Chutney (page 239), *Daqus* (page 238), Dhofari Coconut-Eggplant Chutney (opposite)

DHOFARI COCONUT-EGGPLANT CHUTNEY

1 (2-inch) piece tamarind paste

1 cup hot water

1 medium eggplant, peeled and roughly cubed (about 3½ cups)

½ plum tomato, cored and chopped

½ medium red onion

½ to 1 serrano chile, seeded

¼ large green bell pepper, chopped

¼ cup coconut milk

2 tablespoons plus 1 teaspoon distilled white vinegar

1 teaspoon kosher salt

MAKES ABOUT 3 CUPS

At a roadside *madhbi* stand on the outskirts of Salalah, an old Dhofari woman shared her signature eggplant chutney recipe with us. We slathered the addictive blend of earthy eggplant, rich coconut milk, and hot peppers on everything from smoky *Mishakik* beef skewers (page 26) to crispy, sweet *Khubz Lahooh* bread (page 178). The chutney will keep 3 to 5 days in the refrigerator.

Place the tamarind paste in a small bowl and pour the hot water over it; let sit until the paste has softened and cooled, 20 to 30 minutes.

Using a masher, break up the paste in the water. Using a fine-mesh sieve, strain the tamarind concentrate over a bowl, a little at a time, using a wooden spoon to firmly mash and press the pulp to extract as much liquid as possible, scraping the pulp on the underside of the sieve into the bowl. Discard the fibrous pulp in the sieve and set the tamarind liquid aside.

Bring a few cups of water to a boil in a medium saucepan and boil the eggplant until soft, about 10 minutes; drain and let cool.

Place the eggplant in a blender along with 6 tablespoons of the tamarind liquid, the tomato, onion, both peppers, coconut milk, vinegar, and salt; purée into a smooth sauce. Adjust the seasoning with salt and chile to taste. Chill and store in the refrigerator and use as you would a hot sauce.

OMANI MANGO CHUTNEY

1 tablespoon vegetable oil

½ small yellow onion, minced

2 ripe soft yellow mangos, peeled and cubed (discard skins but reserve pits)

5 cloves garlic, halved

2 Korean green peppers or other small sweet chiles, halved and seeded

1 serrano chile, halved lengthwise, stemmed

¼ cup freshly squeezed lime juice

1 tablespoon distilled white vinegar

2 tablespoons sugar

1 teaspoon kosher salt

¼ teaspoon ground cumin

⅛ teaspoon cayenne

MAKES ABOUT 2 CUPS

In Zanzibari households, fried snacks like *Sambusa* (page 148) and Tuna Croquettes (page 144) are served with a tangy, distinctly Omani adaptation of Indian mango chutney. Subtly piquant, the sweet-savory dip is made with cooked ripe mangos, mild chile peppers, and loads of garlic. It is much faster to make than traditional *achar*, or pickled green mango, and unlike preserved mango, this chutney is best eaten within a week and should be stored in the refrigerator.

Heat the oil in a medium saucepan over medium-low heat and cook the onions until soft, without browing, about 10 minutes. Stir in the mangos, garlic, green peppers, chile, lime juice, vinegar, sugar, salt, cumin, cayenne, and 1 cup water. Bring to a simmer over medium-high heat. Once simmering, decrease the heat to medium and cook, stirring occasionally, until some of the liquid evaporates and the mango breaks down a bit, 25 to 30 minutes. Remove from the heat and let cool completely. The taste will improve as it sits. Store, covered, in the refrigerator up to 1 week.

OMANI OIL
(CUMIN AND CORIANDER INFUSED GHEE)

1 teaspoon cumin seeds

1 teaspoon coriander seeds

1 cup (2 sticks) unsalted butter

MAKES ¾ CUP

Called Omani Oil, this ghee (clarified butter) is infused with cumin and coriander and used to finish savory porridges like *Arseeyah* (page 47) and *Harees* (page 52). Once made, it will keep up to 6 months in the fridge, and it is wonderful for making fried eggs or stirring into mashed potatoes. To make plain ghee, simply omit the cumin and coriander seeds and follow the steps below.

Toast the cumin and coriander seeds in a dry skillet over medium-high heat until they pop and are fragrant, about 2 minutes. Remove from the heat.

Place the butter in a medium cast-iron skillet or other heavy pan and turn the heat to medium-low. It will take 15 to 16 minutes total to make the ghee. The butter will begin to melt and become foamy after about 5 minutes, then start to sputter. Stir the toasted spices into the butter 8 minutes into cooking, then turn the heat to low and cook 7 to 8 minutes more, until the milk solids turn brown in the bottom of the pan. Watch closely so the solids don't burn or caramelize, as that will turn it into brown butter.

Remove from the heat and let sit a couple of minutes before straining into a clean jar using a fine-mesh sieve lined with cheesecloth. Discard the solids. The ghee will keep for 6 months in the refrigerator.

ACKNOWLEDGMENTS

There were countless friends, acquaintances, and total strangers who selflessly helped Dawn and me with this project, and we could not be more grateful to everyone for their time, support, and assistance.

We would like to especially thank our beloved friends Miad Al Balushi, Thuraya Al Said, and Ameer Al Ghammari, who have been a part of this book since its inception, giving freely of their time and support every step of the way.

Thanks also go to:

Riyadh Al Balushi, the writer behind the blog *Omani Cuisine*, whom I never met, but whose help putting me in touch with his friends throughout Muscat was my entry point into Oman. James Oseland, who, as my supportive boss, let me explore this passion to begin with, and as a mentor, taught me to approach culinary storytelling not through words in isolation, but with an eye on the visual narrative as well. Betty Fussell, Dawn's and my adopted grandmother and mentor, whose tireless passion for the world and for the written word has been one of our great inspirations. Dr. Mohammed Al Muqadam of the Sultan Qaboos University, whose insights about Oman and connections with young Omani students throughout the Sultanate made it possible for us to learn about places and foods we would never have had the opportunity to explore so intimately otherwise.

Wonderful Omani home cooks: dear friend Waleed Salim Al Harthy; Noora Al Balushi and Hamida Badai in Muscat; the Al Said family cooks, Shaymeena and Yasmeen; Hamdan Al Saqri and his family in Jabal Akhdar; Bader and the Al Lawati family; Munthar and the Al Shamakhi family in Sur; Fathiya Al Rassady; the women of the Al Abry tribe in Al Hamra; Sheikha Al Hajri and the women of Binat Al Bedu in Sharqiyah; and the women of the Buraimi Women's Association and the Salalah Women's Association.

Chefs and restaurateurs: the prolific Omani celebrity chef Issa Al Lamki, who presents Omani cuisine authentically while taking it to new heights; entrepreneurs Adnan Al Balushi and Souad Al Jabriya Aghsan Al Barakah, the owners of Aghsan Al Barakah Omani Foods, who patiently taught us their craft; and the chefs Shabu Thambi and Raiya Al Sukairy of NHI, who are training the next generation of Omani cooks.

The two talented Omani women who wrote the first English-language Omani cookbooks in Oman, Lamees Abdullah Al Taie with her canonic *Al Azif* and Fawziya Ali Khalifa Al Maskiry, who wrote the practical and beloved *A Taste to Remember*.

Those who officially assisted us, but whose assistance went above and beyond: the Ministry of Information, especially Said Al Hashli, who became a friend and an incredible resource over the past two years; Mubarak Al Rahbi of the Ministry of Social Development; Bader Al Dhuli of the Oman Tourism College and his former colleague, Hans Morokutti;

and the people at the Sultan Qaboos Center for Cultural Understanding.

Friends and artists: Yousef Al Nahawi, whose positivity and eye for beauty exemplifies what I love about Oman; poet and beautiful cook Nasra Al Adawu; and Alia Farsi, whose work reflects an utter rootedness in Omani tradition and heritage and an openness to the world with an eye to the future. And a special thanks to all our Omani friends, especially Sultan Al Shamsi, who took the time to meet us, eat with us, drive us around, and introduce us to their perspectives on Oman.

Back in America: Kellie Evans and Farideh Sadeghin for incredible recipe testing and brainstorming. Michelle Heimerman for her volunteer photo editing and Allie Wist for her styling and design advice and recipe testing. Laura Sant, Sarah Green, and Yewande Komolafe, who worked their asses off in the test kitchen. Volunteer recipe testers Michelle Loayza, Ben Mims, Meghan Boledovich, Justin Kennedy, Karla Giboyeaux, Moira and Eric Sedgwick, Heather Ferguson, Kristen Sabarito Carter, Katie Hards, Helen Baldus, Betsy Andrews, Laura Loesch-

Quintin, Meryl Rosofsky, Zainab Shah, Alex Olsen, Barbara Miller, Jessica Smith, Marie Hoffman, Joey and Denise Freitas. And my dad, Colin Campbell. Also, my mom, Corinne Carlson; my brother, Keith Campbell; Shehzad H. Qazi; and all the other friends and loved ones who listened to me obsess over this project ad nauseam.

Kirsty Melville at Andrews McMeel, who has been a champion of this project from the beginning, and the entire editorial staff, especially my editor, Jean Lucas, and art team Tim Lynch and Holly Ogden, who helped to bring this idea to life. Ariana Lindquist, an incredible photographer who shot the hell out of this book, working every sunlit moment and into the night on some death-march photo shoots.

Most of all, I would like to thank Dawn Mobley, my best friend, co-author, incredible cook and recipe writer, and armchair psychologist. There is no one on earth I would rather have shared this experience with. Her support and talent made it possible to push this project beyond a mere cookbook to a life-altering piece of work that I will be proud of for the rest of my life. We had a hell of a lot of fun.

METRIC CONVERSIONS AND EQUIVALENTS

METRIC CONVERSION FORMULAS

To Convert	Multiply
Ounces to grams	Ounces by 28.35
Pounds to kilograms	Pounds by .454
Teaspoons to milliliters	Teaspoons by 4.93
Tablespoons to milliliters	Tablespoons by 14.79
Fluid ounces to milliliters	Fluid ounces by 29.57
Cups to milliliters	Cups by 236.59
Cups to liters	Cups by .236
Pints to liters	Pints by .473
Quarts to liters	Quarts by .946
Gallons to liters	Gallons by 3.785
Inches to centimeters	Inches by 2.54

APPROXIMATE METRIC EQUIVALENTS

Volume

¼ teaspoon	1 milliliter
½ teaspoon	2.5 milliliters
¾ teaspoon	4 milliliters
1 teaspoon	5 milliliters
1¼ teaspoons	6 milliliters
1½ teaspoons	7.5 milliliters
1¾ teaspoons	8.5 milliliters
2 teaspoons	10 milliliters
1 tablespoon (½ fluid ounce)	15 milliliters
2 tablespoons (1 fluid ounce)	30 milliliters
¼ cup	60 milliliters
⅓ cup	80 milliliters
½ cup (4 fluid ounces)	120 milliliters
⅔ cup	160 milliliters
¾ cup	180 milliliters
1 cup (8 fluid ounces)	240 milliliters
1¼ cups	300 milliliters
1½ cups (12 fluid ounces)	360 milliliters
1⅔ cups	400 milliliters
2 cups (1 pint)	460 milliliters
3 cups	700 milliliters
4 cups (1 quart)	0.95 liter
1 quart plus ¼ cup	1 liter
4 quarts (1 gallon)	3.8 liters

Length

⅛ inch	3 millimeters
¼ inch	6 millimeters
½ inch	1¼ centimeters
1 inch	2½ centimeters
2 inches	5 centimeters
2½ inches	6 centimeters
4 inches	10 centimeters
5 inches	13 centimeters
6 inches	15¼ centimeters
12 inches (1 foot)	30 centimeters

Weight

¼ ounce	7 grams
½ ounce	14 grams
¾ ounce	21 grams
1 ounce	28 grams
1¼ ounces	35 grams
1½ ounces	42.5 grams
1⅔ ounces	45 grams
2 ounces	57 grams
3 ounces	85 grams
4 ounces (¼ pound)	113 grams
5 ounces	142 grams
6 ounces	170 grams
7 ounces	198 grams
8 ounces (½ pound)	227 grams
16 ounces (1 pound)	454 grams
35.25 ounces (2.2 pounds)	1 kilogram

OVEN TEMPERATURES

To convert Fahrenheit to Celsius, subtract 32 from Fahrenheit, multiply the result by 5, then divide by 9.

Description	Fahrenheit	Celsius	British Gas Mark
Very cool	200°	95°	0
Very cool	225°	110°	¼
Very cool	250°	120°	½
Cool	275°	135°	1
Cool	300°	150°	2
Warm	325°	165°	3
Moderate	350°	175°	4
Moderately hot	375°	190°	5
Fairly hot	400°	200°	6
Hot	425°	220°	7
Very hot	450°	230°	8
Very hot	475°	245°	9

COMMON INGREDIENTS
AND THEIR APPROXIMATE EQUIVALENTS

1 cup uncooked white rice = 185 grams

1 cup all-purpose flour = 140 grams

1 stick butter (4 ounces • ½ cup • 8 tablespoons) = 110 grams

1 cup butter (8 ounces • 2 sticks • 16 tablespoons) = 220 grams

1 cup brown sugar, firmly packed = 225 grams

1 cup granulated sugar = 200 grams

Information compiled from a variety of sources, including *Recipes into Type* by Joan Whitman and Dolores Simon (Newton, MA: Biscuit Books, 1993); *The New Food Lover's Companion* by Sharon Tyler Herbst (Hauppauge, NY: Barron's, 2013); and *Rosemary Brown's Big Kitchen Instruction Book* (Kansas City, MO: Andrews McMeel, 1998).

INDEX

A

Al Abry tribe, 154
absorption, for rice, 69
Ad Dakhiliyah Date-Lime
    Refreshment, 231
Al Adawu, Nasra, 63
Aghsan Al Barakah Omani Foods
    restaurant, 54
alcoholic beverages, 215
Amazon, 11
Arab trading ships, xxv
Arabic coffee (*kahwa*). *See* coffee
arooz. See rice
Arseeyah, 47–48
Al Arubi, Sultan bin Saif, xxi
Aseeda, 56–57

B

Badai, Hamida, 130
Balaleet, 196–97
Baluchi people, xvii, 107
Al Balushi, Adnan, xxviii, 34, 54
Al Balushi, Miad, 19, 181, 219
Al Balushi, Noora, 181
Al Balushi, Riyadh, xxix
banana leaves, 43–44
bananas, 130–31
Al Barakah, Souad Al Jabriya Aghsan,
    xxviii, 54
barbecue sauce, 39
Basic Basmati Rice, 69
Basic Omani Stock, 234

basmati rice
    Basic Basmati Rice, 69
    Citrusy Seafood Soup with Basmati
        Rice, 106–7
bay leaf (*ghar*), 4, 5
beans
    Chile-Lime Chickpeas, 134
    Zanzibari Slow-Cooked Coconut
        Beans, 132–33
Bedouin people, xi, xiv–xv, 21, 46,
    100, 189
Bedouin Whole Charred Fish, 24–25
Bedu Samak Mashwi, 24–25
beef
    Beef and Flatbread Stew, 58–59
    Dhofari Fried Black Pepper Beef with
        Rice, 78–79
    Peppery Beef Skewers with Spicy
        Tamarind Sauce, 26–27
    Slow-Cooked Caramelized Beef, 96–97
    substitutions, 13
between meals, 139–243. *See also*
    savory bites
beverages, 215
    Ad Dakhiliyah Date-Lime
        Refreshment, 231
    Black Lime Tea, 224
    Cardamom-Thyme Sweet Milk Tea, 220
    Cinnamon Bark Tea, 226
    Fresh Ginger Tea, 227
    Ginger-Cardamom Omani Breakfast
        Tea, 223
    Hibiscus Juice, 230
    Lemon-Ginger-Mint Juice, 230
    Omani Coffee, 216

    "Red" Mint Tea, 221
    Saffron Sweet Milk Tea, 219
    Spiced Sweet Milk Tea, 218
    Tamarind Juice, 228
bin Abdullah Al Said, Sayyid Jamshid, 67
Bin Atiq, 110
bin Saleh, Harameli, xxiii
bin Taimur, Said, xviii, xx, xxii
Binat al Bedu, 24
biryanis. *See* rice
biscuits, 190–91
black limes (*limoo Omani*)
    Black Lime Tea, 224
    broken black limes, 4, 5
    Dried Black Limes, 236
    flesh only black limes, 4
    halved black limes, 4
    substitutions, 12
    whole black limes, 4
black lime powder. *See* ground black
    limes
black peppercorns (*filfil aswad*), 4, 5
    Dhofari Fried Black Pepper Beef with
        Rice, 78–79
Boga La Nazi, 212–13
breads, 161
    Chapati with Egg, 175
    Crêpes with Date Syrup, 180–81
    Crisp-Fried Dhofari Crêpes, 178–79
    Date Chapati, 169–71
    Dhofari Pan-Fried Flatbread, 182–83
    Nigella Seed and Cardamom
        Crispbread, 184–85
    Omani Bread, 162–65

breads *(continued)*
    Omani Bread with Egg and Cheese, 166–68
    Pan-Fried Flatbread, 174–75
    Sur Fennel "Step" Bread, 186–87
    Sweet Cardamom Zanzibari Fried Bread, 172–73
    Zanzibari Sesame Bread, 176–77
brides, 40–42
Broth-Infused Rice with Chicken and Lentils, 71–73
Buraimi, xv, 45, 56, 139, 141, 191
Buraimi Women's Association, 12, 19, 140
Al-Busaidi, xxi
Al Bustan Palace Hotel, 202

C

cake, 206–7
cardamom *(heel)*, 4, 5
    Cardamom-Thyme Sweet Milk Tea, 220
    Ginger-Cardamom Omani Breakfast Tea, 223
    Nigella Seed and Cardamom Crispbread, 184–85
    Sweet Cardamom Zanzibari Fried Bread, 172–73
    Sweet Pumpkin with Cardamom and Coconut Cream, 212–13
    Vermicelli in Rose Water–Cardamom Milk, 204–5
cassia. *See* cinnamon bark and cassia
celebrations, 16, 40–42
chana dal, 8, 11
Chapati, 174–75
    Chapati with Egg, 175
    Date Chapati, 169–71
charring, 21–23
    Bedouin Whole Charred Fish, 24–25
    Lamb Kebab Sandwiches with Charred Tomato and Onion, 29
Chedi Hotel, 33
The Chedi's Yogurt Tandoori-Spiced Shrimp, 32–33
cheese
    Omani Bread with Egg and Cheese, 166–68
    Puck cheese, 158, 166
Chewy Fried Dough in Saffron Syrup, 192–94
chicken
    Broth-Infused Rice with Chicken and Lentils, 71–73
    Chicken *Kabuli*, 71–73
    Coconut Chicken Curry, 114–15
    Double-Cooked Chicken in Rose Water and Spice-Infused Rice, 88–91
    Fried Triangle Pastries Stuffed with Ground Chicken, 148–51
    Hot Stone Dhofari Chicken, 36–37
    Mashed Chicken and Rice, 50–51

Omani-Spiced Ground Chicken
Kebabs, 30–31
Savory Chicken and Rice Porridge,
47–48
Twice-Fried Chicken Dumplings,
152–53
Yemeni-Style Roasted Chicken and
Saffron Rice, 80–81
chickpeas, 134
chile (*filfil*), 5, 6
Chile-Lime Chickpeas, 134
Fried Potato-Chile Puffs, 146–47
chili
Chili, Lime, and Ghee Corn Cups, 157
Chili-Spiced Potato Chips, 158–59
chutney
Coconut and Mint Yogurt Chutney,
239, 240
Dhofari Coconut-Eggplant Chutney,
240, 241
Omani Mango Chutney, 242
cilantro, 102–3
cinnamon bark and cassia (*qirfa*), 5, 6
Cinnamon Bark Tea, 226
Citrusy Seafood Soup with Basmati
Rice, 106–7
cloves (*qirunfil*), 5, 6
coconut
Coconut and Mint Yogurt Chutney,
239, 240
Coconut Chicken Curry, 114–15
Coconut Cookies, 198–99
Dhofari Coconut-Eggplant Chutney,
240, 241
Fresh Pasta Simmered in Coconut
Cream, 208–9
Swahili Coconut Shrimp Curry,
116–17
Sweet Plantains in Coconut Cream, 195
Sweet Pumpkin with Cardamom and
Coconut Cream, 212–13
Whole Fish in Coconut Sauce, 104–5
Zanzibari Coconut Creamed
Spinach, 129
Zanzibari Slow-Cooked Coconut
Beans, 132–33
coconut milk powder, 6, 7
substitutions, 12
coffee (*kahwa*), xxv, 4, 5
Omani Coffee, 216
coffeepot (*dallah*), 4
condiments, 233
Basic Omani Stock, 234
Coconut and Mint Yogurt Chutney,
239, 240
Cumin and Coriander Infused
Ghee, 243
Dhofari Coconut-Eggplant Chutney,
240, 241
Dried Black Limes, 236
Khaleeji Tomato-Garlic Hot Sauce,
238, 240

Omani Mango Chutney, 242
Omani Oil, 243
Omani Salsa, 238, 240
Spicy Mayo, 239, 240
cookies, 198–99
coriander (*kuzbara*), 6, 7
Cumin and Coriander Infused
Ghee, 243
Omani Oil, 243
corn, 157
crêpes
Crêpes with Date Syrup, 180–81
Crisp-Fried Dhofari Crêpes, 178–79
crispbread, 184–85
Crisp-Fried Dhofari Crêpes, 178–79
Crisp-Sautéed Shark with Turmeric and
Onion, 110–11
croquettes, 144–45
Cucumbers with Salt and Lime, 156
cumin seed (*kamoon*), 6, 7
Cumin and Coriander Infused
Ghee, 243
Omani Oil, 243
curry, 112. *See also marak*
Coconut Chicken Curry, 114–15
Spicy Mirbat Squid Curry, 122–23
Spicy Zanzibari Squid Curry, 118–19
Sur-Style Peppery Fish Steak Tomato
Curry, 120–21
Swahili Coconut Shrimp Curry, 116–17

D
Daftar Kaji, 200–201
dal
chana dal, 8, 11
Omani-Spiced Red Lentils, 126–27
Rice with Red Lentils, 70
dallah (coffeepot), 4
Dango, 134
Daqus, 238, 240
dates (*tamr*), 6, 7, 137
Ad Dakhiliyah Date-Lime
Refreshment, 231
Crêpes with Date Syrup, 180–81
Date and Sesame Biscuits, 190–91
Date Chapati, 169–71
Date Syrup, 7, 180–81
Royal Sticky Date Pudding, 202–3
Sweet and Spicy Lamb and Date Stew,
98–99
desserts, xvii. *See also* sweets
Dhofar, xv, xviii, xxiii, xxv, xxviii, 78, 83,
95, 110, 112, 161, 238, 239
Dhofari Coconut-Eggplant Chutney,
240, 241
Dhofari Fried Black Pepper Beef with
Rice, 78–79
Dhofari *Karak*, 220
Dhofari Pan-Fried Flatbread, 182–83
Dhokri, 60–61
dhows (Arab trading ships), xxv, 86

dishdasha, xi, xxii, 22
Double-Cooked Chicken in Rose Water
and Spice-Infused Rice, 88–91
Dried Black Limes, 236
dumplings
Lawati Lamb and Dumpling Stew,
60–61
Pan-Seared Meat Dumplings, 154–55
Toasted Flour and Ghee Dumpling,
56–57
Twice-Fried Chicken Dumplings,
152–53
dunia ("That's the life"), 139

E
eggplant, 240, 241
eggs
Chapati with Egg, 175
Omani Bread with Egg and Cheese,
166–68
Sweet Vermicelli with Salty Egg,
196–97
Eid al Adha, 16, 40, 43
Eid al Fitr, 40, 43
Empty Quarter, 67

F
fattah. See Thareed
fenjan (handleless cups), 4
fennel (*shumar*), 6, 7
Sur Fennel "Step" Bread, 186–87
Fiery Tamarind Barbecue Sauce, 39
filfil. See chile
filfil aswad. See black peppercorns
Fire-Steamed Seafood and Vegetables,
34–35
fish. *See also* giant fish roe
Bedouin Whole Charred Fish, 24–25
Crisp-Sautéed Shark with Turmeric
and Onion, 110–11
Salalah-Style Seared Fish in Rice, 82–83
Spiced Tuna and Vegetable Rice, 76–77
substitutions, 13
Sur-Style Fried Fish, 108–9
Sur-Style Peppery Fish Steak Tomato
Curry, 120–21
Tuna Croquettes, 144–45
Whole Fish in Coconut Sauce, 104–5
fish marinade, 104–5
flatbread
Beef and Flatbread Stew, 58–59
Dhofari Pan-Fried Flatbread, 182–83
Pan-Fried Flatbread, 174–75
flour, toasted, 56–57
Fresh Ginger Tea, 227
Fresh Pasta Simmered in Coconut
Cream, 208–9
Fried *Mandazi*, 172–73
Fried Potato-Chile Puffs, 146–47
Fried Triangle Pastries Stuffed with
Ground Chicken, 148–51

G

garlic, 238, 240
ul gha'ada. See lunch
Al Ghammari, Ameer, 23, 34, *77*, 139, 140
ghanim. See lamb
ghar (bay leaf), 4, 5
ghee
    Chili, Lime, and Ghee Corn Cups, 157
    Cumin and Coriander Infused
        Ghee, 243
    Omani Oil, 243
    substitutions, 12–13
    Toasted Flour and Ghee Dumpling,
        56–57
Al Ghubra (neighborhood), 33, 46
giant fish roe (*samak beed*), 34
ginger (*zanjabeel*), 7, 9
    Fresh Ginger Tea, 227
    Ginger-Cardamom Omani Breakfast
        Tea, 223
    Gingery Tamarind Yogurt Marinade, 38
    Lemon-Ginger-Mint Juice, 230
Green Mountains, xvii
grilling, 21–23. *See also* roasting; smoking
    The Chedi's Yogurt Tandoori-Spiced
        Shrimp, 32–33
    Fire-Steamed Seafood and Vegetables,
        34–35
    Hot Stone Dhofari Chicken, 36–37
    Lamb Kebab Sandwiches with Charred
        Tomato and Onion, 29
    Omani-Spiced Ground Chicken
        Kebabs, 30–31
    Peppery Beef Skewers with Spicy
        Tamarind Sauce, 26–27
    Whole Fish in Coconut Sauce, 104–5
ground black limes (black lime powder),
    4
Gulf Cooperation Council, xviii

H

halwa, 210–11
Al Hamra, 100, 137, 228
Al Hamra Musanif Lahm, 154–55
handleless cups (*fenjan*), 4
Harees, 8, 9, 52–53
Shorbat Harees, 62–63
Al Harthy, Waleed Salim, 38
Al Hashli, Said Abdullah, 83, 100, 239
heel. See cardamom
Herodotus, xxiii
Hibiscus Juice, 230
Homemade Omani *Halwa*, 210–11
hot sauce
    Daqus, 238, 240
    Khaleeji Tomato-Garlic Hot Sauce,
        238, 240
    Omani Salsa, 238, 240
Hot Stone Dhofari Chicken, 36–37

I

ibn Said, Ahmad, xxi
India, xii, xxii, xxiii, xxiv, xxv, 4, 6, 9, 11,
    12, 45, 46, 67, 84, 93, 112, 114, 125,
    126, 143, 147, 148, 174, 200, 242.
    See also South Asia
ingredients, purchasing and substituting, 3

J

Jabal Akhdar, xvii, xxv, 9, 19, 47, 52, 100,
    125, 141, 199
jooz at-tiib (nutmeg), 7, 9
juice, 228
    Ad Dakhiliyah Date-Lime
        Refreshment, 231
    Hibiscus Juice, 230
    Lemon-Ginger-Mint Juice, 230
    Tamarind Juice, 228

K

Kachori, 146–47
kahwa. See coffee
Kahwa Al Omani, 216
kaimati. See luqaimat
Kak, 184–85
Kalia Kabuli, 78–79
Kamba Wa Nazi, 116–17
kamoon. See cumin seed
Karak "Ghassan," 223
Karas, 208–9
Kargeen Caffe, 226
Katlesi Za Samaki, 144–45
kebabs
    Lamb Kebab Sandwiches with Charred
        Tomato and Onion, 29
    Omani-Spiced Ground Chicken
        Kebabs, 30–31
key dates, xviii
Khaleeji, xi
Khaleeji Tomato-Garlic Hot Sauce,
    238, 240
Khubz al Tawa, 182–83
Khubz Lahooh, 178–79
Khubz Mahallah, 180–81
Khubz Ragag, xv, 162–65
Al Khusaibi, Samar, xxix, 207
Al Khusaibi sisters, xxix
Kuku Paka, 114–15
kurkum. See turmeric
kuzbara. See coriander

L

ladies who lunch, 17–19
lahm. See meat
Lahm Kalia, 96–97
lamb (*ghanim*)
    Lamb and Wheat Berry Soup, 62–63
    Lamb Kebab Sandwiches with Charred
        Tomato and Onion, 29
    Lawati Lamb and Dumpling Stew,
        60–61

    Layered Lamb and Yogurt Masala Rice,
        84–85
    Pit-Roasted Lamb Wrapped in Banana
        Leaves, 43–44
    substitutions, 13
    Sweet and Spicy Lamb and Date Stew,
        98–99
Al Lamki, Issa, xxvii, 19, 50, 52, 63, 74,
    143, 195
Al Lamki, Lubna, 143, 195
languages, xvii
Al Lawati, Adila, 46, 200
Al Lawati, Bader, 46, 60
Lawati Crisp Fried Dough with Sugar,
    200–201
Lawati Lamb and Dumpling Stew, 60–61
Lawati people, 16, 45, 46, 107
Layered Lamb and Yogurt Masala Rice,
    84–85
legumes, 125. *See also* beans; lentils
Lemon-Ginger-Mint Juice, 230
lentils, 8, 9
    Broth-Infused Rice with Chicken and
        Lentils, 71–73
    Omani Lentil Soup, 64–65
    Omani-Spiced Red Lentils, 126–27
    Rice with Red Lentils, 70
limes. *See also* black limes
    Ad Dakhiliyah Date-Lime
        Refreshment, 231
    Chile-Lime Chickpeas, 134
    Chili, Lime, and Ghee Corn Cups, 157
    Cucumbers with Salt and Lime, 156
    Saltfish with Cilantro and Lime, 102–3
Limoo Omani, 236. *See also* black limes
LuLu Hypermarket, 1
lunch, 15, 16, 67
    ladies who lunch, 17–19
    main meal, 67–68
Luqaimat, 189, 192–94

M

maa' al urid. See rose water
madhbi (river-rock grilling), 37
Madhbi Djaj, 36–37
Madrouba, 50–51
Madrouba Malleh, 54–55
Maharagwe Ya Nazi, 132–33
main course. *See* chicken; curry; meat; rice;
    seafood; vegetarian/vegan dishes
Maldouf, 169–71
Malleh, 102–3
Al Mamry, Said Naser, 122
Mandi Djaj, 80–81
mango, 242
Maqboos, 74–75
marak, 93–95, 112
    Marak Dal, 126–27
    Marak Hubar, 122–23
    Marak Samak, 120–21

marinades
 fish, 104–5
 Gingery Tamarind Yogurt Marinade, 38
masala rice, 84–85
Mashed Chicken and Rice, 50–51
Al Maskiry, Fawziya Ali Khalifa, xxvi
masoor dal. See red lentils
mayonnaise, 239, 240
Mchicha Wa Nazi, 129
meat (*lahm*), 93–95
 Beef and Flatbread Stew, 58–59
 Dhofari Fried Black Pepper Beef with
  Rice, 78–79
 Lamb and Wheat Berry Soup, 62–63
 Lamb Kebab Sandwiches with Charred
  Tomato and Onion, 29
 Lawati Lamb and Dumpling Stew,
  60–61
 Layered Lamb and Yogurt Masala Rice,
  84–85
 Pan-Seared Meat Dumplings, 154–55
 Peppery Beef Skewers with Spicy
  Tamarind Sauce, 26–27
 Pit-Roasted Lamb Wrapped in Banana
  Leaves, 43–44
 Slow-Cooked Caramelized Beef, 96–97
 Sweet and Spicy Lamb and Date Stew,
  98–99
Mina Seafood, 122

mint
 Coconut and Mint Yogurt Chutney,
  239, 240
 Lemon-Ginger-Mint Juice, 230
 "Red" Mint Tea, 221
Mirbat, 122–23
mishak, 22, 23
Mishakik, 26–27
Mkate Wa Ufuta, 176–77
Mobley, Dawn, xv, xvi, 1, 12, 17, 19, 68,
 69, 143, 166–68, 202, 236
Mohammed (prophet), 137
mountains, xvii
Muradef, 186–87
Musanif Djaj, 152–53
Muscat, xi, xvii, xviii, xxii, 1, 15, 33, 45, 54,
 80, 100, 141, 143, 158, 161, 228, 239
 food scene, xxvi–xxix
mussar turbans, xi
Mutrah, xxvii, 46, 93, 107, 141, 200

N
Naheemah, 22
Naseeb, Rasmiya, 182
National Hospitality Institute,
 xxvi–xxvii, 177
Ndizi Mbichi, 130–31
Ndizi Mbivu, 195

Nigella Seed and Cardamom Crispbread,
 184–85
nutmeg (*jooz at-tiib*), 7, 9

O
Oman, xi–xvi
 celebrations, 16, 40–42
 food importance in, 16
 history of, xx–xxvi
 key dates, xviii
 ladies who lunch, 17–19
 lunch as main meal, 67–68
 quick facts, xvii
 relationships and food, 15–16
 sultanate of, xvii, xix
 togetherness of meals, 19
 women, 12, 17–19, 140
Oman LNG (Liquified Natural Gas), 121
Oman Vegetable Oil & Derivatives, 99
Omani Bread, 162–65
Omani Bread with Egg and Cheese,
 166–68
Omani Coffee, 216
Omani Curry, 112
Omani Halwa Factory, 210
Omani *Lamb Biryani*, 84–85
Omani Lentil Soup, 64–65
Omani Mango Chutney, 242
Omani *Marak*, 112

Omani Oil, 243
Omani Salsa, 238, 240
Omani-Spiced Ground Chicken Kebabs, 30–31
Omani-Spiced Red Lentils, 126–27
Omani Vegetable Plate, The, 136
onions
  Crisp-Sautéed Shark with Turmeric and Onion, 110–11
  Lamb Kebab Sandwiches with Charred Tomato and Onion, 29
  Red Onion and Tomato Spiced Rice, 74–75
Oseland, James, ix–x

P

Pakistan, xxii, xxiv, xxv, 9, 93, 107. See also South Asia
palm oil, 99
Pan-Fried Flatbread, 174–75
Pan-Seared Meat Dumplings, 154–55
pantry, 1, 233
  Basic Omani Stock, 234
  Coconut and Mint Yogurt Chutney, 239, 240
  Cumin and Coriander Infused Ghee, 243
  Dhofari Coconut-Eggplant Chutney, 240, 241
  Dried Black Limes, 236
  Omani Mango Chutney, 242
  Omani Oil, 243
  Omani Salsa, 238, 240
  Spicy Mayo, 239, 240
pasta, 208–9. See also vermicelli
Peppery Beef Skewers with Spicy Tamarind Sauce, 26–27
Persia, xi, xviii, xxii, 4, 9, 11, 16, 21, 45, 46, 67, 93. See also South Asia
Petroleum Development Oman, 38
Pit-Roasted Lamb Wrapped in Banana Leaves, 43–44
plantains, 195
porridge, 45–46
  Mashed Chicken and Rice, 50–51
  Savory Chicken and Rice Porridge, 47–48
  Savory Turmeric-Scented Saltfish and Rice Porridge, 54–55
  Savory Wheat Porridge, 52–53
  Toasted Flour and Ghee Dumpling, 56–57
potatoes
  Chili-Spiced Potato Chips, 158–59
  Fried Potato-Chile Puffs, 146–47
  Tuna Croquettes, 144–45
produce, 125. See also vegetables
Puck cheese, 158, 166
pudding, 202–3
pumpkin, 212–13

Q

Qashat Bil Nargil, 198–99
qirfa (cinnamon bark and cassia), 5, 6
qirunfil (cloves), 5, 6
Queen of Sheba, xxv
quick boil method, for rice, 69

R

Rabees, 110–11
Ragag Ma Beed Wa Jibne, 166–68
Ramadan, xvi, 16, 22, 26, 40, 45, 46, 52, 137, 143
Al Rasbi, Sulaf, 121
red lentils (masoor dal), 8, 9
  Omani-Spiced Red Lentils, 126–27
  Rice with Red Lentils, 70
"Red" Mint Tea, 221
Red Onion and Tomato Spiced Rice, 74–75
relationships and food, 15–16
religion, xvii
rice (arooz), 9, 66
  Basic Basmati Rice, 69
  Broth-Infused Rice with Chicken and Lentils, 71–73
  Citrusy Seafood Soup with Basmati Rice, 106–7
  Dhofari Fried Black Pepper Beef with Rice, 78–79
  Double-Cooked Chicken in Rose Water and Spice-Infused Rice, 88–91
  Layered Lamb and Yogurt Masala Rice, 84–85
  as main meal, 67–68
  Mashed Chicken and Rice, 50–51
  Red Onion and Tomato Spiced Rice, 74–75
  Rice with Red Lentils, 70
  Salalah-Style Seared Fish in Rice, 82–83
  Savory Chicken and Rice Porridge, 47–48
  Savory Turmeric-Scented Saltfish and Rice Porridge, 54–55
  Spiced Tuna and Vegetable Rice, 76–77
  Spicy Layered Vegetables and Rice, 86–87
  Yemeni-Style Roasted Chicken and Saffron Rice, 80–81
river-rock grilling (madhbi), 37
roasting
  Lamb Kebab Sandwiches with Charred Tomato and Onion, 29
  Pit-Roasted Lamb Wrapped in Banana Leaves, 43–44
  Whole Fish in Coconut Sauce, 104–5
  Yemeni-Style Roasted Chicken and Saffron Rice, 80–81
rose water (maa' al urid), 9
  Double-Cooked Chicken in Rose Water and Spice-Infused Rice, 88–91

Vermicelli in Rose Water–Cardamom Milk, 204–5
Royal Sticky Date Pudding, 202–3

S

sacred spaces, 15–16
saffron (za'affaron), 8, 9
  Saffron Karak, 219
  Saffron Sweet Milk Tea, 219
  Saffron Syrup, 192–94
  Yemeni-Style Roasted Chicken and Saffron Rice, 80–81
Al Said, Qaboos bin Said, xviii, xx, xxii, xxvi
Al Said, Thuraya, 12, 17, 18, 19, 21, 41, 47, 50, 67, 189, 192
Salalah, xi, 21, 37, 45, 68, 78, 94, 100, 125, 141, 157, 178, 184, 239
Salalah-Style Seared Fish in Rice, 82–83
saloonat, 45, 112
salsa, 238, 240
saltfish
  Saltfish with Cilantro and Lime, 102–3
  Savory Turmeric-Scented Saltfish and Rice Porridge, 54–55
samak beed (giant fish roe), 34
Samaki Maqli, 108–9
Samaki Wa Kupaka, 104–5
Samar's Date Cake, 206–7
Sambusa, 148–51
sandwiches, 29
Al Saqri family, 199
sauce, 38–39, 89, 208–9. See also hot sauce; marinades
  Coconut Sauce, 104–5
  Fiery Tamarind Barbecue Sauce, 39
  Spicy Tamarind Sauce, 26–27
savory bites, 143
  Chili, Lime, and Ghee Corn Cups, 157
  Chili-Spiced Potato Chips, 158–59
  Cucumbers with Salt and Lime, 156
  Fried Potato-Chile Puffs, 146–47
  Fried Triangle Pastries Stuffed with Ground Chicken, 148–51
  Pan-Seared Meat Dumplings, 154–55
  Tuna Croquettes, 144–45
  Twice-Fried Chicken Dumplings, 152–53
Savory Chicken and Rice Porridge, 47–48
Savory Turmeric-Scented Saltfish and Rice Porridge, 54–55
Savory Wheat Porridge, 52–53
Saweeyah Bil Haleeb, 204–5
Sayadiyah, 82–83
sea, xvii
seafarers, xx–xvi
seafood, 93–95, 100
  Bedouin Whole Charred Fish, 24–25
  The Chedi's Yogurt Tandoori-Spiced Shrimp, 32–33

Citrusy Seafood Soup with Basmati Rice, 106–7
Crisp-Sautéed Shark with Turmeric and Onion, 110–11
Fire-Steamed Seafood and Vegetables, 34–35
Salalah-Style Seared Fish in Rice, 82–83
Saltfish with Cilantro and Lime, 102–3
Savory Turmeric-Scented Saltfish and Rice Porridge, 54–55
Spiced Tuna and Vegetable Rice, 76–77
Spicy Mirbat Squid Curry, 122–23
Spicy Zanzibari Squid Curry, 118–19
Sur-Style Fried Fish, 108–9
Sur-Style Peppery Fish Steak Tomato Curry, 120–21
Swahili Coconut Shrimp Curry, 116–17
Tuna Croquettes, 144–45
Whole Fish in Coconut Sauce, 104–5
sesame
    Date and Sesame Biscuits, 190–91
    Zanzibari Sesame Bread, 176–77
Al Shamakhi, Ghassan, 223
Al Shamakhi, Wafa'a, 86, 108–9, 187, 223
Shanaliza, 21–22
shark, 110–11
Sharqiyah, xiv–xv, 21, 24, 67, 100
Shaymeena (cook), 12, 17, 18, 47
Sheikha, 24
shopping guide, for specialty ingredients, 11
Shorbat Harees, 62–63
shrimp
    The Chedi's Yogurt Tandoori-Spiced Shrimp, 32–33
    Swahili Coconut Shrimp Curry, 116–17
shumar. See fennel
shuwa, 40
skewers, 26–27
Slow-Cooked Caramelized Beef, 96–97
smoking, 21–23
    Pit-Roasted Lamb Wrapped in Banana Leaves, 43–44
snacks. See savory bites
soups, 45–46. See also porridge; stew
    Citrusy Seafood Soup with Basmati Rice, 106–7
    Lamb and Wheat Berry Soup, 62–63
    Omani Lentil Soup, 64–65
South Asia, xi, xiv, xxiii, xxvi, xxix, 9, 16, 45, 84, 107, 114, 125, 148, 169, 174, 205, 215, 218
Special Karak, 218
specialty ingredients, 11
Spiced Sweet Milk Tea, 218
Spiced Tuna and Vegetable Rice, 76–77
spices, 3, 4–9, 11
    blend, 89
    paste, 43–44
    trade, xxii–xxiv
Spicy Layered Vegetables and Rice, 86–87

Spicy Mayo, 239, 240
Spicy Mirbat Squid Curry, 122–23
Spicy Tamarind Sauce, 26–27
Spicy Zanzibari Squid Curry, 118–19
spinach, 129
squash, 213
squid
    Spicy Mirbat Squid Curry, 122–23
    Spicy Zanzibari Squid Curry, 118–19
stew, 45–46. See also porridge; soups
    Beef and Flatbread Stew, 58–59
    Lawati Lamb and Dumpling Stew, 60–61
    Sweet and Spicy Lamb and Date Stew, 98–99
stock, 234
substitutions, 12–13
Al Sukairy, Raiya, 177
Sultan (friend), 139
Sultanate of Oman, xvi, xvii, xviii, xix, xxi, xxii, xxv, xxvi, xxix, 6, 12, 16, 46, 64, 67, 84, 141, 157, 158, 189, 192, 215
sultans, xx–xvi
Sur, xxv–xxvi, 19, 93, 100, 112
Sur Fennel "Step" Bread, 186–87
Sur Vegetable Biryani, 86–87
Sur-Style Fried Fish, 108–9
Sur-Style Peppery Fish Steak Tomato Curry, 120–21
Swahili Coconut Shrimp Curry, 116–17
Sweet and Spicy Lamb and Date Stew, 98–99
Sweet Cardamom Zanzibari Fried Bread, 172–73
Sweet Plantains in Coconut Cream, 195
Sweet Pumpkin with Cardamom and Coconut Cream, 212–13
Sweet Vermicelli with Salty Egg, 196–97
sweetened condensed milk
    Cardamom-Thyme Sweet Milk Tea, 220
    Saffron Sweet Milk Tea, 219
    Spiced Sweet Milk Tea, 218
sweets, 189
    Chewy Fried Dough in Saffron Syrup, 192–94
    Coconut Cookies, 198–99
    Date and Sesame Biscuits, 190–91
    Fresh Pasta Simmered in Coconut Cream, 208–9
    Homemade Omani Halwa, 210–11
    Lawati Crisp Fried Dough with Sugar, 200–201
    Royal Sticky Date Pudding, 202–3
    Samar's Date Cake, 206–7
    Sweet Plantains in Coconut Cream, 195
    Sweet Pumpkin with Cardamom and Coconut Cream, 212–13
    Sweet Vermicelli with Salty Egg, 196–97
    Vermicelli in Rose Water–Cardamom Milk, 204–5

syrup
    Date Syrup, 180–81
    Saffron Syrup, 192–94

T
Al Taie, Lamees Abdullah, xxvi
tamarind (tamir hindi), 8, 9
    Fiery Tamarind Barbecue Sauce, 39
    Gingery Tamarind Yogurt Marinade, 38
    Spicy Tamarind Sauce, 26–27
    Tamarind Juice, 228
tamr. See dates
tandoori-spiced shrimp, 32–33
tea
    Black Lime Tea, 224
    Cardamom-Thyme Sweet Milk Tea, 220
    Cinnamon Bark Tea, 226
    Fresh Ginger Tea, 227
    Ginger-Cardamom Omani Breakfast Tea, 223
    "Red" Mint Tea, 221
    Saffron Sweet Milk Tea, 219
    Spiced Sweet Milk Tea, 218
Thareed, 58–59
"That's the life" (dunia), 139
thyme. See also wild thyme
    Cardamom-Thyme Sweet Milk Tea, 220
Toasted Flour and Ghee Dumpling, 56–57
tomatoes
    Khaleeji Tomato-Garlic Hot Sauce, 238, 240
    Lamb Kebab Sandwiches with Charred Tomato and Onion, 29
    Red Onion and Tomato Spiced Rice, 74–75
    Sur-Style Peppery Fish Steak Tomato Curry, 120–21
tuna
    Spiced Tuna and Vegetable Rice, 76–77
    Tuna Croquettes, 144–45
    Tuna Kabuli, 76–77
turmeric (kurkum), 8, 9
    Crisp-Sautéed Shark with Turmeric and Onion, 110–11
    Savory Turmeric-Scented Saltfish and Rice Porridge, 54–55
Twice-Fried Chicken Dumplings, 152–53

V
vegetables. See also fennel
    Fire-Steamed Seafood and Vegetables, 34–35
    The Omani Vegetable Plate, 136
    Spiced Tuna and Vegetable Rice, 76–77
    Spicy Layered Vegetables and Rice, 86–87
    Zanzibari Coconut Creamed Spinach, 129
    Zanzibari Savory Mashed Green Bananas, 130–31

vegetarian/vegan dishes. *See also* rice
 Chile-Lime Chickpeas, 134
 Chili, Lime, and Ghee Corn Cups, 157
 Chili-Spiced Potato Chips, 158–59
 Cucumbers with Salt and Lime, 156
 Fried Potato-Chile Puffs, 146–47
 Omani Lentil Soup, 64–65
 The Omani Vegetable Plate, 136
 Omani-Spiced Red Lentils, 126–27
 Toasted Flour and Ghee Dumpling,
   56–57
 Zanzibari Coconut Creamed
   Spinach, 129
 Zanzibari Savory Mashed Green
   Bananas, 130–31
 Zanzibari Slow-Cooked Coconut
   Beans, 132–33
vermicelli, 8, 9
 Sweet Vermicelli with Salty Egg,
   196–97
 Vermicelli in Rose Water–Cardamom
   Milk, 204–5

W

Al Wadi Al Kabir (neighborhood), 158
Al Wahiba tribe, 24
wedding celebrations, 40–42
wheat berries (*harees*), 8, 9
 Lamb and Wheat Berry Soup, 62–63
 Savory Wheat Porridge, 52–53
Whole Fish in Coconut Sauce, 104–5
Whole Foods, 11
whole pierced black limes, 4
wild thyme (*za'atar*), 8, 9, 11
women
 brides, 40–42
 Buraimi Women's Association, 12,
   19, 140
 ladies who lunch, 17–19

Y

yellow split peas, 8, 11, 71–73
Yemeni-Style Roasted Chicken and
 Saffron Rice, 80–81

yogurt
 The Chedi's Yogurt Tandoori-Spiced
   Shrimp, 32–33
 Coconut and Mint Yogurt Chutney,
   239, 240
 Gingery Tamarind Yogurt Marinade, 38
 Layered Lamb and Yogurt Masala Rice,
   84–85
Al Yousuf, Ghada, xxvii

Z

za'affaron. See saffron
za'atar (wild thyme), 8, 9, 11
zanjabeel. See ginger
Zanzibar, xviii, xxi, xxii, xxiii, 104
Zanzibari Biryani, 88–91
Zanzibari Coconut Creamed Spinach, 129
Zanzibari Savory Mashed Green
 Bananas, 130–31
Zanzibari Sesame Bread, 176–77
Zanzibari Slow-Cooked Coconut Beans,
 132–33

ARTIST BIOGRAPHIES

ARIANA LINDQUIST

Ariana Lindquist is an international documentary photographer, focusing on the interaction between culture and economy, whose work has been honored with first place awards by World Press Photo, NPPA: Best of Photojournalism, and the White House News Photographers Association as well as with a Fulbright to China. Her images are published by *Time*, the *New York Times*, and the *Atlantic*, among others. Ms. Lindquist has visually documented global cuisine for many years as a contributing photographer for *Saveur* magazine. arianalindquist.com

FARIDEH SADEGHIN

Farideh Sadeghin spent seven years as a chef in New Zealand before turning her attention to the editorial side of food and moving to New York City, where she oversees the *Saveur* test kitchen, writes, and develops recipes in addition to styling and photographing food. She has developed recipes, styled, and shot for publications such as the *Fried & True* cookbook, Eater.com, *Lucky Peach*, *Departures*, and *Saveur* magazines. sadeghin.photoshelter.com

KATIE MCBRIDE

Katie McBride is an illustrator and designer in Richmond, Virginia. Her work spans a range of tones and themes—from whimsical, children's book–style images of animals doing people things to conceptual editorial illustration, maps, infographics, and beer labels. She holds a BFA from Virginia Commonwealth University, served as a co-chair of the Richmond Illustrators Club, and taught at the Visual Arts Center of Richmond. katiemcbride.com

JOSIE PORTILLO

Josie Portillo was born, raised, and currently works in Los Angeles, California, as a freelance illustrator. She received a BFA in illustration with a focus in entertainment arts at Art Center College of Design. She draws inspiration from mid-century design, vintage children's animation, folk art, nature, and traveling. portilloillustration.com

LAURA SANT

Laura Sant began her career as a designer and illustrator before deciding her job didn't involve nearly enough eating. After a brief stint working in kitchens as a pastry chef, she landed at *Saveur* magazine in New York, where she now writes, edits, illustrates, and occasionally makes biscuits. mizsant.net

Andrews McMeel Publishing, LLC
an Andrews McMeel Universal company
1130 Walnut Street, Kansas City, Missouri 64106

www.andrewsmcmeel.com

15 16 17 18 19 20 SDB 10 9 8 7 6 5 4 3 2 1

ISBN: 978-1-4494-6082-2

Library of Congress Control Number: 2015938223

www.feliciacampbell.com

Photographer: Ariana Lindquist
Photography: Farideh Sadeghin: (Omani
    ingredients-24) p. 5, 7, 8; (saweeyah) p. 204;
    (coffee service) p. 217; (saffron karak) p. 219;
    (Omani condiments) p. 240. Dawn Mobley:
    (coconut cookies) p. 198. Felicia Campbell: (Old
    Muscat) p. xxi, (bags of spices) p. 2, (sea and
    palms) p. 18, (mint juice) p. 230.
Recipe developer and writer: Dawn Mobley
Recipe testers: Kellie Evans and Farideh Sadeghin
Testing assistants: Laura Sant, Yewande Komolafe,
    and Sarah Green
Illustrator: Katie McBride (Oman map, page xviv)
Illustrator: Josie Portillo (Indian Ocean map,
    endpapers)
Illustrator: Laura Sant (step-by-step illustrations,
    pages 151, 164–165, 168, and 171)
Editor: Jean Z. Lucas
Designer: Holly Ogden
Art director: Tim Lynch
Production editor: Maureen Sullivan
Production manager: Cliff Koehler
Demand planner: Sue Eikos